How the West Was Su

MW00583810

How the West
Was Sung

Music in the Westerns of John Ford

Kathryn Kalinak

UNIVERSITY OF CALIFORNIA PRESS
Berkeley · Los Angeles · London

University of California Press, one of the most distin-
guished university presses in the United States, enriches
lives around the world by advancing scholarship in the
humanities, social sciences, and natural sciences. Its activities are supported by the UC Press Foundation and
by philanthropic contributions from individuals and
institutions. For more information, visit
www.ucpress.edu.

University of California Press
Berkeley and Los Angeles, California

University of California Press, Ltd.
London, England

Library of Congress Cataloging-in-Publication Data

Kalinak, Kathryn Marie, 1952–.
  How the West was sung : music in the westerns of
John Ford / Kathryn Kalinak.
      p.   cm.
  Includes bibliographical references and index.
  ISBN-13: 978-0-520-25233-2 (cloth : alk. paper)
  ISBN-13: 978-0-520-25234-9 (pbk. : alk. paper)
    1. Ford, John, 1894–1973—Criticism and interpreta-
tion.   2. Motion picture music—United States—History
and criticism.   I. Title.

PN1998.3.F65K35   2007
781.5'42—dc22   2006037036

Manufactured in the United States of America

16   15   14   13   12   11   10   09   08   07
10   9   8   7   6   5   4   3   2   1

This book is printed on New Leaf EcoBook 50, a
100% recycled fiber of which 50% is de-inked post-
consumer waste, processed chlorine-free. EcoBook 50
is acid-free and meets the minimum requirements of
ANSI/ASTM D5634–01 (Permanence of Paper).

For Ralph and Emily

Contents

Acknowledgments

This book would not have been possible without the inspiration, input, encouragement, and support of many people: Matthew Bernstein and Gaylyn Studlar, who first asked me to think about the music in John Ford's westerns; Janet Walker, who first challenged me to consider the impact of minstrel music, and who offered insight and encouragement on the manuscript; and Arthur Eckstein and Peter Lehman, who first nudged me to investigate *The Searchers*. Dan Ford met with me and provided many unique insights into his grandfather's life and work. His contribution shaped this book in important ways, and I am honored to have made his acquaintance. Harry Carey Jr. and his wife Marilyn graciously shared memories of *3 Godfathers* with me. Krin Gabbard supplied his critical attention to the manuscript, Caryl Flinn prompted me to "get it done," as Tyree says in *Rio Grande,* and Sandy Flitterman-Lewis offered her intelligence and support.

The research for this book was facilitated by librarians, archivists, and scholars from all over the country: Charles Silver of the Museum of Modern Art; Lauren Buisson of Arts Special Collections at UCLA; Ned Comstock of the Cinema-Television Library and Haden Guest of the Warner Bros. Archive, both at USC; James D'Arc of the L. Tom Perry Special Collections and Dean Duncan, both of Brigham Young University; the staff of the Lilly Library at Indiana University; Stacy Behlmer, Barbara Hall, and Warren Sherk of the Margaret Herrick Library of the Academy of Motion Picture Arts and Sciences in Beverly Hills; the staff of the Lincoln Center Library for the Performing Arts, New York Public Library; Rosemary Cullen of the John Hay Library at Brown University; Kathryn Miller of the Center for American Music at the University of Pittsburgh; Anthony Vaver of the Robert D. Farber University Archives and Special Collections at Brandeis University; and James Hoy of Emporia State University, Rudy Behlmer, and Larry Hopper.

Many others have lent their ears to this project. I had no idea when I started how difficult it would be to track down and identify the songs in Ford westerns. Thanks here go to Rita Clark and Haydn James of the Welsh Association of London, Thomas O'Grady of the University of Massachusetts, Boston, Seamus Connolly of Boston College, Ralph Bravaco, Emil Kalinak, and Robert Shaw. Any errors in attribution, however, are all my own.

A Helms Fellowship from the Lilly Library allowed me to see John Ford's papers. Here at Rhode Island College, I wish to thank Dean Rich Weiner for the sabbatical to finish writing this book; the Faculty Research Fund for several grants to support my research; the staff of Adams Library for service above and beyond the call of duty; Robert Shein of the Multicultural Media Center for media support; and my colleagues in the Film Studies Program, Joan Dagle and Claudia Springer, for their interest and encouragement, and the late Mark Estrin, who continues to inspire me.

California has been my home away from home in writing this book, and I would like to thank Jon and Janice Jerde for the use of their beautiful Stone House, just up the road from Harry Carey's last residence, and as perfect a place to write a book on John Ford as anyone could possibly imagine. I also thank Peter Dreyer, for giving the manuscript precision and polish, and Mary Francis for guiding the project to fruition at the University of California Press.

Finally, my deepest gratitude goes to my husband, Ralph, and my daughter, Emily, who went on this journey with me, literally and figuratively: sharing my ups and downs, accommodating my deadlines, and bringing me the joy that comes from sharing something you love with someone you love. Thank you both.

Introduction

Huw Morgan in John Ford's *How Green Was My Valley* (1941) describes his Welsh village as ringing "with the sound of many voices, for singing is in my people as sight is in the eye." Something very similar might be written about all the films of John Ford (1894–1973). Ford is unique among directors in the Hollywood studio system in his insistence on song, both vocal and instrumental, diegetic (i.e., heard by the characters and often with a source visible on screen) and nondiegetic (i.e., heard by the audience but inaudible to the film's characters), in war films, social and political dramas, historical epics, comedies, and literary adaptations, genres not accustomed to accommodating such performances.

This book focuses on music in the western, a genre that Ford both defined and dominated. In fact, the preponderance of song is one of the most distinctive features of Ford's imprint on the genre. Perhaps this is why so many memories of Ford westerns hinge on their production numbers: "The Girl I Left Behind Me" and "She Wore a Yellow Ribbon," sung by soldiers in *Fort Apache* (1948) and *She Wore a Yellow Ribbon* (1949); "All Praise to St. Patrick," played for the Grande Marche, and "Garry Owen," played by the regimental band in *Fort Apache*; "The Streets of Laredo," sung as a lullaby in *3 Godfathers* (1948); "Drill, Ye Terriers, Drill," sung by the railroad workers in *The Iron Horse* (1924), and "Sweet Genevieve," sung by the protagonists of *Hellbent* (1918) (two of Ford's "silent" westerns); "I'll Take You Home Again, Kathleen," heard on a music box in *Rio Grande* (1950); "Shall We Gather at the River?" in just about everything. And this is just the beginning of a list of songs performed, in one way or another, in Ford westerns. No wonder one of Ford's biographers, Tag Gallagher, observes: "Ford's cinema can, without too much exaggeration, at times be likened to a trailer for a musical."[1]

Song crosses the diegesis in Ford westerns, too. If these moments are less immediately audible than the diegetic performances, they are no less characteristic of music's operation in Ford westerns: "Jeanie with the Light Brown Hair," as a leitmotif for Hatfield in *Stagecoach* (1939); "Lorena," as a leitmotif for Martha in *The Searchers* (1956); "Oh, Bury Me Not on the Lone Prairie," as an aural marker for the stagecoach in *Stagecoach, Fort Apache, She Wore a Yellow Ribbon,* and *3 Godfathers;* "Battle Hymn of the Republic," underscoring Captain York's last speech in *Fort Apache;* "The Battle-cry of Freedom" as the cavalry charges to the rescue in *Stagecoach.*

Ford's predilection for American folk song, hymnody, and period music is more than a stylistic gesture. Songs authenticate historical era and geographic place and contribute to narrative trajectory, character development, and thematic exposition. In Ford, song also carries the ideological payload. Ford westerns focus on the settling of the American West and the function of community in that enterprise. Given this agenda, it is not surprising that the films engage with the relationship between history and myth, the definitions of nation and nationality, and matters of class, ethnicity, race, and gender. Song plays a vital role in creation of such ideologically loaded concepts, tapping into emotionally laden and culturally determined responses powerfully and, for most spectators, subconsciously. In fact, one can chart the ideological terrain of a Ford western through its songs.

Song has been mentioned as a feature of Ford's work by most critics and scholars, from the initial wave of auteurist analysis in the 1960s to recent reevaluation in the 1990s and beyond.[2] But few have addressed the music in Ford westerns in detail. Claudia Gorbman writes about the musical representation of Indians in "Drums along the L.A. River: Scoring the Indian" and includes some analysis of *Stagecoach;* K. J. Donnelly writes about the construction of ethnicity in the film score and references several Ford westerns in *The Spectre of Sound: Music in Film and Television;* William Darby analyzes the musical confluences among three Ford films in "Musical Links in *Young Mr. Lincoln, My Darling Clementine* and *The Man Who Shot Liberty Valance*"; Lane Roth discusses implications of some folk songs in selected Ford westerns in "Folk Song

Lyrics as Communication in John Ford's Films"; and Edward Buscombe treats the score in depth in his British Film Institute monographs on *Stagecoach* and *The Searchers*.[3] I have contributed "The Sound of Many Voices: Music in John Ford's Westerns" to the anthology *John Ford Made Westerns: Filming the Legend in the Sound Era* and "'Typically American': Music for *The Searchers*," in *The Searchers: Essays and Reflections on John Ford's Classic Western*, both of which find their way, in one form or another, into the pages of this book.[4] All of Ford's major biographers, Ronald L. Davis, Scott Eyman, Dan Ford, Tag Gallagher, and Joseph McBride include some consideration of music, with Gallagher offering the most sustained attention to the subject.[5]

Yet there has been no systematic analysis of the music in Ford's westerns, no clear reckoning of which songs appear in which films, scant critical analysis of how the film score in general and songs in particular operate narratively, thematically, structurally, and ideologically; few attempts to recreate the cultural contexts in which the songs were produced and received, and little investigation into the production histories of the scores. There is also a surprising amount of misinformation about the music in Ford westerns. This book is an attempt to rectify the situation, to fill a gap in the scholarship on Ford, by addressing a powerful system of meaning circulating through the westerns, one Ford recognized and, to an amazing degree controlled.

How the film score in general and songs in particular operate in Ford westerns is a rich site for investigation, encompassing a number of questions. How does the classical Hollywood film score function, and how do songs affect its operation? How does music operate in and through culture, and what happens to music's function when it becomes channeled through a film score? Song creates meaning through its simultaneous construction as music and text. How do songs function in individual films to anchor and amplify meaning? How do songs contribute to narrative construction, character development, and thematic enterprise? How do songs function as a form of cultural transmission, providing an access point into a film's ideological level? How have the changes in the cultural landscape since the heyday of the western influenced our understanding of the music in Ford's films and what it contributes to their meaning? What part do music and song play in the processes, both conscious and unconscious, that shape the way we experience these films? To what extent did Ford control the sound track, and what form did his participation take from film to film? I believe that answering these questions is essential to a full understanding of John Ford's westerns, given the key role their music plays and Ford's own direct participation in its selection and use.

To provide some answers, my inquiry has spread out in a number of critical directions, including cultural studies, feminist theory, masculinity studies, African American studies, ethnic studies, and discourses of authorship, and my research has encompassed a variety of sources in addition to the voluminous scholarship on Ford: production and music files and business records at RKO, Warner Bros., Twentieth Century–Fox, Paramount, Republic, and Argosy Pictures; archives or personal papers of John Ford, and several composers who worked for him, Erno Rapee, Louis Gruenberg, Victor Young, Max Steiner, George Duning, and Alex North; the holograph scores of Richard Hageman, George Duning, Alex North, and Max Steiner; and interviews and correspondence with many people, here and abroad, who have generously shared their knowledge of music and memories of John Ford with me. I hope I have been able to bring this wealth of material to bear on the issue of why it matters to pay attention to the music.

The book is organized around the films themselves, with some chapters devoted to individual films and others encompassing related titles as well. I treat all of Ford's sound westerns and the key extant silent westerns. As far as the surviving records permitted, I have reconstructed the production history of the score of each film, analyzing the musical score in general and the use of songs in detail. Providing the titles of the songs heard in each film proved to be a formidable task. The cue sheets for Ford's westerns, listing the titles of the music, have not all survived, and even when the cue sheets are available, they do not always list the songs by title, especially songs that were in the public domain, or thought to be by the studio. Thus I have in many cases had to rely on my own ears and those of others to identify the songs performed in the films or that find their way into the background score. I feel confident that the diegetic songs are all properly identified. When it comes to the nondiegetic score, however, and subtle allusions to, extremely brief quotations of, and homages to songs, I fear that sometimes Ford and his composers may be one step ahead of me. I think I've run a good race, though.

Each chapter has an individual focus as well, briefly summarized below, which connects the films through their music to larger cultural contexts. For purposes of full disclosure, I should state that I define the western as a film that takes place in the geographic space of the American West. Thus three films sometimes treated as westerns are not specifically considered here: *Drums Along the Mohawk* (1939), which although shot in Utah, takes place in New York, and *The Horse Soldiers* (1959) and "The Civil War" segment of *How the West Was Won* (1962), both of which transpire on the battlefields of the Civil War.

Chapter 1 tackles the question of authorship and argues that a consideration of the musical scores of John Ford's westerns demands a nuanced definition of authorship. This chapter addresses Ford's participation in the creation of the scores for his films, outlining Ford's relationship to music on and off the set and tracing the development of his musical aesthetic, forged in the silent era and tempered by the early years of sound film. Song is a particular kind of cultural transmission, rooted in historical, institutional, economic, aesthetic, and cultural practices, and its use reminds us that definitions of authorship need always be grounded within these larger contexts to fully understand the production of meaning.

Chapter 2 is devoted to Ford's silent films, focusing on two feature westerns, *The Iron Horse* and *3 Bad Men* (1926). For Ford, music was anything but incidental. He exploited the power of music, and especially song, to the full extent of the limited technology available to him in the silent era. The presence of music, and especially the performance of song, was an integral part of even his earliest films. An analysis of *The Iron Horse* focuses on the ways in which song in Ford's westerns is intertwined with the production of meaning. The performance of "Drill, Ye Terriers, Drill," for instance, reinforces the film's explicit message of assimilation as it taps into discourses about race, ethnicity, and national character and identity beneath the surface of the film. Song also provides an important access point to *3 Bad Men*. One of its male protagonists is associated with song, and his music makes him so sexually alluring that, at one point, he is almost overcome by an unintended listener made amorous by his performance. The relationship between music and masculinity, so central to Ford, and especially to the westerns, is sketched out here, and my comments prefigure an argument I make in greater depth in chapter 6.

Chapter 3 is devoted to Ford's first sound western, *Stagecoach,* and I have used the chapter as an opportunity to focus on song: its impact on the operation of the classical Hollywood film score, its simultaneous constitution as music and text, its function as cultural currency, its relationship to musical stereotyping, and its part in the processes, both conscious and unconscious, that shape filmic reception. The credits for *Stagecoach* announce that the score is "based on American Folk Songs." In staking a claim to a particular kind of musical heritage, *Stagecoach* converged with larger cultural currents of the era, especially in American art music, that were to shape the future of both American music and the genre of the western.

Chapter 4 pairs two films not typically connected: *My Darling Clementine* (1946) and *The Man Who Shot Liberty Valance* (1962). *My Darling Clementine* continues the musical trajectory of *Stagecoach*. Ford envisioned the sound track as a series of folk and period songs, but more simply arranged and orchestrated, and largely produced diegetically. Darryl F. Zanuck, production chief at Twentieth Century–Fox, had different ideas and not only recut and reshot some of the film but added orchestral cues, altering the musical design. This chapter reconstructs Ford's original intentions vis-à-vis the music and demonstrates the limits of Ford's considerable power in the Hollywood studio system.

If *My Darling Clementine* is the most Fordian of the western film scores, *The Man Who Shot Liberty Valance* runs a close second. Characterized by the same sparse musical textures and dependent upon source music, including many of Ford's favorite songs, *The Man Who Shot Liberty Valance* represents a return to Ford's musical roots. Standard readings of *The Man Who Shot Liberty Valance* position the film as a revisionist western. The musical score compels reconsideration. The film indeed looks backwards, but at least musically speaking, it is with as much nostalgia as critique, complicating the thorny issues of history and mythology with which the film grapples.

Chapter 5 focuses on two Argosy productions, *3 Godfathers* and *Wagon Master* (1950), films in which Ford had more direct control over the forces of production than he had in his studio work. Ironically, owning the company didn't make filmmaking any easier for Ford, and market forces would sometimes prove as difficult to negotiate as the power of studio executives. Nevertheless, Argosy was responsible for some of Ford's most popular films, as well as a significant portion of his westerns. Argosy also afforded him the opportunity to develop a relationship with the composer Richard Hageman, who was to score four Argosy westerns.

Ethnicity and its representation is a recurrent aspect of Ford's westerns, and in *3 Godfathers,* the clash and combination of Mexican and Anglo cultures finds interesting analogues in the music. In *Wagon Master,* Ford decided to use originally composed contemporary songs for the first time, and the celebrated country-and-western vocal and instrumental group Sons of the Pioneers provide several songs for the sound track. They were also to lend their distinctive sound to two other Ford westerns, *Rio Grande* and, most famously, *The Searchers.*

Chapter 6 is devoted to the cavalry trilogy: *Fort Apache, She Wore a Yellow Ribbon,* and *Rio Grande.* Although Ford did not conceive of these films as a trilogy, there is good reason, from a musical standpoint, to do so, since several songs (as well as characters, settings, and narratives) traverse all three films. Men and music have figured importantly in other Ford films and in other Ford westerns, but it is in the cavalry trilogy where the nuances of this pairing are played out the most fully against conventional cultural stereotypes of masculinity and femininity. Ethnicity, as it does in many Ford westerns, also figures prominently in the cavalry trilogy, but here it is Ford's own ethnic origins that take center stage. Ford has a complex relationship to his Irishness. Songs both complicate and enrich its representation. Sons of the Pioneers reappear in the last of the trilogy, *Rio Grande,* again bringing contemporary country-and-western music with them. This time, their songs function as an emotional undercurrent to the film, voicing, literally, the repressed desires of the characters.

Chapter 7 takes as its subject the film most Ford scholars cite as his masterpiece, *The Searchers.* A number of issues central to the film revolve around song: the formation and breakdown of community, the role of the archetypal western protagonist, and the place and function of gender, ethnicity, and race on the frontier. In *The Searchers,* these ideologically fraught issues are defined through music. Song also enters into the relationship between the film and contemporaneous social history. Given the central function of song in *The Searchers,* and its powerful cultural contexts, neglecting the score clearly diminishes our understanding of the film.

Chapter 8 treats *Two Rode Together* (1961) and *Sergeant Rutledge* (1960), films in the shadow of *The Searchers.* Like *The Searchers, Two Rode Together* is a captivity narrative that gave Ford the opportunity to reexamine the confrontation between Anglos and Indians in America's past. Unlike *The Searchers,* however, the musical score largely abandons folk and period music, although its use of the guitar raises interesting issues in the representation of ethnicity and anticipates later developments in the western film score.

When Ford made *The Searchers,* he thought he had made a socially conscious film with a progressive message about race. At the time of the film's release, critics and audiences seem to have missed the point. With *Sergeant Rutledge,* Ford highlighted race, and no one who saw the film could doubt Ford's intentions. Musically, however, *Sergeant Rutledge* has more in common with *Two Rode Together* than with *The Searchers,* and it contains little in the way of the characteristic folk and period music so intrinsic to earlier Ford westerns. But the score does have its one big moment, producing interesting echoes of *The Searchers*.

Chapter 9, the book's conclusion, focuses on Ford's last western, *Cheyenne Autumn* (1964). Ford's westerns are traversed by a variety of musical aesthetics positioned along a musical continuum: on the one end, the lean sparse sound of *My Darling Clementine*, with its virtual dependence upon the diegetic use of folk song, hymnody, and period music, and, on the other, the lush sound of the classical score in a film like *The Searchers*, in which folk song, hymnody, and period music are embedded. It seems somehow fitting that *Cheyenne Autumn* should absorb both ends of this spectrum, from the wall-to-wall aesthetic of Alex North's nondiegetic score to the virtually diegetic use of music in the central Dodge City sequence. As a conclusion to Ford's career, the score holds a few surprises too. For the first time, Ford initiated research on native American music, and in his attempt to incorporate it into the film, he anticipates Hollywood's discovery of world and ethnic music.

Late in his life, Ford told an interviewer, "I've always used a great deal of music in my pictures, although I don't have a good ear."[6] Mr. Ford, I beg to differ, and in the forthcoming pages, I hope to make my case.

CHAPTER I

How the West Was Sung

Music in the Life and Films of John Ford

There were two pianos in the Ford household, but neither John Ford nor anyone else in his immediate family played them.[1] Among the notable directors of Hollywood's classical studio era, Ford took the most active and sustained control of the music for his films, and yet he couldn't read music, he couldn't play an instrument, and he sang aloud only when drunk (and then only Irish songs), his grandson Dan told me.[2] Yet professional musicians listened to what he had to say about the music. Much is made and rightly so of Ford's extraordinary visual sense, an eye for composition that seldom failed him. Ford had a musical sense, too, an instinctive feeling for when to use music and an encyclopedic knowledge of what music to use. For the westerns, he liked folk songs, nineteenth-century popular tunes, and Protestant hymnody. Ford treated music in much the same way he treated dialogue: pared it down to its essence, eliminated the irrelevant, and delivered it simply and without affectation. Such a minimalist approach, of course, depends upon choosing exactly the right line of dialogue and exactly the right piece of music. Repeatedly, and with a remarkable consistency, given Hollywood's mode of production, this is what Ford was able to do.

Born John Martin Feeney in 1894 (although he claimed otherwise) near Portland, Maine, to Irish immigrant parents, John Ford was the youngest of six surviving children. A sensitive child, and a reader, he was also a tough football player who earned an athletic scholarship to the University of Maine. After a difficult entry into college life, Jack "Bull"

Feeney followed his brother Frank to Hollywood. Billed as Francis Ford (it was Frank who adopted the less ethnic surname), Frank had become a silent film actor and director. Eventually, he founded his own production company. He was thus in a position to provide his brother with an apprenticeship in the business, and he did. Jack Ford began directing in 1917.

A reversal of fortunes visited the Ford brothers in the 1920s. Under the tutelage of the cowboy star Harry Carey, Jack produced a series of successful contemporary westerns, and, as John Ford, was catapulted to international acclaim for *The Iron Horse.* Frank was plagued by domestic woes, alcoholism, and business problems and hit bottom. He would find work as a character actor in his brother's films for the rest of his life.

Ford plugged away through the transition to sound and eventually became Twentieth Century–Fox's most dependable director. With a string of critical and box office successes in the late 1930s and 1940s, he was Hollywood's most prestigious filmmaker, winning four Academy Awards as Best Director, and two more for his documentaries, a total unmatched to this day. Powerful, difficult, and cantankerous, he worked within the studio system but managed to go his own way nonetheless, butting heads with studio executives but generally thriving in Hollywood. It would be 1939 before he returned to the westerns that had been his entry into the industry and made *Stagecoach,* a film in which he cast his young friend John Wayne. Westerns would be a central thread in the fabric of Ford's opus, and several of his last films were westerns, but he never won an Academy Award for his work in the genre by which he is now defined.

Any book that devotes itself to the work of a single director needs to confront its own assumptions about authorship and at very least make them explicit for its readers. The field of film studies has been marked since its inception as an academic discipline in the 1960s by auteurism, a romantic and powerful definition of the director as a visionary artist and the source of filmic meaning. Not all directors were deemed auteurs, only those who were able to leave their personal imprint on a film. Ford was fairly early on championed as an auteur; Andrew Sarris in *The American Cinema* (1968) placed him in his legendary pantheon of directors,[3] and there is a prodigious industry still devoted to this view of Ford today.[4] Auteur status was largely equated with control over the mise-en-scène in these early formulations, influenced no doubt by *Cahiers du cinema,* the journal in whose pages the notion of the director as auteur first appeared. Ford's status was seen as the result of his ability to render story, character, and theme in visual terms. Even the structuralist approaches to authorship that followed, notably Peter Wollen's work on Ford in *Signs and Meaning in the Cinema* (1969) tended to privilege visual language.[5] Music was ignored in shaping these arguments.

Ford was able to exert control over an aspect of film production to which few directors in the studio system even had access, and his relationship to the music challenges traditional notions of what constitutes film authorship. Of the American directors elevated to auteur status by the critics, few directly became involved with the score (D. W. Griffith, King Vidor, and Charles Chaplin, in the silent era, and Orson Welles in his limited collaborations with Bernard Herrmann, in the sound era, are notable exceptions). Most directors left the music in the capable hands of composers. Ford, however, generally chose the songs for his films himself, and since their scores largely consist of songs, and are sometimes even limited to songs, surely this complicates things. Does Ford deserve special status in the pantheon of directors? Or is the concept of auteurism unable to accommodate a director who controlled more than just the visual field? Ignoring the score may be the least of traditional auteurism's problems, and it has long since been put to rest in academic film studies as a viable approach to understanding meaning production. But auteurism is not alone in its short-sightedness.

Under the influence of the poststructuralist revolution of the 1970s, more recent theories have repositioned authorship within a network of meaning production that exceeds the director. John Ford is no longer simply seen as an individual artist working within an assembly-line mode of production who was able to transcend the system and mark his films with personal meaning. Rather, "John Ford" is a site determined by a variety of industrial, institutional, economic, social, legal, cultural, and psychic practices that have the power to govern the ways in which films are interpreted. At its most extreme, directors are regarded as the products of psychic and cultural forces that leave them little or no control over meaning. Although these theories posit more sophisticated models for meaning production in film, they often share the visual bias of traditional auteurism.

My own theory of authorship, evolved over the course of writing this book, is situated somewhere between the positions briefly sketched in the two preceding paragraphs. Studying the musical scores of films has made it impossible for me to ignore the impact of culture on filmic meaning. Music is a form of cultural transmission, trailing preestablished responses that influence filmic meaning in powerful ways. These responses can be exploited for specific reasons, but they do not originate with the director. Cultural meaning has a life of its own, and it always exceeds the individual.

At the same time, I find it difficult to turn my back on the individual. Business and production records indicate that Ford directly influenced the scores of the films that bear his name. He was notorious for collaborating on all aspects of a film's production, including the musical score. He had a prodigious knowledge of nineteenth-century American history, and he knew the music of the period. In the end, I realize that I think about authorship in cultural and individual terms, however uncomfortably those two concepts co-exist. I fear that in erasing the individual author from authorship, the discipline has unduly narrowed its understanding of meaning production. (And perhaps this is why auteur theory has had such a long shelf life outside academia.) Or maybe I just cannot give up on human agency and the idea that the power of culture ultimately finds its expression through individuals. I am neither the first to point out the power to govern meaning contained in the signature of a powerful director nor the last to throw up my hands in frustration in attempting to ascertain the source of filmic meaning. Considering the musical score and tracing its impact in John Ford westerns has convinced me that definitions of authorship are central to our discipline; that "old-fashioned" ideas of authorship can offer useful theoretical and methodological strategies when grounded in industrial, economic, aesthetic, social, cultural, and psychic contexts; that production history and biography have important perspectives to impart to our understanding of filmic meaning; and that a recognition of the importance of the musical score enriches our understanding of John Ford's westerns.

To put those perspectives in perspective, if you will, I devote the remainder of this chapter to Ford and music, to his collaboration on the musical scores for his films, to the evolution of his musical aesthetic from his earliest silent westerns through the early years of sound, and to the part music played in his life on and off the set. The similarities among the scores of Ford's westerns, the striking recurrence of the same songs, across numerous genres, produced by different studios in different eras and scored by different composers, as well as the extent to which many of the songs are not typical or used conventionally, has convinced me that there is a kind of music that I am prepared to describe as Fordian. How else to account for "Ten Thousand Cattle" being cut from *Stagecoach* only to reappear in *My Darling Clementine*; the appearance of

"Red River Valley" in *The Grapes of Wrath* (1940), *They Were Expendable* (1945), *Wagon Master,* and *My Darling Clementine;* "Oh, Bury Me Not on the Lone Prairie" in *Stagecoach, Fort Apache, She Wore a Yellow Ribbon* and *3 Godfathers;* "The Cuckoo Waltz" in *Young Mr. Lincoln* (1939), *My Darling Clementine,* and *The Sun Shines Bright* (1953); "Garry Owen" in *The Long Voyage Home* (1940), *Fort Apache, She Wore a Yellow Ribbon, The Long Gray Line* (1955), and *The Searchers;* "Sweet Genevieve" in *Hell Bent, Fort Apache,* and *The Man Who Shot Liberty Valance;* "Shall We Gather at the River?" in *Stagecoach, The Grapes of Wrath, Tobacco Road* (1941), *My Darling Clementine, 3 Godfathers, Wagon Master, The Searchers,* and *7 Women* (1965); "The Battle-cry of Freedom" in *The Prisoner of Shark Island* (1936), *Young Mr. Lincoln, Stagecoach,* and *They Were Expendable* (1945), "Lorena" in *The Searchers* and *The Horse Soldiers;* and "Battle Hymn of the Republic" and "Dixie" in Ford films too numerous to mention here. And this list is by no means inclusive.[6] Years after the completion of a film, Ford could still recall its songs, correcting interviewers who misremembered song titles or the films in which they were heard.

Furthermore, while the song choices in Ford's films may now seem typical, what anyone might use in a similar situation, I would point out that there is nothing obvious about a Texas cowboy tune representing the forced migration of Okies to California during the Great Depression or a western dirge accompanying the progress of a stagecoach. Songs in Ford westerns can be obscure, anachronistic, used out of context. That they now seem obvious choices is largely a function of hindsight and the powerful connections in Ford between music and visual images.

Ford was involved in every aspect of a film's production. Although he never took screen credit, he supervised the writing of the screenplay and often created dialogue on the set. He described himself as "a cameraman rather than a director,"[7] and there is plenty of evidence that he determined and set up the shots for his films. Ford exerted a large measure of control over the editing process too. "I cut in the camera and that's it."[8] Ford would shoot so economically, generally aiming for only one take, that studio editors were left with few options but to follow his editing plan. Darryl F. Zanuck at Twentieth Century–Fox seems to have been the most successful at trimming Ford's work; others, like Herbert Yates at Republic, got nowhere.

Ford also collaborated on the sound track. Through the power and prestige he had accrued in Hollywood, his knowledge of music, and the force of his combustible personality, he was in a unique position for a

Hollywood director of his era. He wasn't always invested in the musical score per se (this may be because he worked with composers he trusted), but he cared about the songs, and he was in a position to select them himself, both those performed in the film and those heard in the background score. Correspondence about song choice and even song lyrics turns up in Ford's files, not in the composer's, and Ford even wrote custom lyrics for some of the period songs heard in his films.

The process of selecting songs differed from film to film. Ford sometimes had very specific ideas about the music very early on in the production process. Some diegetic songs are clearly noted in the scenarios of the silent era and the screenplays of his sound films. More often they are not. The business of choosing songs could be an ongoing process, extending into the shooting schedule, with final selections sometimes made as late as the location shooting in some cases, surprising the very actors called upon to perform. It is important and revealing to note that the songs heard in Ford's films do not appear in the source material, with one exception: "The Holy City" in Peter Kyne's book *The Three Godfathers* also figures in Ford's *3 Godfathers*.[9]

Ford liked to work with composers that he knew and trusted. He didn't always choose the composer, and sometimes he wasn't satisfied with the score even when he did. But when afforded the opportunity to choose, he did so. Richard Hageman became virtually the house composer at Argosy Pictures, Ford's production company. And when Hageman wanted a job on a Ford film, he wrote to Ford. Even as late as *Cheyenne Autumn,* at a time when Ford's power in Hollywood was waning, Warner Bros. waited to hire the composer Alex North until Ford had approved the choice. Although evaluating the quality of a film score is a notoriously subjective process, I am willing to assert that many of the composers who worked for Ford did their best work for him. If you have any doubt, listen to the score for, say, *Angel and the Badman* (James Edward Grant, 1947) alongside *She Wore a Yellow Ribbon* to hear the difference Ford made to the career of Richard Hageman. Or compare *Shane* (George Stevens, 1953) to *Rio Grande,* both scored by Victor Young. After *Angel and the Badman,* Hageman confessed to Ford that he would never score another western, but Ford could be very persuasive. Hageman scored four more for Ford.

From the beginning, Ford understood music's power, and he included songs even in his earliest films. Musical performances were anything but incidental for him, and songs, in particular, fulfilled clear dramatic functions in his silent westerns. In *Straight Shooting* (1917), the cowboys relax listening to phonograph records, and when their boss arrives, he orders the music stopped. In *Bucking Broadway* (1918), the cowboys gather around a piano to sing "Home, Sweet Home" after the protagonist, Cheyenne Harry (Harry Carey), learns that he has been jilted by the woman he loves, the song an audible expression of his loss. In *Hell Bent,* Cheyenne Harry (Harry Carey) and Cimarron Bill (Duke Lee) drunkenly sing "Sweet Genevieve," but their singing and the sentiment attached to it differentiates them from the rest of the drunken rabble in the saloon. In *The Iron Horse,* the Union Pacific and Central Pacific rail gangs sing "Drill, Ye Terriers, Drill," whose lyrics encapsulate the film's theme of cooperation and assimilation and whose rhythms force the men to work together. In *3 Bad Men,* Dan (George O'Brien) sings "All the Way from Ireland" and later serenades his love with a harmonica, expressing the seductive power often attached to song in Ford.

Ford not only understood music's power, he exploited it to the full extent of the technology available to him. Direct cueing, the practice of inserting song lyrics into the intertitles during the visual performance of music, was a recognizable feature of silent cinema's golden age, exploited in some of the era's most successful films: "Kashmiri Song," aka "Pale Hands I Loved," in *The Sheik* (George Medford, 1921); "Oh! Susannah" in *The Covered Wagon* (James Cruze, 1923); "You're in the Army Now" in *The Big Parade* (King Vidor, 1925), and "Prisoner's Song" in *Steamboat Bill, Jr.* (Charles Reisner, 1928). Ford appears to have been using direct cues even earlier, however, inserting song lyrics into routine westerns, not the typical genre for such a sophisticated practice. Rick Altman points out that the song lyrics spelled trouble for accompanists, who could no longer use the intertitles for transitions between pieces, a common practice at the time to ensure musical continuity.[10] In an era when directors had virtually no control over the musical accompaniment, Ford was using direct cues to manage at least some of the songs that accompanists chose, resulting in the occasional but identifiable synchronization between music and image during screenings.

In *Bucking Broadway,* the performance of "Home, Sweet Home" is initiated by a close-up of a cowboy picking out the melody on a piano. For those in the audience who play the instrument, this shot functions as a direct and unmistakable cue for a specific song. The intertitles dispel any ambiguity: the lyrics of "Home, Sweet Home" appear on the screen as the cowboys sing. Ford has, in effect, tied accompanists' hands. And this was in 1917. In *Hell Bent,* the lyrics of "Sweet Genevieve" appear on the screen, intercut with shots of the singing. It's hard to imag-

ine an accompanist choosing anything else. In *The Iron Horse*, characters clearly mouth the lyrics to "Drill, Ye Terriers, Drill," which again
appear as intertitles. Here the sequence is actually edited to the rhythms
of the song. Erno Rapee, who scored for the film for its New York premiere, used "Drill, Ye Terriers Drill" so often that reviewers left
whistling the tune.

Ford hated interviews and was a notoriously difficult subject; his lack
of cooperation with journalists and film critics is legendary. But sometimes his seemingly unresponsive answers can be revelatory, as in this
reply to a critic's question about "'what happened when sound came in':
'Nothing. We made them with sound.'"[11] There is more than a grain of
truth here for, in fact, Ford employed many of the same strategies he had
used in the silent era to control the music in his first sound-on-film feature, *Mother Machree* (1928).[12] The single surviving sequence of synchronized sound in the film is a song, "Mother Machree." Its performance follows a direct cue: a close-up of the sheet music on the piano, with
the clearly visible music and lyrics of the song.

Ford would soon develop more sophisticated techniques for incorporating musical performance, but it must have been liberating, in those
early years of sound production, to be able to determine the aural as well
as the visual performances. Ford inserted songs into bleak melodramas
like *Four Sons* (1928), comedies like *Riley the Cop* (1928), action-
adventure films like *The Black Watch* (1929) and *Seas Beneath* (1931),
prison pictures like *Up the River* (1930), and literary adaptations, like
Arrowsmith (1931).

Ford's musical aesthetic was born in the silent era and was based on
an understanding of music's power and the development of strategies for
controlling it. Direct cues, close-ups, and specific editing patterns would
help get accompanists to use the songs Ford chose. With the advent of
mechanically reproduced sound, Ford could ensure that his choices
would be heard. By including many of the songs as diegetic performances, he could more directly control their use, selecting the songs and
filming the performances sometimes before a composer was even assigned to the film. Many of the musical performances were recorded live
on the set, including the singing. This sometimes put composers in the
position of having to ask Ford what music he had already chosen for
"their" scores.

Ford's musical aesthetic evolved during the late 1920s to the mid
1930s, when he learned a certain economy of means with regard to the
music. Most typical Hollywood films from this era limit the performance

of music to visible sources, such as dance bands, radios, and wandering violinists, banishing nondiegetic background music, which compromised the realist aesthetic promoted in these early years of sound production. (Where was the music coming from?) The first successful inclusion of nondiegetic background music is generally credited to *King Kong* (Ernst B. Schoedsack and Merian C. Cooper, 1933), scored by Max Steiner, although there were certainly earlier, limited experiments in nondiegetic background scoring. With 75 minutes of the film's 100-minute running time filled with lush orchestral music, *King Kong* dramatically altered Hollywood's approach to the sound track, and by 1935, films were filled with lush nondiegetic film scores. Despite the fact that Steiner scored three films for Ford in the mid 1930s, Ford resisted the wall-to-wall scoring and the orchestral sounds of late romanticism that soon became a hallmark of studio production.

Ford liked music simply orchestrated and sparingly used. "Generally, I hate music in pictures—a little bit now and then, at the end or at the start," he told Peter Bogdanovich. Ford wasn't opposed to the use of nondiegetic music per se, however, and he went on to say: "but something like the Ann Rutledge theme *belongs*."[13] But he was certainly wary of too much of it. Robert Parrish, a child actor and later editor, remembered Ford's response to finishing *Young Mr. Lincoln*: "Look, the picture's finished now. I know you're going to try to louse it up—you're going to put in too much music, or over-cut or under-cut it or something—but try not to spoil this for me because I think it's a good picture."[14] As Parrish's recollection indicates, Ford was not always in a position to fully realize his musical ambitions, and the score would thus prove to be something of a battlefield, as the production histories of several films, such as *They Were Expendable* and *My Darling Clementine,* demonstrate.

In the early sound era, Ford worked as a contract director. He quickly learned to adapt to the new medium and increasingly managed to include the performance of songs: "Little Mother" in *Four Sons;* "Auld Lang Syne" in *The Black Watch;* "Girl of My Dreams," "M-O-T-H-E-R," and "Red, White, and Blue" in *Up the River;* "The Monkeys Have No Tails in Zamboanga" in *Seas Beneath;* "Silent Night" in *Airmail* (1932); "Rose of Tralee," "The Minstrel Boy," and "Believe Me, If All Those Endearing Young Charms" in *The Informer* (1935). The trilogy Ford made with Will Rogers is loaded with music, memorably "My Old Kentucky Home" sung by Hattie McDaniel in *Judge Priest* (1934) and "There's No Place Like Home" played on a saw in *Steamboat Round the Bend*

(1936). "Dixie" is played for President Lincoln in *The Prisoner of Shark Island* (1936), William Priest has it played to influence the jury in *Judge Priest*, and Lincoln plays it himself in *Young Mr. Lincoln.*

By the 1940s, when Ford was Hollywood's most prestigious director, the diegetic performance of hymns, folk songs, and period music became something of a trademark: "Red River Valley" played on the accordion by Danny Borzage and sung, briefly, by Henry Fonda in *The Grapes of Wrath,* "Garry Owen," played on an accordion (Danny Borzage again), and "Shenandoah" and "When Irish Eyes Are Smiling" sung in *The Long Voyage Home,* "Cwm Rhondda" sung in Welsh and "God Save the Queen" in English in *How Green Was My Valley,* "Red River Valley" (again on Danny Borzage's accordion) in *The Battle of Midway* (1942), and "The Monkeys Have No Tails in Zamboanga" and "Dear Old Girl" sung by sailors in *They Were Expendable.* But it was in Ford's westerns where the use of song took on iconic proportions. *Stagecoach* alone includes fifteen pieces of period music, many of them songs, and all of the sound westerns that followed incorporate period song in one form or another.

Harry Carey Jr., a regular in Ford's stock company of actors in the late 1940s and 1950s, has clear memories of the music: "There was a very special feeling on every John Ford set. It was the feeling that something great was happening, a feeling of reverence. It wasn't a feeling of reverence for John Ford; it was a feeling of reverence for art. It was like being in church. Maybe the music had something to do with it."[15] Maybe it did. There certainly was enough of it on a Ford set. In 1924, the accordionist Danny Borzage, brother of the director Frank Borzage, signed on to provide mood music on his accordion for *The Iron Horse,* and he continued to do so for Ford on and off the set for the next forty years. The day would start with the arrival of cast and crew, each of the major players accompanied by a theme song, selected by Borzage: John Wayne eventually acquired "Maquita" from *They Were Expendable;* Ward Bond, "Wagons West" from *Wagon Master,* Henry Fonda, "Red River Valley" from *The Grapes of Wrath,* and Harry Carey Jr., "The Streets of Laredo" from 3 *Godfathers.* John Ford entered to "Bringing in the Sheaves," one of his favorite hymns.

There was plenty of singing on location too, after the day's shooting was over, when cast and crew assembled to wind down and find amusement. Drinking was *verboten,* but sing-alongs were encouraged. On *The Iron Horse,* the singing started as the train bearing cast and crew left Union Station in Los Angeles, with "My Darling Clementine" and "The

Yellow Rose of Texas" sung that first night. Ford joined in the singing and told some stories of his own.[16] Singing appears to have continued unabated throughout the production. The circus train pressed into service as sleeping quarters had a separate car dubbed "Camp Ford Theatre," devoted to entertainments such as sing-alongs, minstrel shows, Indian war chants and dances, jazz performances, and even a talent show to benefit Children's Hospital in Hollywood. (Ford had taken to warming his feet on location by tearing off "a few steps of the Indian War Dance.")[17] "Drill, Ye Terriers, Drill" caused a minor sensation when members of the cast would launch into it for "spasmodic outbursts of vocal exercise many times during the day."[18]

According to Maureen O'Hara, "Oh, we had to do concerts every night."[19] Singing was so much a part of a Ford location that to amuse themselves, cast and crew would sometimes make up new songs to familiar melodies. For *Two Rode Together*, Ken Curtis created special lyrics, which Ford loved, for "Bringing in the Sheaves." During *How Green Was My Valley*, Ford himself composed some for "The Farmer in the Dell" to accompany the appearance on the set of the writer Philip Dunne: "We haven't changed a line / We haven't changed a line / It's just the way you wro-ote it, / We haven't changed a line."

Like most directors of the silent era, Ford used live music on the set to create mood and atmosphere, but Ford would continue the practice throughout his entire career, an exceptional perhaps if not unique practice during the sound era! In the silent era, live music could be played during filming; in the sound era, music was played on Ford's sets, both on location and in the studio, as the scene was being readied for action and during rehearsals. Usually, Dan Borzage would play the accordion, and sometimes he would be joined by others. Rudy Behlmer reports that "Oh, Bury Me Not on the Lone Prairie" was played on location during the shooting of *Stagecoach*.[20] Pippa Scott describes how music was used on the set of *The Searchers*. "Pappy [Ford] did something very very special which I've never really encountered again. And that was that straight through your dialogue, straight through important moments in the picture, he let Borzage play all kinds of music that he thought was emotionally correct for the moment, which profoundly affected the actors."[21] John Wayne remembered just such "soft music on the set," putting him in the mood for some of the more difficult, emotional scenes in *The Searchers*.[22] Although Wayne does not identify the tunes he heard, it is not hard to imagine Borzage playing the same songs that would later turn up on the sound track.

Figure 1. Singing at the Field Photo Farm. Front row, from left: Ken Curtis,
John Ford, John Wayne at the microphone, Harry Carey Jr., and Danny
Borzage on the accordion. Courtesy Lilly Library, Indiana University, Bloom-
ington, IN, and Dan Ford.

Borzage's mood music was not limited, however, to off-camera moments. His accordion can be heard in *The Grapes of Wrath* ("Red River
Valley"), *The Long Voyage Home* ("Garry Owen"), *The Battle of Midway* ("Red River Valley" again), *My Darling Clementine* ("My Darling
Clementine"), *The Searchers* ("Shall We Gather at the River?"), and *The
Man Who Shot Liberty Valance* (Ann Rutledge's theme). Borzage plays
the accordion on camera in *3 Godfathers* ("Silent Night"), *Wagon Master* ("Come, Come Ye Saints") and *The Searchers* ("The Yellow Rose of
Texas"),[23] and he appears as an extra in films too numerous to mention.

Off the set, music was an important part of Ford's life as well. To
begin with, Ford was very knowledgeable about music, and he didn't listen indiscriminately. Despite living above the Hollywood Bowl, he never
attended a concert there, and he didn't listen to the radio. But he liked
live music. Many of the same performers who appear in Ford westerns
appeared in Ford's living room, among them the Sons of the Pioneers, the
former Pioneer and Ford's son-in-law Ken Curtis, Harry Carey Jr., and
Stan Jones. Live music was also an important part of the Field Photo
Farm in the San Fernando Valley, Ford's home away from home after the

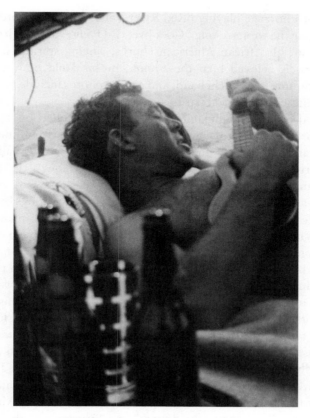

Figure 2. Ward Bond and ukulele aboard the *Araner*.
Courtesy Lilly Library, Indiana University, Bloomington, IN, and Dan Ford.

war, which provided a clubhouse for veterans of the Field Photographic
branch that Ford had commanded. Holiday and other get-togethers there
were always accompanied by music. Sometimes Harry Carey Jr. would
sing (he remembers "The Streets of Laredo" and "Come, Come Ye
Saints," as well as unnamed songs with John Wayne) or Sons of the Pioneers would perform. At Christmastime, Jimmy Stewart played "Jingle
Bells" on the accordion. Ford's grandson Dan remembers the music as
distinctly multicultural, decades before the term began to be used, with
country-and-western music interspersed with Hawaiian music (not generally known outside of Hawaii at that time), gospel music, and conventional popular songs. Harry Carey Jr. remembers bagpipers. Harry
Carey Sr.'s funeral was held at the Field Photo Farm, orchestrated by

Ford, with Borzage playing "Red River Valley" on his accordion, Burl
Ives singing the western song "Goodbye, Old Paint," and the Jester Hairston Choir, an African American chorus, singing spirituals. Even on
board Ford's beloved boat the *Araner,* music could be heard: home
movies capture a mariachi band, and candid photos include plenty of informal music-making on board.

Ford also owned and maintained an extensive collection of commercial recordings, which included classics of eighteenth- and nineteenth-
century art music; opera and original cast recordings of Broadway musicals; Irish, Welsh, Italian, and Mexican folk songs; Tahitian and
Hawaiian music; American folk songs; spirituals; cowboy songs and
country-and-western music, including numerous recordings by the Sons
of the Pioneers; military music; bugle calls; John Phillip Sousa marches;
religious music; Christmas music; big band music; Latin big band music;
and recordings by popular singers such as the Andrews Sisters, Frank
Sinatra, Bing Crosby, and Rudy Vallee.[24] Ford would listen to his collection during the preproduction and scripting stages of a new film. According to Patrick Ford, the director's son, "He'd lock himself in his
'den,' with his old 'victrola' and play records to put himself in a scene-
creating mood."[25] That the scores for Ford westerns include the some of
the same songs that are catalogued in Ford's surviving record collection
can hardly be a coincidence: "Oh, Bury Me Out on the Lone Prairie,"[26]
"Red River Valley," Home, Sweet Home," "[I Dream of] Jeanie with the
Light Brown Hair," "The Girl I Left Behind Me," "Carry Me Back to
Old Virginny," "Home on the Range," and "The Irish Washerwoman."

According to Dan Ford, John Ford's grandson and first biographer,
the music was Ford's top and sometimes only priority during postproduction. Dan had the opportunity of working with his grandfather on
only one occasion, on the 1971 CBS documentary *The American West
of John Ford.* Ford, he recalled, "really was paying attention when we
did the music, when we scored it."[27] The documentary largely consists
of clips from the westerns, but John Ford proved surprisingly uninter-
ested in the editing. In fact, the only postproduction appearance he made
was at the scoring session. "For John Ford, there was no need for dialogue," James Stewart observes in *The American West of John Ford.*
"The music said it all." That might well serve as the thesis of this book.

CHAPTER 2

Hearing the Music in John Ford's Silents

The Iron Horse and *3 Bad Men*

It may seem rather odd to begin the analysis of music in John Ford westerns with silent examples. But as I note in chapter 1, Ford's musical aesthetic was forged in the silent era and tempered in the early years of sound. Thus the two surviving feature-length westerns generally regarded as Ford's silent masterpieces, *The Iron Horse* and *3 Bad Men*, merit more than passing mention. I am interested in the privileging of songs in these westerns, the production numbers—their function in terms of the construction of narrative, character, and theme, and their impact on the ideological undercurrents of these films. Both *The Iron Horse* and *3 Bad Men* exploit song, and they share themes that would prove central to later Ford westerns—manifest destiny, national identity, and the definition of masculinity. Taken together, *The Iron Horse* and *3 Bad Men* provide a model, in microcosm, for the ways in which song functions in Ford's westerns.

The Iron Horse tells the story of the building of the transcontinental railroad, largely focusing on the Union Pacific moving westward. Steeped in the optimism of the 1920s, the film unproblematically presents the doctrine of Manifest Destiny. When Ford conceived *The Iron Horse*, the impact of the railroad's construction was a distant memory, and the ambivalent reception initially accorded it had been blunted by nostalgia. For most Americans, the transcontinental railroad had created civilization out of the wilderness, provided jobs, and opened new territories for exploration. Inaugurated during the Civil War in 1862, and completed seven years ahead of schedule, the railroad seemed nothing less than a miracle of technology. It was "a monument to American energy."[1] Robert Louis Stevenson would write of its construction, "if it be heroism that we require, what was Troy to this?"[2] It would be left to later decades to point out that the transcontinental railroad not only displaced the Native Americans[3] whose tribal lands the rails intersected but destroyed their hunting grounds and the vast herds of buffalo that inhabited them. The railroad exploited its labor force—largely freed slaves and immigrants, including thousands of Chinese imported for the arduous work of the Central Pacific and abandoned when the work was complete. Pneumonia, poisoning, drowning, and sun- and heatstroke beset the laborers. Strikes for better conditions and pay were common. Exploitation of labor and rampant corruption made a number of white men extremely rich. By 1900, almost half of the millionaires in the United States had made their fortunes on the railroad.

To most Americans in the 1920s, however, when railroads are said to have employed one out of every twenty workers in this country, the train stood for something overwhelmingly positive and uniquely American.[4] As Lynne Kirby points out in her study of the train in cinema, crossing geographic barriers became linked in the public consciousness with crossing social barriers. The transcontinental railway, in particular, came to be regarded as a symbol of democracy and an expression of national identity.[5] By the 1920s, train travel was already on the decline,[6] however, and *The Iron Horse* would benefit from the nostalgia that was beginning to attach to the railroad. In fact, the film rode that nostalgia all the way to the bank.

The Iron Horse, one of the top-grossing films of the 1920s, also proved to be Ford's first international success.[7] But its production was plagued by problems. Uncharacteristically over budget and behind schedule, Ford infuriated studio executives at William Fox Pictures, who watched costs soar to $280,000. Relegated to the sidelines by location shooting in the Sierra Nevada near Wadsworth, Nevada, in winter, Fox executives threatened Ford by telegram. Ford ignored them, holding up one of their telegrams for Pardner Jones, a crew member and crack shot, to put a bullet through it. One legendary anecdote has Ford answering a production manager's complaint about shooting delays by tearing ten pages out of the script: "Now we're three days ahead of schedule."[8] Such stories should be taken with a grain of salt, however—especially when Ford is telling them, and I've seen this anecdote attributed to any number of different Ford films and even different directors. It may be apocryphal, but Ford stuck to it, and as late as 1964, he was still repeating it. The production chief, Sol Wurtzel, was sent to rein Ford in, but was lured instead into a three-day crap game. "He never did get around to inspecting the books," Ford recalled.[9] Ultimately, Wurtzel came to Ford's defense, interceding for him with the New York office. William Fox himself demanded to see the footage. He liked what he saw and gave Ford the go-ahead, hoping the film would rival Paramount's successful western of the previous year, *The Covered Wagon* (1923). It did. *The Iron Horse* turned out to be Ford's "crowning triumph," and the studio promoted it in a massive publicity campaign: "A Regiment of United States Troops and Cavalry; 3,000 Railway Workmen; 1,000 Chinese laborers; 800 Pawnee, Sioux and Cheyenne Indians; 2,800 Horses; 1,300 Buffaloes; 10,000 Texas Steers . . . [and] the actual old-time locomotives 'Jupiter' of the old Central Pacific line and '116' of the Union Pacific."[10] This last part actually turned out to be true.

Scholars of the western have generally argued that, as a genre, the western is occupied with defining the nation by circulating generative myths about the formation of the nation and its national character. Westerns are thus concerned, if only implicitly, with questions of who or what is an American. This issue emerges in the genre as early as the 1920s, and *The Iron Horse* is a prime example. The film both narrativizes the doctrine of Manifest Destiny, hinging the happiness of the main characters on the successful completion of the railroad, and mythologizes assimilation as the democratic entry point into American identity. Music plays a key role in that myth.

The plot of *The Iron Horse* concerns childhood sweethearts, Davy Brandon (George O'Brien) and Miriam (Marge Bellamy), separated by time and circumstance and reunited by the transcontinental railroad. Davy, a surveyor, goes to work for Miriam's father, a contractor for the Union Pacific, and befriends a group of Irish immigrants. Miriam's father is desperate to find a pass through the Black Hills to keep on schedule; Davy knows of such a pass but is betrayed and left for dead by the railroad's chief engineer, Miriam's fiancé, Peter Jesson (Cyril Chadwick). Missed opportunities and misunderstandings keep the lovers apart, and Davy defects to the Central Pacific. When the railroads are united at Promontory Point, Utah, so, too, are Davy and Miriam. The union of the country through the railroad is mirrored in the joining of the couple.

Part of the explicit message of the film is the need for tolerance and cooperation. This is played out among the immigrant laborers, who must learn to put aside their cultural differences, accept one another, and work together to become a powerful, coordinated labor force. Their ability to do so, reflected in the rhythm in which they learn to work, enables the completion of the railroad. The joining of Davy and Miriam at the end of the film mirrors and reinforces a number of unions: the joining of the East Coast to the West Coast; the uniting of Civil War veterans, "ex-soldiers of the North and South working peacefully side by side"; the marriage of Tony, an Italian laborer, and Nora Hogan, an Irishwoman; and the wedding of the rails themselves, celebrated in a ceremony with the driving of a golden spike. The formation of the couple and the completion of the railroad converge. Tony and Nora get caught up in the bargain; now assimilated, they ride the coattails of America's destiny. Of Ford's work on *The Iron Horse,* Dan Ford would write: "His vision was never more optimistic."[11] As Ford's vision darkened, however, it also deepened. His later films would be peopled with a diverse collection of ethnic types who resist cultural homogenization. But *The Iron Horse* has no such complications. Song plays a key role in its optimism, a musical evocation of unity and cooperation, a reminder of the necessity of both tolerance and fitting in, and homage to the value of hard work.

There were several sources for the film. A surviving version of the scenario references Edwin L. Sabin's monumental study *Building the Pacific Railroad* (1919). Another source, clearly, were the photographs of Alexander Gardener documenting the railroad's construction. Ford's ending tableau duplicates Gardener's widely reproduced photograph of the ceremony at Promontory Point. The railroad novel, a popular subgenre in western fiction well into the twentieth century, was an important and even determining influence as well. From 1890 to 1910, railroad fiction was one of the most popular genres in American fiction.[12] Rail-roading novels had their own stock types, such as the brash and brawny young protagonist out to make his fortune in the West, a beautiful and unattached young woman, and immigrant workers, largely Irish, who serve as comic foils, along with formulaic plot devices such as the search for the pass, the Indian attack, the singing of the work crews, and convergence of heterosexual romance and the completion of the railroad. These generic elements figure prominently in Zane Grey's popular *The U. P. Trail* (1918), which features a handsome, brawny young surveyor, a trio of Irish immigrants whom he befriends, an on-again-off-again romance between the surveyor and the woman he loves, and a dramatic reunion between them at the joining of the rails at Promontory Point.[13]

A third source for *The Iron Horse* may have been Ford himself: "I was always interested in the railroad and wanted to make a picture about it," he said.[14] He recalled that his Uncle Mike, an Irish immigrant who had labored on the Union Pacific, had "told me stories about it and taught me the songs they had sung."[15] Of course, this was the same Uncle Mike who supposedly quipped that Gettysburg "was horrible. I went six whole days without a drink."[16] Various railroading songs of the era, including "Drill, Ye Terriers, Drill," may have been taught to Ford by his Uncle Mike, but Ford always knew how to tell a good story, and he could be full of blarney.[17]

"Drill, Ye Terriers, Drill" (aka "Drill, Ye Tarriers, Drill" aka "Drill You Tarriers Drill") is a song whose historical origins are clouded, and whether or not it is a genuine folk ballad actually sung by railroad workers is an open question.[18] Most of the great transcontinental railroad ballads emerged in the 1870s and 1880s, after construction was complete. In fact, "Drill, Ye Terriers, Drill" enjoyed its most widespread popularity when it was introduced in New York by the Irish comic singer Thomas Casey in the late 1880s under the title "Drill You Tarriers Drill." Casey had himself been a laborer excavating beneath the streets of New York and had firsthand experience of drilling into hard rock. His performances of "Drill You Tarriers Drill," first at political rallies for Tammany Hall and later on the vaudeville stage, were a huge hit. The song has several verses, each followed by a chorus (which we hear in *The Iron Horse*). Casey played numerous parts on stage, among them the boss and the foreman, and he interpolated lines of dialogue to lend verisimilitude to his performance: "Stand back there. Blast! Fire!" and "Where's the fuse, McGinty?"[19] The song, played for laughs by Casey, was soon inserted into Charles K. Hoyt's hit comedy *A Brass Monkey*, but not before Casey had copyrighted it. Casey's name does not appear on the original printing as the author, a not unusual practice for unknowns—Stephen Foster's name did not appear on the first editions of "Oh! Susannah" either—but Casey's name would appear on subsequent editions beginning in 1888.

"Drill, Ye Terriers, Drill" sounds like an authentic work song, and it is easy to see how it slipped into the folk repertoire. It was widely anthologized during the rise of the folk movement in the 1930s, when it was recorded by the Weavers, a popular folk group, and Burl Ives, among others. Copyright, however, is not always an accurate indicator of a song's origins, and there is some evidence to suggest that "Drill, Ye Terriers, Drill" is considerably older than Thomas Casey's published version and was indeed sung by Irish laborers on the transcontinental railroad. Casey, after all, worked as a driller in the 1870s and 1880s and

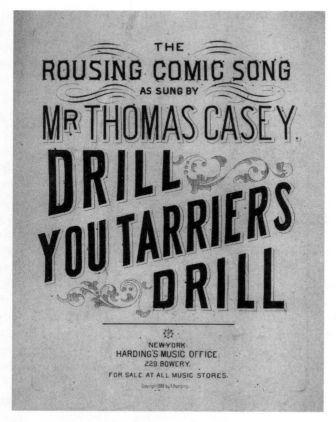

Figure 3. Cover of the sheet music for "Drill You Tarriers Drill." Courtesy Brown University Library.

may have learned the song from other Irishmen on the job. Did Casey see the song's potential and bring it with him when he made the move from day laborer to entertainer? The fact that there are multiple published variants of "Drill, Ye Terriers, Drill," even in the nineteenth century, could also point to an origin predating Casey. Given that the key term in the title, "terriers," is said to have been British slang for manual laborers, the song may be based on a British antecedent. There is, unfortunately, no unequivocal evidence that the song existed before Thomas Casey put it in print, although the source I consider to be the most reliable, Norm Cohen's *Long Steel Rail: The Railroad in American*

Folk Song, "strongly suggests" that the song "is considerably older" than Casey's version.[20]

I doubt that Ford knew of the song's thorny history, and he never revealed the songs his Uncle Mike taught him, if indeed his Uncle Mike taught him any at all. More than likely, Ford assumed that "Drill, Ye Terriers, Drill" was a song sung by Irish rail gangs on the Union Pacific, which it may well have been. The song also commonly figures in railroad novels. In Zane Grey's *The U. P. Trail,* for instance, Irish tracklayers repeatedly sing it.[21] That "Drill, Ye Terriers, Drill" found its way into *The Iron Horse* is not surprising. But it didn't get there by default. Ford was heavily invested in this material, his first opportunity at a large-scale, prestige production, and he involved himself, even more than usual, in every aspect of the film's production. Given Ford's combative nature (he came to blows with his brother Eddie O'Fearna on the set), the level of compliance he expected from those he worked with, especially the writers, and the general importance that he accorded music, both on the set and off, I think it highly unlikely that "Drill, Ye Terriers, Drill," the most clearly identifiable Irish song about working on the railroad, was put there by anyone other than Ford himself.

Music in the silent film was a highly variable enterprise. Accompaniment ranged from live to recorded music, and sometimes included both, from improvisatory to fully scored, from solo instrumentation, usually piano or organ, to the resources of a symphony orchestra and almost everything in between. Typically, it hinged on the cue sheet, a series of musical cues coordinated with the images, usually with some musical notation to cue the accompanist. Original orchestral scores for silent films were rare, and many of these were compiled from nineteenth-century art music, the popular music of the day, and tunes composed expressly for film accompaniment. Some directors, such as D. W. Griffith and King Vidor, were able to exert a measure of control over these orchestral scores, choosing musical selections for specific scenes. Griffith even composed themes for *The Birth of a Nation* (1915).[22] Control, however, could be ephemeral. When *The Birth of a Nation* was reissued in 1920, it was given a new score.[23] More typically, the director was not involved with the musical accompaniment to a film. In the case of *The Iron Horse,* William Fox himself selected Erno Rapee to create an orchestral score for the New York premiere.[24] In large venues, however, the performance of such orchestral scores was dependent upon the musical director, who could choose to ignore the score and substitute music of his or her own, and in the smaller theaters, it was limited by a lack of musical resources. Typical of John Ford, he nonetheless found a way to exert his wishes.

William Fox distributed *The Iron Horse* as an exclusive road show engagement. It premiered in New York at the Lyric Theater on August 28, 1924, but did not open in Los Angeles until the following February. The orchestral score created by Rapee was first heard at the New York premiere. Rapee was Hungarian, among a flood of Europeans to relocate to this country in the 1910s. Trained as a composer of art music, a conductor, and an arranger, he was the director of the Hungarian Opera Company in New York and a vaudeville pianist when, in 1917, he was appointed musical director at the Rialto, the first film theater to boast a resident symphony orchestra. Rapee made his mark on the world of silent film accompaniment in a number of ways: as the premiere music director in New York, working at the Rivoli, the Capitol, the Roxy, and, finally, Radio City Music Hall; and as the author of two extremely influential books that shaped the sound of silent film accompaniment: *Motion Picture Moods for Pianists and Organists* in 1924 and *Erno Rapee's Encyclopedia of Music for Pictures* in 1925. At a time when the typical film score consisted of popular music combined with cues culled from the standard literature of accompaniment, and the occasional reference from the classical repertoire, Rapee advocated the use of art music, especially that of the nineteenth century. Declaring that the American moviegoing public was "culturally starved,"[25] Rapee embarked on an ambitious program of education in his job as musical director in a series of New York theaters. Determined "that motion-picture audiences could be reclaimed from Tin Pan Alley and induced to absorb symphonic orchestrations,"[26] Rapee might follow "Old Black Joe," say, with a piece from Gounod's *Faust* and sneak in some Tchaikovsky. Rapee would later claim that "the two factors . . . responsible for America's present musically awakened condition are Rapee and radio, in that order."[27] William Fox lured Rapee to Philadelphia when his flagship theater, the Fox, opened there in 1924 with an orchestra of fifty-five players. It was not to prove a felicitous pairing. Rapee soon tired of the westerns that were Fox's bread and butter, experimenting with jazz "[o]ut of pure boredom."[28] Even worse, the patrons for Fox westerns were, to Rapee's chagrin, "not quite ready for the classics."[29] Rapee and Fox soon parted, but not before Fox hired Rapee to score *The Iron Horse* for its premiere in New York.[30]

Rapee's score has not survived,[31] but related musical material provides a tracing of its form. An original piece of music, "The March of the Iron

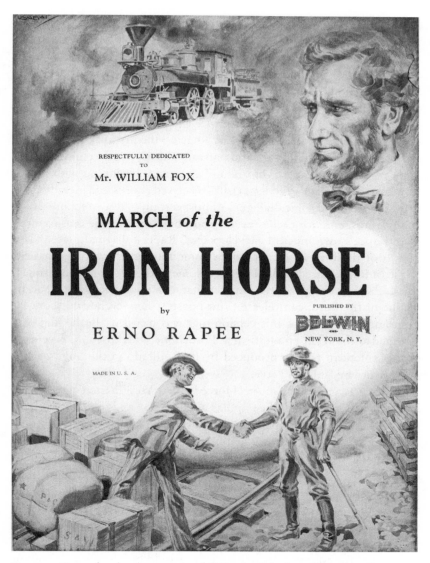

Figure 4. Cover for the sheet music of "March of the Iron Horse" by Erno Rapee. Original music from silent film scores was sometimes published as sheet music, especially if the music proved popular. © 1925 Belwin Music Publishing. All rights reserved. International copyright secured. Used by permission of Alfred Publishing Co, Inc. Courtesy Library of Congress.

Horse," was published as sheet music, an indication of its popularity, in 1925. The central melody was probably used as a leitmotif for the train, and I suspect the piece in its entirety to be a piano reduction of the main title sequence. Two disks entitled "Echoes from *The Iron Horse*," totaling about six and a half minutes, are part of John Ford's phonograph disk collection at Brigham Young University. These appear to be recordings of the music played by Grauman's Theatre Orchestra for the stage show preceding the screening in Los Angeles; the first disk is a pastiche of minstrel songs, folk tunes, and patriotic music,[32] the second, a recreation of the Indian attack on the railway gang, beginning with a performance of "Drill, Ye Terriers, Drill" by mixed chorus and including Indian war cries and some dialogue. Almost certainly, Rapee's score was a compilation score for orchestra incorporating some movie music culled from Rapee's own musical encyclopedias, Rapee's original piece, "The March of the Iron Horse," perhaps some nineteenth-century classical music (if Rapee dared), and, I suspect, some of the very same folk tunes, minstrel songs, and patriotic numbers that turn up on the disks. A recent reissue of the European release print boasts a new orchestral score by John Lanchbery; it was this version that was heard when the film was screened at the silent film festival at Pordenone, Italy in 1998. A version of the American release produced by Paul Killiam in the 1970s has a piano score by William Perry.

Rapee was a powerful musical force in New York in the 1920s, "with his finger on the pulse of the popular audience,"[33] and thus it is not surprising that the reviews mention the music. The *New York Times* commented favorably on Rapee's score, and *Variety,* in its inimitable style, claimed the score "added considerably to the thrill moments."[34] No doubt the war whoops provided by orchestra members whenever Indians appeared on screen were a contributing factor. Another review claimed that "Rapee's musical achievement is just as big in its field as is that of Director Ford in making the story a great film entity."[35] There would be no guarantee, however, that Rapee's score would be used as the film toured the country. Accompaniment would be left to the discretion of theater management, as this admonition from the trade paper *Film Daily* indicates: "By all means secure Erno Rapee's score to use with the showing. It's very important and mighty fine."[36] When the film opened in Los Angeles at Grauman's Egyptian on February 21, 1925, it did indeed play with Rapee's score.

There is no indication that Ford had any access to Rapee, who worked exclusively in New York at this time. Ford remained on the West

Coast until shortly before the film's New York premiere. Yet, by 1924, Ford had learned how to control musical moments that were important to him. In *The Iron Horse*, Ford made sure that "Drill, Ye Terriers, Drill" would be heard in the cinematic auditorium by exploiting some of the same techniques he had developed early in his career for the incorporation of song: close-ups of the music's production, including the work crews singing and the appearance of song lyrics in the intertitles. In *The Iron Horse,* footage was edited to conform to the rhythms of song. An extant scenario indicates that movements of the laborers should be synchronized with their song: "Sledges land on spikes in rythm *[sic]*"; "Sledges hitting spikes in time to the words"; "Close shot of the gang laying track and singing as they work." This note appears at the end of the first singing sequence: ". . . get over that the rythm *[sic]* of the work and the singing is never lost, even in spite of the Indians."[37] That these details were addressed in the scenario before filming started indicates that music was an important element of the production. Clearly, the easiest option for scoring these sequences would be to use the song that Ford had used in filming them, "Drill, Ye Terriers, Drill."[38] In fact, Rapee did use "Drill, Ye Terriers, Drill" in these sequences, and apparently elsewhere too.

"Drill, Ye Terriers, Drill" is embedded in both the film's narrative and its ideological core. It is heard the first time we see the Union Pacific laborers at work, coordinating their movements to the rhythms of the song they sing. "Drill, Ye Terriers, Drill" facilitates the work by bonding the men to each other, young to old, Italians to Irish, Union to Confederate. Song, which both produces and symbolizes cooperation and unity, becomes itself a metaphor for the film's central message of overcoming difference and working together. The lyrics both allude to the hardships and deprivation of railway life—"sure it's work all day with no sugar in yer tay"—and offer a strong work ethic in response—"Drill, ye terriers, drill. . . . An' work and shwe-a-t.'" Even the advent of an Indian attack does not stop the Union Pacific workers, who exchange sledges for guns, song for shouts, and drive the Indians off, returning to their work and song without missing a beat. An extant version of the scenario takes pains to describe this effect: "the appearance of the Indians [should] be as brief and casual as it is written."[39] There is another brief reprise of the song following Davy and Casey's departure from the Union Pacific. Without them, the work won't flow, and not even the song can get the rail gang, whose rhythms have been disrupted, back in sync.

The final and extended use of "Drill, Ye Terriers, Drill" can be heard

later in the film, sung by the Chinese on the Central Pacific. Taught to
them by the Irishman Casey, the song facilitates the work of the Chinese
laborers as it had earlier for the mix of the Irish and Italian on the Union
Pacific. Song unites Union Pacific and Central Pacific, Caucasian and
Asian work crews, featured characters and nameless extras. Of course,
there are some subtle changes in both the song and the representation of
the Chinese laborers. More on this later.

The optimism of the Jazz Age covered over many deep contradictions
in American life: in an era of unprecedented prosperity, there were racial
unrest, anti-immigrant sentiment, a continued backlash against women
after the introduction of universal suffrage, and changing definitions of
masculinity, occasioned by the new status of women and exacerbated by
the cinema. Some of these issues, especially the status of the immigrant
in America, are part of the ideological backdrop to *The Iron Horse,*
which depicts a nation struggling to redefine itself, asking what it meant
to be an American and how to work out the deep divisions in American
social life. These struggles complicate the film's surface optimism and illuminate the underside of American social history in the early twentieth
century.

By the 1910s, pressure was mounting to close the door to immigration, which Congress severely restricted in 1921. Competition for jobs
and housing could be fierce among the newly arrived, and the American
social fabric was strained at the seams by a massive influx of diverse cultures. Limiting future immigration and assimilating those already here
would be the nation's response, although assimilation was not univer-
sally advocated. Northern Europeans were more acceptable than the
johnny-come-latelys from southern and eastern Europe. Asian immigration had by and large been eliminated decades earlier. For a nation
whose Statue of Liberty greeted immigrants with "Give me your tired,
your poor, your huddled masses yearning to be free," immigration was
a conflicted issue, to say the least. So was race. Native Americans and
African Americans were not considered part of the mix.

In *The Iron Horse,* the population that follows the railroad track
forms its own community. It can be seen as a microcosm of America itself. Management is white, the labor force is immigrant, and threats
come from nonwhite outsiders (savage Indians and a swarthy villain who
passes for an Indian). The native-born, white protagonist, Davy Brandon, is the only character allowed upward mobility. Although coded as
working class, he is able to upgrade by the end of the film, his new status signaled by the suit and ornate vest that replace his work clothes and

the daughter of the railroad boss on his arm. When the building of the railroad is complete, he will go on to management, while his immigrant cronies will need to find another job.

Who will and will not be assimilated into the fabric of American life is clearly indicated in the film. The Irish are at the top of the food chain, already assimilated into American culture. Italians have a thing or two to learn before they can be absorbed. The Chinese, while not represented negatively, are nonetheless not assimilated. Nor are the Indians. And despite the fact that African Americans made up a significant portion of the Union Pacific work force, there are none in the film.

The immigrants singled out to befriend the protagonist, Davy, are coded as already assimilated by their first appearance. They wear "their old uniforms of the Civil War," according to the intertitles, and three of them are identified by their military rank: Sergeant Slattery (Francis Powers), Corporal Casey (J. Farrell McDonald), and Private Shultz (James Welch). Those Civil War uniforms are, of course, Union Army issue, and the trio of immigrant laborers who wear them are Irish and German.[40] Later, Davy bonds with another Irish laborer, Dinny (Jack O'Brien). The Irish are hard workers, loyal, and cooperative; Casey is the boss of the rail gang, overseeing the Italians on the Union Pacific and later the Chinese on the Central Pacific. Ford's privileging of the Irish reflects more than just his own Irish heritage; historically, the Irish were a significant portion of the railroad's labor force, often functioning as the gang bosses. Still, as the Irish American novelist Thomas Flanagan notes, "At times [the film] seems to imply that the railroad that linked east and west was built by Irishmen, with Chinese and Italian laborers offering subordinate and comical assistance."[41]

Northern Europeans were among the first wave of immigrants to pour into America in the late nineteenth century. Eastern and southern immigrants arrived later; by the 1920s, they were the focus of much of the discrimination against immigrants, a substantial portion of it from other immigrants who had arrived earlier. In *The Iron Horse,* "eyetalian" laborers appear as troublemakers ("All work—no pay—snow and chilbains—buffalo meat make' us seek—Indians shoot like hell—everything no good—we quit!"), coded as different by their costumes and their pidgin English ("Tony he build the beeg ra'lroad all by heemself—alone"). The intertitles identify them as "shirkers," and according to Casey, these "furriners" won't work. The Irish and the Italians are at odds for most of the film; they reconcile only after Tony has announced his marriage to Nora Hogan—"Me, I Irish now, too." In fact, Irishness is so identified with Americanness in the film that Tony's statement is tantamount to a declaration of American citizenship. Intermarriage holds the key to acceptance, the work ethic of the Irish counterbalancing the indolence of the southern Europeans.

Congress closed the door to Chinese immigration in 1882, fully forty years before it officially limited other immigrants. Discrimination against the Chinese who came to work on the railroad, both during their stint as employees of the Central Pacific Railway and afterwards as they attempted to settle permanently in this country, was ugly. Leland Stanford, one of the owners and president of the Central Pacific, attempted to defuse the racism, publicly stating that the Chinese laborers were "as efficient as white laborers. . . . without them it would be impossible to complete . . . this great National highway."[42] But Chinese continued to be the victims of prejudice by other immigrant laborers and by locals. In Truckee, California, the film's mountain location, and a former site of Central Pacific construction, Chinese workers had been lynched by vigilantes.[43] An early version of the scenario included a sequence depicting the inauguration of construction on the Central Pacific attended by various dignitaries such as Leland Stanford, as well as by "gangs of chinamen." A number of "roughnecks get together and begin throwing eggs" at the "coolies," until they are blocked by the crowd.[44] This version of the scenario depicts the workforce on the Central Pacific as segregated: "gangs of Chinamen" construct the roadbed; Davy, wielding his sledge is depicted in a separate shot "with the white track-layers."[45]

Ford, with his characteristic sympathy for the outsider and his own background as the child of immigrants, must have chafed at these sequences. They're gone from the completed film. The sequence in which the Chinese are pelted with eggs was dropped; the Irishman Casey, although the rail boss, works alongside the Chinese and shares his tobacco with them; and Davy, although not shown in the same shot with Chinese workers, is clearly a part of their integrated rail gang. The opening sequence of railroad work in the film depicts the Chinese labor force and the hardships they faced blasting and tunneling their way through the Sierra Nevada. In one of the film's most memorable sequences, it is the Chinese workers who haul a locomotive up a mountainside, a reminder that the building of the Central Pacific was more dangerous and produced more fatalities than the Union Pacific. After the railroad was completed, the general consensus was that the Central Pacific was better built,[46] the project's completion seven years ahead of schedule being largely attributed to the efficiency of the Chinese workers. The Chinese can be seen at the end of the film, present at the ceremony to drive the golden spike.

Yet the Chinese remain outside the possibility of assimilation. With their traditional clothing, long pigtails, and foreign food, they are clearly coded as Other. Song provides a powerful reminder of their difference. Casey and Davy defect to the Central Pacific, where the Chinese cannot seem to learn to work together. (How did they manage to get the railroad built before Casey arrived?) Casey teaches them "Drill, Ye Terriers, Drill" in an effort to coordinate their movements and get them to work together. Casey's frustration is palpable. Their movements do not match the rhythms of "Drill, Ye Terriers, Drill," and their pikes bob up and down in erratic patterns. Maybe tobacco will help? (It doesn't.) Davy looks on paternalistically, then returns to swinging his axe with assured power. There are also new lyrics for the Chinese, too, provided by Casey: "Drill, ye Chineymen, Drill" and "Drill, ye Haythens, Drill." Back in Springfield, Illinois, in the opening sequence of the film, Davy's father envisions the future of a transcontinental railroad and dedicates himself to its realization, "with the help of God." Apparently, God is on the side of the railroad; the Chinese "haythens" never truly had a chance of becoming part of the new Eden the train transverses.

Long-term discrimination against Asian immigrants had made them more insulated than other immigrant groups, and many Asians lived quite separate lives from the dominant culture of their adopted homeland. Something of this historical reality is reflected in the situation of the Chinese extras both on and off-screen. The Chinese were not a part of Camp Ford. The cast and crew lived in an old circus train that could be moved along the tracks. Indians lived in teepees and the Chinese in tents.[47] Indians (and some whites in yellowface, it looks to me) doubled for Chinese when Ford ran short of Chinese extras, and Chinese doubled for Indians when necessary. Yet, as he did throughout his career in sound film, Ford hired Indians as extras, providing well-paying work, which was otherwise difficult if not impossible to come by, and was made an honorary chief. Conveniently, the Nevada location was part of the Paiute reservation; ironically, the Paiute were one of the tribes displaced by the railroad.

The depiction of the Indians in the film is as complicated as the representation of the Chinese. In Ford's westerns, it generally is. At the very least, the Indians are represented as having a legitimate interest in destroying the rails. It's their culture against Manifest Destiny, and the film doesn't blame them for putting up a fight. The white villain who disguises himself as an Indian, Deroux (Fred Kohler),[48] is evil incarnate. He blocks the railroad for personal gain, the film's nod to the rampant corruption that surrounded the railroad's construction. In fact, the most savage act in the film is reserved for Deroux, who, disguised as an Indian, ruthlessly murders Davy's father. Some of the most thrilling cinematography is used in photographing the Indians, and an emotional vignette is accorded the death of a brave, his loyal dog lying across his body. And it is the Pawnees, enlisted as scouts by the Union Pacific, who ride heroically to the rescue of the besieged train: "like a sweeping wind the Pawnee Scouts rush to the rescue." Yet Indians are ultimately Other, although sometimes nobly so; the film doesn't really know what to do with them; assimilation is never a possibility, and the Indians simply disappear as the railroad nears completion. At least the film resists the formulaic ending of railroad novels: the defeated Indians standing in awe of the iron horse. Zane Grey ends *The U. P. Trail* with the Indians on a bluff watching the train move across their tribal lands, "a symbol of the destiny of the Indian—vanishing—vanishing—vanishing—."[49]

Missing from the film's melting pot of race and ethnicity are African Americans, who make no appearance in *The Iron Horse*. Freed and escaped slaves were a major part of the work force on the Union Pacific, and their work songs are an important part of American cultural history. In fact, the single most recognizable song about the building of the railroad is "I've Been Working on the Railroad," adapted from a song traditionally sung by slaves in the South, with lyrics customized to railroad work. It is not known whether Rapee used "I've Been Working on the Railroad" in his score; John Lanchbery does in his recent score, where, provocatively, it accompanies the Chinese workers.

Another part of the ideological core of *The Iron Horse* is masculinity. The complexities of the representations of masculinity in Ford westerns and the relationship of music to those representations are played out more consciously and in greater depth in Ford's 1926 western, *3 Bad Men,* to which I turn next. With regard to *The Iron Horse,* however, the conscious display of Davy's body is worth noting, as is the intensity of male friendships: the trio of Irish immigrants who befriend Davy, and the bond between Davy and the younger, burly, handsome Dinny. It's always important to remember that audiences in the twenty-first century view the film through a different lens than audiences of the 1920s. What may strike viewers today as patently homoerotic (I've heard my students actually gasp when Davy and Dinny embrace) may have been read quite differently in 1924. Even given changing cultural perspectives, however, there remains a noticeable difference between the ardor of the emotion played out among the men and the pallid and unconvincing heterosexual romance.

Male bonding in the western has generally been understood as repressed homoeroticism. Virginia Wright Wexman, in analyzing the historical function of homoeroticism in the genre, argues that its "fundamental significance is to position homosexuality as a contrasting tendency that can be used to highlight the sexual propriety associated with the Western's valorization of dynastic marriage."[50] It is interesting to consider how often westerns are not entirely successful in doing so. While *The Iron Horse* clearly privileges the heterosexual couple, it cannot quite contain the eroticism circulating around the men in the film. The passion of Davy and Dinny's reunion at the joining of the rails (Davy, bare-chested, embraces Dinny, and for one brief moment it seems as if the two will passionately kiss) surpasses anything transpiring between Davy and Miriam. Even reviewers in the 1920s noted something unconvincing. "Certainly there were more glorious romances breathing beneath the fury of that day than has [sic] been pictured here," one wrote.[51] Contemporaneous reviews also noted, with discomfort, the attention to O'Brien's body: "The producers have permitted him to have too much of the show at certain junctures, especially when he heaves his manly chest. . . . His shirt sleeves are tucked up high enough to give one a good view of his biceps, which appear to be frequently strained for effect."[52]

The film that explicitly treats masculinity is *3 Bad Men,* a film that defines the kind of man that is needed in the West, both to tame and to settle it. (In *3 Bad Men,* this is not necessarily the same thing.) "[I]t shows a time when men were men," a contemporary reviewer wrote.[53] But there is more than one definition of masculinity on offer in the film. Song speaks to those definitions and enters into a complex relationship with representations of masculinity that would become a distinctive component of Ford's later westerns.

Like *The Iron Horse, 3 Bad Men* takes as its subject Manifest Destiny: in this case, the Dakota land rush of 1878. This mammoth giveaway (twenty-four million acres were claimed by 1887) was precipitated by the discovery of gold in the Black Hills following the completion of the transcontinental railroad. The film does acknowledge that the Dakotas belonged to the Indians, but never explains how and why disposal of that land is transferred to the discretion of President U. S. Grant, who "set a day when settlers might race for possession of the rich lands." Manifest Destiny trumps all. As an opening intertitle majestically puts it: "Westward the course of Empire takes its way." Irish, Italian, and Jewish immigrants journey west from overcrowded eastern cities and converge with the native-born on the frontier.

Ford's crew built a replica of the frontier town of Custer in the Grand Teton Mountains, near Jackson Hole, Wyoming; the land rush was shot in the Mojave Desert, about fifty miles from Victorville, California. The production seems to have been calmer than that of *The Iron Horse:* no bullets flying at telegrams or cast and crew; no reported fistfights; everyone housed and fed efficiently. But a Ford location shoot was never uneventful. A baby was hurriedly borrowed and its mother spirited off the set for the memorable stunt where it is left on the ground and rescued moments before a stampede of horses and wagons reach it. Ford did the scene in one take and with no rehearsal.[54] "The Ford outfit was the roughest, god damnedest outfit you ever saw!" the property master, Lefty Hough, exclaimed.[55] Previews reportedly went badly, and, much to Ford's frustration, Fox recut the film. It was neither the first time nor the last that studio executives would tamper with Ford's work.[56]

A score for *3 Bad Men* has not survived. But one was created for the premiere by Erno Rapee's successor at the Fox Theater in Philadelphia, Adolph Kornspan. By 1926, Rapee had resigned his job with Fox and returned to Europe to head UFA's music department.[57] A European émigré like Rapee, Kornspan would prove more successful at the Fox Theater, overseeing its transition to sound and, as its musical director, conducting the live stage shows that accompanied screenings through World War II. In 1926, however, Kornspan had neither Rapee's stature nor his influence, and his score may not have circulated widely or even been heard at all outside of Philadelphia. But like *The Iron Horse, 3 Bad Men* contains a privileged performance of a specific piece of music complete with lyrics in the intertitles: "All the Way from Ireland." A review of the film that mentions the score suggests that, like Rapee, Kornspan found it expedient to reproduce the song alluded to in the intertitles.

The plot of *3 Bad Men* revolves around the eponymous three bad men: Bull Stanley (Tom Santschi), Mike Costigan (J. Farrell McDonald, reprising his gruff but lovable Irishman from *The Iron Horse*), and Spade Allen (Frank Campeau). This trio of outlaws, on the lam from the law for robbery and horse theft, befriend a young woman, Lee Carlton (Olive Borden), moments after her father has been murdered. Settling down with her three rescuers, Lee awaits the day of the land rush with a map marking gold deposits. Genuinely caring for Lee and concerned about her welfare, the three men go husband hunting, after first ascertaining that none of them fit the bill. They settle on Dan O'Malley, a charming Irishman (George O'Brien, now an established matinee idol), a handsome young settler looking for work. A subplot involving Bull's sister, Millie (Priscilla Bonner), seduced and abandoned by the town's sexual predator, Layne Hunter (Lou Tellegen), its corrupt sheriff, serves as a warning of the dangers awaiting single women on the frontier and underscores the necessity of finding a husband. Narrative complications include Layne Hunter's designs on both Lee and the same piece of land she wants. The three bad men ultimately sacrifice their lives so that Lee and Dan can reach their promised land. A flash-forward to the couple's happy future includes a ranch (what happened to the gold?) and a young son, watched over by the ghosts of his namesakes.

Despite the fact that many commentators deem it Ford's silent masterpiece and one of the great films of the 1920s, *3 Bad Men* is woefully neglected. It is less overtly optimistic and grittier than *The Iron Horse*. The land rush is fueled as much by greed as it is by the promise of a fresh start in the wilderness, the sheriff is corrupt, women are sexually exploited, and settlers are more at risk from white men than from red. *3 Bad Men* seems more western than *The Iron Horse*, too; its plot is more tied to the frontier itself, and its characters are more focused on settling the land. Jean Mitry notes: "*The Iron Horse* could have taken place in another locale as long as there were railroad construction and attacks by the natives. In *Three Bad Men* [sic] the American West not only justifies the story and gives it its movement, color and setting, but it also justifies the psychological makeup of the characters."[58] *The Iron Horse* focuses on the melting pot and the assimilation of diverse ethnicities and cultures into an American nation. In *3 Bad Men*, immigrants once again converge on the frontier as the Irish, Scotch, Jews, Chinese, and Italians "seek the reality of their dreams in America." But the film focuses more on the forging of national character by the men who tamed and settled the frontier.

The noble outlaw Bull Stanley distills the qualities necessary to tame the frontier. Ford's vision of the West was inherently democratic; he valued his characters, not according to legal standards, but his own moral code. Appearances can be deceiving in Ford's West: outlaws could prove trustworthy and loyal, virtuous and selfless; representatives of the law could be corrupt and self-serving. In the final analysis, it is what you do that counts, not who or what you are. Bull Stanley, wanted for robbery, and fully capable of it and more (he is about to kill Lee when he realizes that she is a woman), is ultimately judged by the actions we see him perform in the film and not by his notorious criminal past.

A significant part of *The Iron Horse*'s ideological backdrop was the racial unrest and anti-immigrant sentiment of the 1920s, and these issues find their way into *3 Bad Men* in the form of representations of the Irish (utterly charming), Indians (a benign nonpresence), and a Jewish merchant (comic foil). Gender was another of the era's ideological flashpoints. Traditional definitions of masculinity had already been rocked earlier in the century by urbanization, industrialization, and immigration. In response, masculinity recentered itself around athleticism and a regression to a pastoral world where physical prowess mattered. To be manly now meant to be strong and in control of a powerful body, and if this new body couldn't materially affect the course of daily existence, it would at least come in handy in the wilderness, under construction in the early twentieth century as a geographic and ideological space. Theodore Roosevelt embodied this new masculinity in his writings about his life on the frontier, in his rugged, muscular, outdoorsy persona, and in his public policy as president of the United States. To some extent, the founding of the national parks system under Roosevelt is a direct consequence of changing definitions of masculinity that imagined access to virgin wilderness as the ultimate means to carve out or renew a masculine identity. Given these parameters, it should come as no surprise that these new "manly qualities"[59] found their archetypal representation in the figure of the cowboy. Owen Wister's *The Virginian* (1902), perhaps the most famous western novel of the twentieth century, is dedicated to Theodore Roosevelt, who proclaims in his western manifesto *Ranch Life and the Hunting Trail* (1888):

> Civilization seems as remote as if we were living in an age long past. The whole existence is patriarchal in character; it is the life of men who live in the open, who tend their herds on horseback, who go armed and ready to guard their lives by their own prowess, whose wants are very simple, and who call no man master. Ranching is an occupation like those of vigorous, primitive pastoral people, having little in common with the humdrum, workaday business world of the nineteenth century.[60]

The granting of the right to vote to American women in 1920 marked the loosening of strictures on women's political, economic, social, and sexual lives. But it was in the cinema that the most aggressive challenge to conventional definitions of masculinity was mounted. In response to changing definitions of women and their social roles, a new type of man began to appear on the screen in the 1910s, descended from matinee idols of the stage such as John Barrymore and Lou Tellegen: nonmuscular and slight, sexual, sensual, even feminine (although definitely not a "sissy"), beautiful, exotic, erotic, often coded as racially or ethnically Other, and, above all, attentive to women's needs. Gaylyn Studlar, in her study of masculinity in 1920s cinema, describes this new model of masculinity as "sexually troublesome, ideologically transgressive."[61] The Italian-born Rudolph Valentino is the hyperexample, but he was preceded by the Japanese-born Hollywood star Sessue Hayakawa and followed by the Mexican-born Ramon Navarro. And as Miriam Hansen points out, Valentino paid the price: "The perceived deviations from dominant standards of social and sexual identity that troubled and perhaps destroyed his career were the very qualities that made him an object of unprecedented fascination."[62]

Disturbingly, at least for men, female audiences were drawn to this new model of masculinity. *3 Bad Men* considers various forms of masculinity, both explicitly, in the husband-hunting sequence and implicitly in the representation of its male characters. Song pays a part in articulating the differences among them and endorsing a particular manifestation of masculinity for the settling of the West and for the new social reality that was transforming America.

The husband-hunting sequence consciously foregrounds masculinity and what its proper form should be. Midway through the film, the three bad men go looking for marriageable men, considering and rejecting a number of candidates before deciding upon Dan O'Malley. The first candidate is too masculine. Like Bull, he is big, hairy, and belligerent, coded by his dress as a backwoodsman. He is rejected outright, as is candidate #2—a Chinese man. "They get shot too easily," Mike says. The third candidate, dapper in suit, bowler hat, and cane, is coded as homosexual. "I've just reached manhood," he explains. "Then you'd better reach again," Mike responds. This candidate is terrified of Mike and Spade, and a girl he attempts to dance with tries to steal his pocket watch. She gestures to the crowd with her limp wrists, telegraphing what she thinks of him. He is so effeminate that Mike and Spade worry about leaving him alone! But the pickings are slim in Custer, and "If a man's heart is in the right place, it don't matter what sex he belongs to." When Dan appears, after defending himself admirably in a barroom brawl, he is the unanimous choice. "I found a *man!*" Bull shouts.

Bull Stanley, played by the established screen cowboy Tom Santschi, presents us with a kind of unreformed masculinity. Big, unshaven, aggressive, mature—Santschi was pushing forty—and with a propensity to violence, Bull is aptly named. He represents a kind of retrograde masculinity that may have been necessary to tame the frontier, but that positions him as an outsider in the film's narrative economy. Bull never imagines himself as Lee's husband, although he is attracted to her and she to him. The film can't either. It is as if he has too much masculinity and the wrong kind to settle down and become a husband and father. He is a man cut out for life on the edge of society, ultimately destined either to move on or die. By the 1920s, his style of masculinity was becoming outmoded. Despite the fact that he has the largest male role in the film, Santschi did not dominate the publicity.

Lou Tellegen, thin, fashionable, in clinging pants and exotic bolero jackets, and beautifully coifed, plays the sexual predator Layne Hunter. Almost totally forgotten now, Tellegen was a major star on stage and screen and had a notorious and well-publicized private life, details from which exemplified the character he was asked to play in *3 Bad Men*. Tellegen was a glamorous figure in his day, a European matinee idol first in Paris on stage and screen (he co-starred in several *Film d'Art* productions) and then on the New York stage before coming to Hollywood. He was leading man to Sarah Bernhardt in more ways than one, married four times, and was famed as "the perfect lover."[63] His first-person memoir was entitled *Women Have Been Kind*.[64] "No woman can resist him," his publicity proclaimed,[65] and his powers of seduction do seem to have been formidable. Wife # 2 was the illustrious diva of the Metropolitan Opera and screen star Geraldine Farrar. A self-professed New Woman, Farrar publicly renounced marriage, vowing never to compromise her career.[66] Legions of her female fans, called Gerryflappers, vowed the same. Thus it must have come as something of a shock to all of them when Farrar wed Tellegen. The marriage ended badly, but Tellegen "took love as he found it."[67] He moved on. Thus when cast, or rather typecast, as a western lounge lizard in *3 Bad Men*, Tellegen brought a wealth of personal baggage to the role.

As he is depicted in the film, Hunter epitomizes the dangers of the new model of masculinity. Although attentive to females, Layne Hunter is a predator, using his sensuality to seduce innocent women like Millie, Bull's sister, and leave them to a degraded fate. He has the same plans for Lee Carlton, and his designs motivate the three bad men to find a husband for her fast. In *3 Bad Men*, Layne's brand of masculinity is suspect; the very qualities that establish him as attractive to women in the film (his attentiveness, his dress, his good looks, his sensuality) call his sexuality into question. He becomes associated with the town dandy, coded as a homosexual. At one point, the dandy dresses up exactly like Hunter. The latter, who senses the threat, is not amused.

Figure 5. Geraldine Farrar and Lou Tellegen. Farrar, an avowed New Woman, had publicly sworn off marriage to dedicate herself to her career in opera and film, and her marriage to Lou Tellegen was thus something of a surprise to her legion of female fans. Courtesy Academy of Motion Picture Arts and Sciences.

It is George O'Brien who represents the definition of masculinity that the film endorses and who dominated the film's publicity. O'Brien embodied the athletic masculinity represented by Douglas Fairbanks Sr. before him. A World War I veteran and the light heavyweight champ of the Pacific Fleet in 1919, O'Brien found his way to Hollywood soon after the war, but he had a hard time breaking into the movies, initially working as a cameraman, stuntman, and extra. He was a virtual unknown when Ford cast him as Davy in *The Iron Horse;* his audition proved to be a test of his riding skills. O'Brien would do many of his own stunts, practically all of them involving athletics, including his spectacular entrance in *The Iron Horse,* where he stops a galloping horse and jumps onto a moving train. Known for his imposing physique, O'Brien had a personal gym built for him by Fox when he went on location to New York in 1927. The headline of his obituary in the *Los Angeles Times* identified him as "Athlete and Film Actor."[68] He embodied, literally, a definition of masculinity built upon athleticism, strength, and physical prowess.

Although one of O'Brien's earliest appearances on the screen was as an extra in *White Hands* (1922), the kind of swashbuckler that made Valentino famous, studio publicity at Fox made sure that O'Brien would be never be confused with Valentino and the new definition of masculinity. A Fox publicity release for *3 Bad Men* pointedly differentiates O'Brien from Valentino with an unmistakable reference to Valentino's most famous film: "O'Brien's not a sheik or a caveman or lounge lizard—he's a Man's Man and an idol of women." Sustaining this particular image of masculinity was a precarious enterprise for male screen stars. In order to becomes stars, men had to become passive spectacles on display for the pleasure of audiences, but that very act of display challenged their masculinity. Stardom was thus a double bind. The general uneasiness in the national press to the sustained attention to O'Brien's body in *The Iron Horse* gives some indication of the difficulties studios faced in promoting their male stars. Studio publicity sought to ensure that its stars were read the right way: O'Brien was promoted for his manliness; he was "more at home with a punching bag than with mascara and greasepaint."[69] Press releases highlighted his athleticism.[70] Studio publicists dubbed him "The Chest."[71] Posters for *The Iron Horse* featured him fighting.

For a variety of reasons, musical performance complicates the representation of masculinity. Music traditionally has been associated with the feminine in Anglo culture, causing gender trouble for men who have performed it. And yet Ford's cowboys sing and his cavalry troops dance

Figure 6. George O'Brien publicity still. The light heavyweight boxing champ of the Pacific Fleet during World War I, O'Brien was promoted by Fox Pictures for his athleticism. Courtesy Academy of Motion Picture Arts and Sciences.

without compromising their manliness. I develop my argument about masculinity and music in much greater detail in chapter 6. Here I would simply point out that as early as the silent period, Ford gave his cowboys songs to sing, and such musical performances become part of their manliness. In a sense, Ford would colonize music for the sound western, making it safe for his male western protagonists to sing.

Dan O'Malley, an Irish immigrant, sings the only song in *3 Bad Men*: "All the Way from Ireland." Here we see Ford's hand. In the source novel, Herman Whitaker's *Over the Border*, Dan is not an Irish immigrant but a Princeton graduate, and nowhere does he sing, play an instrument, or have anything to do with music.[72] In the film, however, Dan is introduced to the audience through song. In medium and close shots, he plays his harmonica as he heads West. The intertitles present the lyrics, in which a displaced Irishman seeks his fortune and his true love in the Dakotas. The song is an adaptation of a rather obscure Irish ballad, "All the Way from Ireland," about a young Irish girl, Molly, who hails from Tralee. Its lyrics were rewritten to accommodate the narrative of the film, and I think it quite likely that Ford rewrote them himself.

In *3 Bad Men,* music is associated with Dan, not Lee, and that connection does not compromise his masculinity. Moments after singing his song, he tackles the strenuous job of fixing the broken wheel of a Conestoga wagon, and flirts with Lee, trying to steal a kiss. Dan's embrace of his softer side makes him more sexually attractive. In a telling scene late in the film, Dan accidentally intrudes into Lee's tent while she is bathing. Embarrassed and apologetic, he leaves, but he decides to serenade Lee with his harmonica. His playing is so seductive that one of the dance hall girls from town is drawn to him, embracing him from behind. "Do you like that tune, Miss Lee?" he asks. Lee is attracted to the song as well but peers out from her tent only to find Dan being kissed by a rival. Dan decides that his predicament is entirely due to the harmonica playing, which has escalated his sexual allure. In *3 Bad Men,* Dan's masculinity becomes the version that the film endorses, and it is his sensitivity, as evidenced through song, that tips the balance in his favor.

The Iron Horse and *3 Bad Men,* although silent, illuminate the importance of music to the work of John Ford. Even in a silent film, Ford attended to matters of music: using music on the set to create mood and atmosphere; including musical performances in his films' narrative construction; choosing particular songs to be included in the films; using direct cues in the form of song lyrics in intertitles ensuring that the songs would be heard when his films were screened; editing footage to song rhythms; and utilizing music as a window into both character and theme. *The Iron Horse* and *3 Bad Men* point the way to the distinctive and memorable uses of music in the westerns of the sound period.

CHAPTER 3

"Based on American Folk Songs"

Scoring the West in *Stagecoach*

The opening credits for *Stagecoach* announce intriguingly that the musical score is "based on American Folk Songs." It was not a particularly obvious proclamation to make in 1939, the year *Stagecoach* was produced. Although there are some exceptions, notably Cecil B. DeMille's *The Plainsman* (1936),[1] the vast majority of westerns at the time were B pictures, series westerns designed for the bottom of a double bill.[2] They were filled with the country-and-western music that was proving so popular on the radio and records. *Stagecoach,* part of the wave of A westerns that revived the genre as a prestige product, turned to another kind of musical heritage. How and why did folk song come to be regarded as the quintessential American musical form? How did it find its way into the western, replacing the music that had come to be associated with the genre?

Ford had always liked American folk song, hymnody, and period music and used them in his Americana films of the 1930s, such as *Judge Priest* and *Steamboat Round the Bend,* as he had earlier in the silent era. But it was *Stagecoach* that gave Ford his first opportunity to "score" a sound western. The film not only set a pattern for the way Ford would use music in his westerns, its score, an Academy Award winner, provided an important model for the studio western. *My Darling Clementine* may have the most Fordian western film score, but it was *Stagecoach* that blazed the trail. In asserting a connection to American folk song, *Stagecoach* belonged to the broad cultural convergence of national identity and the American West that was to shape both American art music and the genre of the western film.

Aaron Copland, Virgil Thomson, and Louis Gruenberg, important members of art music circles in New York in the 1920s and 1930s, and among the first wave of composers from the concert world to find film work, provided a road map for film composers seeking ways to identify their music as American. That road map became increasingly important to composers of the western. Because the genre as a whole focuses so transparently on American values, its composers have tended to favor musical forms defined as American. The score of *Stagecoach* thus found itself part of a defining movement in American art music dedicated to the quest for a national identity that reached Hollywood in the 1930s from East Coast concert halls.

The name that may come as a bit of a surprise in the preceding paragraph is that of Louis Gruenberg, perhaps the most important composer of the early twentieth century that you've never heard of. Yet Gruenberg literally traversed the trajectory described above: he was a leading figure in New York in the movement to discover and promote a uniquely American music, insisting upon the necessity of recognizing America's own indigenous music in order to do so; he moved to Hollywood in the late 1930s to score films; and he was supposed to score *Stagecoach*. His name remains on the film as one of five composers credited with the music.

The search for an American music certainly predated the 1930s. During George Washington's presidency, William Billings promoted his fugueing tunes as "American music."[3] At the turn of the twentieth century, however, the quest began in earnest as composers experimented with a variety of sources to impart an American flavor to their music, in pieces such as Edward MacDowell's *Suite No. 2* (the *"Indian"*) in 1896 and Henry F. Gilbert's *Comedy Overture on Negro Themes* in 1905. Although the inspiration was European, the idiom romantic, and the authenticity suspect, this American music inaugurated a lively dialogue about national identity in music that was to extend throughout the first half of the twentieth century. At its center was the question of what constituted American music. By the 1920s, composers had decided that the answer was jazz.

Jazz was not only a uniquely indigenous American form, it resonated with modernity, giving American composers, who were still largely trained in Europe, the opportunity to use the cutting-edge compositional techniques they had studied. Jazz became the vernacular music of choice. As Krin Gabbard reminds us, the term "jazz" had a rather elastic meaning in the 1920s;[4] it covered a variety of music practices derived from the original African American form, especially jazzy rhythms and instrumentations. Paul Whiteman was known as the King of Jazz, and the 1927 film *The Jazz Singer* was about the son of a Jewish cantor who wanted to sing popular music. The improvisation at the heart of African American jazz was largely absent, the lyrics of its songs laundered. Yet there could be little question that jazz, however defined, was now considered uniquely American.

There were three "rich veins indigenous to America alone: Jazz, Negro Spirituals, and Indian themes," Gruenberg proclaimed.[5] He was himself the preeminent composer of jazz-inflected concert hall music in the 1920s and early 1930s, including a cantata, *Daniel Jazz* (1923), *Jazzettes* (1924) for violin and piano, *Jazzberries* (1926) for piano, and a *Jazz Suite* (1927) for orchestra, as well as several volumes of spirituals arranged for voice and piano in 1926 and an opera, *The Emperor Jones*, based on the play by Eugene O'Neill, which was part of New York's Metropolitan Opera season in 1933.

But the jazz age eventually ended.[6] Jazz continued to prosper, needless to say, both outside and inside the concert hall, and composers of art music did not wholly abandon the form. But during the 1930s, jazz began to be dislodged from its preeminence as the quintessential American musical form, making way for folk music. The Depression ushered in an era of social consciousness in the arts; composers, visual artists, writers, playwrights, directors, and actors, largely in New York, turned to the Left, seeking a socially relevant medium and idiom that could both express the issues of the age and speak to "the common man," a phrase that ran through the discourse of the era and found its apotheosis in Aaron Copland's *Fanfare for the Common Man* (1942). To do so, composers explored the mediums of radio and film; turning away from the abstraction of European modernism, they discovered a new authentic American form—Anglo American folk song—and the rhythms, harmonies and musical textures derived from it. And as Timothy Scheurer points out, musicians adopted "traditional" musical instruments to go along with the new idiom, among them the guitar, the banjo, and the mandolin.[7]

Composers seeking to create American music had a new vocabulary, what the musicologist Beth E. Levy describes as a "catalogue of composerly whiteness,"[8] pruned of jazz and other ethnically and racially inflected forms. Even Virgil Thomson, who was at the center of the movement, voiced concern that one single musical heritage had now come to represent a diverse and varied nation. "The melting pot theory of American life is not, it would seem, a true picture," Thomson surmised.[9] This music flourished in American art music circles in the 1930s and 1940s and has been heard in concert halls ever since. This is a music that found its audience, and its particular definition of Americanness continues to be a powerful determinant of what sounds American in music to this day.

Embedded within this musical movement was a primal connection between American music and the geographic space of the West, a sense that no music was more American than the folk songs, hymns, and ballads associated with the settling of the West by Anglo Americans. This discourse coalesced most potently in the work of Roy Harris, America's most popular classical composer in the 1930s.[10] Born in Oklahoma and raised in California, Harris gave shape to the quest to capture the intrinsically American in music in dozens of works with the West as a framework, among them *Symphony—American Portrait* (1929), *A Farewell to Pioneers* (1935), *Folksong Symphony* (1940), *Cimarron* (1941), and, most important, his *Third Symphony* (1939). Harris's background gave him a kind of "music and moral authority,"[11] and he endorsed a turn in American music, both on the Left and the Right, away from the urban, the intellectual, the racially and ethnically diverse, and the regionally specific, and toward Anglo American folk song and hymnody. The West, with its wide open spaces and mythic archetypes (the cowboy, the farmer, the pioneer), unfettered by European modernism and untarnished by corrupt urban genres like jazz, came to stand for the quintessential American identity in music, largely superseding other regions' claims. It inspired a host of works: Ferde Grofé's *Grand Canyon Suite* (1931); Copland's *Billy the Kid* (1936), *Music for Radio: Saga of the Prairie* (1937), and *Rodeo* (1942); Thomson's *Symphony on a Hymn Tune* (1928); Gruenberg's *Americana Suite* (1945); and Morton Gould's *A Cowboy Rhapsody* (1942). Even an émigré like Lukas Foss knew how to play the game, composing *The Prairie* (1944).[12]

The birth of the singing cowboy can also be traced to this cultural moment. The new country-and-western music finding its way into the series western functioned as a kind of shadow discourse to the redefinition of American music transpiring in New York, translating similar cultural imperatives about American identity, the geographic space of the West, and the figure of the westerner into forms more accessible to blue-collar audiences. As Peter Stanfield has demonstrated, series westerns were marketed to the working class and typically focused on stories "that were either covertly or overtly concerned with the struggle between labor and capital." Country-and-western music, whose greatest appeal during the Depression was to this same audience, reinforced a "class-specific address."[13] And I think this is part of the explanation why the major studios ignored country-and-western music when they rediscovered the genre of the western and promoted it as a prestige product. Folk song crossed this class divide, however, constituting as distinctly an American form for country-and-western artists as it did for New York intellectuals. In fact, folk song became something of a touchstone for singing cowboys trying to steer clear of jazz's "cultural dissonance" and create a distinctly country, that is, rural, musical identity.[14] Many a folk tune can thus be found interspersed among the original country-and-western songs that formed the backbone of the repertoire of singing cowboys.

Several concert hall composers who took their inspiration from the West actually came West in the 1930s when, for a brief time, Hollywood studios were interested in serious art music composers and those composers were interested in working in Hollywood. Radio, the recording industry, and especially film engaged composers of the era; Copland described film scoring itself as "a revolutionizing force in today's music."[15] Thomson scored documentaries. Copland, Gruenberg, and others (but notably not Harris) actually came to Hollywood, bringing a reliance upon Anglo American folk sources, hymnody, and the distinctive rhythms, harmonies, and musical textures derived from them. Thomson's scores for the documentary films *The Plow That Broke the Plains* (Pare Lorentz, 1936) and *The River* (Pare Lorentz, 1938), Copland's for *The City* (Ralph Steiner and Willard Van Dyke, 1939), *Of Mice and Men* (Lewis Milestone, 1939), and *The Red Pony* (Lewis Milestone, 1939), and Gruenberg's for *The Fight for Life* (Pare Lorentz, 1940) stood in contradistinction to the lush postromantic sound of the classical Hollywood era, garnering critical kudos and lending prestige to the films they accompanied. Hollywood's love affair with art music proved to be brief, and by the 1940s, a successful career in the New York concert hall was no longer an entrée into the world of film. But the legacy of these composers can be found in the lingering connection between Americanness, the West, and Anglo American folk music and hymnody that would eventually find its way into the genre of the western. The score of *Stagecoach* helped to point the way. The success of the film, directed by Hollywood's most prestigious director, and its score, winner of the Academy Award for Best Score over nine entries, including scores by the influential Erich Wolfgang Korngold and Alfred Newman, provided a model for the way the genre would use music. By the 1940s, folk song, generally overorchestrated and used to the point of saturation, had become de rigeur in big-budget studio westerns.

Stagecoach was neither a big-budget production nor a studio film in the traditional sense of the word. Produced by Walter Wanger for his production company,[16] and released through United Artists, the production had a tight production schedule and a very modest budget of $546,000. Ford came in $14,626 under budget. "In Hollywood, that's the price of a good cigar," he quipped.[17] United Artists was not a studio in the conventional sense and had no music department, so the score was farmed out to Paramount, where Wanger had an office. Details of the score's genesis and development remain murky, because some pieces of the puzzle are missing. The evidence, however, points to Gruenberg as the original choice to score the film.[18] Boris Morros, the head of Paramount's music department, was known to promote concert composers (he courted both Igor Stravinsky and Arnold Schoenberg and was the force behind George Antheil's tenure at the studio), and he is the likely source of Gruenberg's being hired. Ultimately, however, Gruenberg's music was discarded. Gruenberg composed, according to his count, about eighteen minutes of music for the film, thirteen of which were "not needed anymore" and returned to him almost immediately. The remaining five minutes were eventually rejected, too. As he wrote of his experience, it was "not a very exciting beginning for a new career." On the cause of Gruenberg's dismissal, history is silent. Whether Gruenberg ran out of time (he described it as a "rush job") or whether his music was deemed inadequate ("not needed any more and returned"), Gruenberg is not the composer of record.[19] One manuscript page of music for *Stagecoach* can be found among Gruenberg's papers. It bears the title "March of the Outcasts (Parody on: 'Shall we gather at the River')" and was intended for the sequence in which Dallas and Doc are marched out of town. Gruenberg argued with Paramount about one remaining cue that he claimed he had worked on, and he signed an affidavit to that effect. Paramount did not see it his way, and he is not credited on the cue sheet. Yet he retains screen credit, which he shares with four other composers, most likely the result of his demonstrated willingness to fight for authorship and, presumably, screen credit.

Boris Morros put a team of composers and arrangers together to finish the job. It wouldn't be the first time or the last that Morros would be called upon to save the score. Hollywood's production of the musical score encompassed a variety of models, from the exceptional single-authored practice of Bernard Herrmann, who composed and orches-

Example 1. Louis Gruenberg's musical sketch "March of the Outcasts" (a parody of "Shall We Gather at the River?"), intended for *Stagecoach*. Used by permission of Joan Gruenberg Cominos. Courtesy New York Public Library.

trated his own film scores, to the more collaborative practice of a composer-orchestrator team such as Erich Wolfgang Korngold and Hugo Friedhofer, to most typical practice in the early studio years, multiauthored texts that depend upon several composers and arrangers working simultaneously. What Roy Prendergast has called "scissors-and-paste-pot scores" were not exceptional in 1939, but what was unusual about *Stagecoach* is the extent to which that collaboration was openly acknowledged.[20] Morros gets a credit for musical direction, routine for the head of the music department, and five composers share screen credit: Richard Hageman, W. Franke Harling (aka Frank Harling), John Leipold, Leo Shuken, and Louis Gruenberg. There was also significant input from Gerard Carbonara, who wrote cues for the Indians, and Stephan Pasternacki, who arranged music for the Lordsburg segment.[21]

This musical team was a mix of experienced staff composer-arrangers and émigrés from the world of art music, some very recent. Harling, Leipold, Shuken, and Pasternacki were Paramount staff composer-arrangers, largely working without screen credit. Gruenberg, Hageman, and Carbonara came from a different world. Gruenberg had recently relocated from New York, and *Stagecoach* was his first film work. Hageman had composed operas and conducted at New York's Metropolitan Opera for nearly twenty years before arriving in Hollywood in 1938. With his work on *Stagecoach*, he began a collaboration with John Ford that would include some of Ford's most distinctive scores. Carbonara, an opera coach, conductor, and concert violinist in both Europe and the United States, had migrated to Hollywood a decade earlier to score silent films. But the experience of the concert hall composers was, in significant ways, not materially different from that of the longtime studio employees. Neither Carbonara nor Pasternacki received screen credit for *Stagecoach*, although their input seems significant. Gruenberg did receive screen credit but did not receive an Academy Award with the composing team, because Walter Wanger left Gruenberg's name off the list of nominees he submitted to the Academy.[22] All of this was standard operating procedure in Hollywood but the results clearly dismayed Gruenberg.

Stagecoach, as has been noted, proclaims itself to be "based on American Folk Songs." I'd like to digress briefly to unpack that term a bit. Folk song, by its very nature, is a slippery entity characterized by a high degree of variation, ranging from simple embellishments of the melodic line to actual alternative melodies and lyrics that themselves contain substantial variations, depending on the era, geographic location, and performance setting. Often folk songs have their roots in older published music that entered the oral tradition and reemerged in altered form. As I have argued elsewhere, many of the tunes we assume to be folk songs, especially those connected to the West, lack historical provenance and turn out have been composed by writers on the East Coast who had little or no experience of the frontier.[23] Many of the folk songs in western film scores are not authentic in the way we have supposed them to be. Often they are minstrel songs, a misrecognition not without import, as I explore in more depth in chapter 7.

The score for *Stagecoach* is more accurately described as "based on" period music. It was Ford's prerogative to choose the songs for his films. The particulars of *Stagecoach*'s production (a rush job, farmed out, as we have seen, to Paramount's music department) kept a team of composers at Paramount, as well as its legal department, scurrying to please Ford and meet the film's release date. Studio publicity claimed that seventeen American folk tunes were used in the film, a bit of an exaggeration by my count. I suspect these seventeen songs may have been Ford's initial list of suggestions. The press book, probably produced at a later date, lists thirteen. I count fifteen songs, or portions thereof in the film: "The Trail to Mexico," aka "Oh, Bury Me Not on the Lone Prairie";[24] "Shall We Gather at the River?"; "Carry Me Back to Old Virginny"; "Jeanie with the Light Brown Hair"; "Careless Love"; "The Battle-cry of Freedom"; "Little Joe the Wrangler"; "Gentle Annie"; "Joe Bowers"; "Rosa Lee"; "Lilly Dale"; "She Is More to Be Pitied Than Censured" (mistakenly referred to in Paramount records as "She's More to be Pitied Than Censored"); "Up in a Balloon"; "I Love You"; and "Al pensar en ti." Other songs were considered, then dropped: "She May Have Seen Better Days"; "My Lulu"; "All around the Mulberry Bush"; and "Red Light Sadie." "Ten Thousand Cattle" was actually filmed as a "vocal visual" with instrumental background but was deleted from the final release print.

"Little Joe the Wrangler" is a traditional Texas song, and "Al pensar en ti," a traditional Mexican song. "Shall We Gather at the River?" is a nineteenth-century Methodist hymn. "The Battle-cry of Freedom" was a Union rallying song during the Civil War; "Jeanie with the Light Brown Hair" and "Gentle Annie" were composed by none other than Stephen Foster, examples of the very few parlor ballads Foster composed to break out of the minstrel circuit.[25] "Careless Love" is a Tin Pan Alley song by W. C. Handy. "Carry Me Back to Old Virginny" by James K. Bland, "Lilly Dale" by H. S. Thompson, and "Rosa Lee," published by the

Ethiopian Serenaders, are minstrel songs. So is "Joe Bowers."[26] As these
songs are used in *Stagecoach,* however, largely as source music in the saloon and bordello sequences in Lordsburg, there is clear narrative justification for their use. But they are not exactly folk songs.

Ford was himself a great student of American history, but he played
fast and loose with it in his westerns. Historical accuracy would often
take a back seat to dramatic necessity. *Stagecoach* takes place sometime
during the years 1881 to 1886, when Geronimo was on the warpath in
the American Southwest. But several songs postdate that era: "She Is
More to Be Pitied Than Censured" (1898), "Careless Love" (1914), and
"I Love You," from the Broadway musical, *Little Jesse James* (1923).[27]
The song that was used for the stagecoach theme, however, has a clear
nineteenth-century lineage, although which song provides it poses an interesting question. Edward Buscombe in his British Film Institute mono-
graph identifies the probable source of the stagecoach theme as "The
Trail to Mexico." Rudy Behlmer cites a "somewhat altered" version of
"Oh, Bury Me Not on the Lone Prairie" as the source.[28] I think they are
both right.

Archival records at Paramount's music department are not much help
in determining the source of the stagecoach theme. The cue sheet does
not indicate the titles of the period music. Since this material was presumed to be in the public domain, there was no need to indicate titles;
instead, cues were labeled by narrative situation such as "Apache Wells
Arrival" or "Geronimo Threatens." The press book is no help either. It
does list "The Trail to Mexico" as one of the songs used in the film, but
is unreliable: it lists songs not used in the film and fails to list some that
are. An interim cue sheet from Walter Wanger Productions does list the
titles of some of the source music but lists "In Old Mexico" as the title
of the stagecoach music. "In Old Mexico," aka "It Happened in Mon-
terey," was a popular song recorded by both Paul Whiteman and Ruth
Etting in 1930 and bears no resemblance to the stagecoach music. I believe this to be an error on the Wanger cue sheet; it was intended to be
"The Trail to Mexico."

Enter Carson S. Robison, who, along with his country-and-western
group, the Buckeroos, had a big success in 1934 with "Carry Me Back
to the Lone Prairie." Robison's song had the same melody as "Oh, Bury
Me Not on the Lone Prairie" but slightly altered lyrics.[29] Robison not
only popularized the song, he copyrighted it. "The Trail to Mexico" and
"Oh, Bury Me Not on the Lone Prairie" have different lyrics, performance tempi, and tone, but they share the same melody, having been de-

rived from the same source, an English song, "The Ocean Burial," copyrighted in 1850 by George Allen, which begins: "Oh bury me not in the deep, deep sea." I believe that Paramount seized upon the similarities between "The Trail to Mexico" and "Oh, Bury Me Not on the Lone Prairie" in order to avoid a copyright battle with Robison, using "The Trail to Mexico" in their legal documents, such as the cue sheet, but actually considering "Oh, Bury Me Not on the Lone Prairie" as the source and counting on the fact that most of the audience would identify it as such. I believe that the error on the Wanger interim cue sheet ("In Old Mexico" instead of "The Trail to Mexico") is an indication that no one was paying attention to the accuracy of the "cover" title. Richard Hageman, who was responsible, in part, for arranging the stagecoach theme, annotated the title of the same tune in the conductor copy of *She Wore A Yellow Ribbon* as "O Bury Me Not on the Lone Prairie."[30]

American song, of whatever lineage, functions in a variety of ways in *Stagecoach*: to flesh out thematic concerns, aid in characterization, and support the film's ideological framework. Some of this transpires on a conscious level and some of it doesn't. What may be a conscious referent for one listener may be unrecognizable to another. It is impossible to draw a clear line between the songs that are perceived consciously and those that are not. Songs can even be perceived on multiple levels of consciousness, with certain types of meaning perceived consciously and other less conscious levels operating beneath them. The use of period music in *Stagecoach*, as with most film music, draws upon various forms of perception to affect audience response.

The most consciously recognizable melodies in the score, to my mind, are "Jeanie with the Light Brown Hair" and "Shall We Gather at the River?" These songs anchor meaning directly by tapping into the reliable, ready-made cultural associations attached to them. "Shall We Gather at the River?" instantly connotes religion; many listeners would be able to identify it as a Protestant hymn. In *Stagecoach*, it is played for humor. Heard initially on an organ, stressing its religious connotation, it is then recast in weird instrumentation as accompaniment to the outraged womenfolk of Tonto. This parodic version of a familiar tune casts ridicule on the Ladies' Law and Order League and arouses our sympathies against them. The song reappears in *My Darling Clementine*.

"Jeanie with the Light Brown Hair," a Stephen Foster parlor ballad associated with the antebellum South, is used as a leitmotif for the southerners Mrs. Mallory and Hatfield. On the conscious level, the song, with its beautiful melody and refined origins as a parlor ballad, reinforces Mrs.

Mallory's social status as a lady and confirms Hatfield's as a gentleman, despite his new occupation. The song also serves as a reminder that they are the outsiders in the new order of the American West. On a less conscious, more deeply buried level, "Jeanie with the Light Brown Hair" evokes nostalgia for a bygone way of life in the antebellum South and effectively softens Mrs. Mallory's snootiness and Hatfield's rigid persona when we are in danger of becoming totally alienated from them. Another familiar melody works the same way. Listen for the strains of "Carry Me Back to Old Virginny" as a clue to Hatfield's identity. It can be heard when Mrs. Mallory notices the crest on his silver drinking cup and moments before this southern gentleman is about to shoot her in the head.

The ways in which folk song, hymnody, and popular music of the era are used in *Stagecoach*'s score, however, largely work on a less than conscious level. Often heard in fragments, cast into unfamiliar harmonic modes, integrated into larger original compositions, or not easily recognizable (Can you recognize the tune of "Gentle Annie"? Could the 1939 audience?), period music is often positioned to affect response without the audience's conscious recognition, giving the film a wash of authenticity without directly calling attention to itself.

Consider the stagecoach theme. My guess is that those few listeners who recognize the tune, or think they do, connect the stagecoach theme to "Oh, Bury Me Not on the Lone Prairie," an enduring cowboy ballad reproduced in endless school songbooks and folk anthologies. Few listeners, if any, will identify it as "The Trail to Mexico." I think the composers of the score were counting on that misrecognition. But whether or not audience members recognize the title, they would respond to the musical cues of westernness infused throughout the song. The loping rhythms and simple harmonies function to connote a sense of western geography without the listener actually knowing the source or even being conscious of the presence of music.

The song used as a love theme for Dallas and Ringo works along these lines as well, and is probably the most striking example in the film of the ways in which cultural associations change over time. The leitmotif is taken from the chorus of the song "I Love You" from the 1923 Broadway production *Little Jesse James*. "I Love You," originally sung by John Boles, was the hit of the show and enjoyed a long shelf life as a popular love song. The Harmonicats successfully revived it as late as the 1940s. In the 1930s, the song was highly recognizable and its associations were very immediate. The title of the song obviously points to heartfelt, romantic love and the lyrics of the chorus, although not used in *Stage-*

coach, would readily be recalled by those who recognized the tune: "I love you, I love you / That's all that I can say." Associations attached to the song and especially to the lyrics are harnessed to the images, anchoring their meaning in a particular way. Dallas and Ringo are validated as a couple, their love true and their commitment eternal. Today, few listeners would recognize the music for Dallas and Ringo as "I Love You." However, listeners unaware of the song's cultural history can still get the point, because violins, upward leaps in the melody, and lyrical performance connote romantic love.

Earlier in their relationship, Dallas and Ringo are accompanied by excerpts from W. C. Handy's bluesy song "Careless Love." Listen for it when Dallas and Ringo first meet at Dry Fork, when they share a drink from the same canteen, and when they bundle up during the snowstorm. "Careless Love" encodes transgression, both sexual (and "Careless Love" means just what you think it means) and racial (it was composed by the African American songwriter W. C. Handy and recorded by African American artists such as Bessie Smith.) Again, listeners do not need to know the origins of the song or its lyrics: the bluesy melody signifies its transgressive nature. Once Dallas and Ringo declare their love for each other, "Careless Love" disappears from the soundtrack and is replaced by the classier "I Love You." Gary Wills argues that "the subsidiary nature of Wayne's role as written can be seen in the vague and misleading assignment of a musical theme to him and the prostitute."[31] I disagree. Changing the musical theme for Dallas and Ringo from "Careless Love" to "I Love You" has a clear narrative and ideological purpose.

"The Battle-cry of Freedom," heard accompanying the cavalry's ride to the rescue, works in the same way. The number two best-selling song in the Union during the Civil War, trailing only "Battle Hymn of the Republic" in sales, "The Battle-cry of Freedom" might have been recognized by far more viewers in 1939 than it is today. But like "I Love You," it encodes its meaning through musical signifiers and does not depend upon conscious recognition of the melody or lyrics to make its point. "The Battle-cry of Freedom" with its martial instrumentation and short clarion-call phrases connotes the military. For listeners who recognize the song and possibly the stirring lyrics of the chorus, there is also another level of meaning. One of the tensions in the film is the lingering animosity between Union and Confederate veterans. By connecting the Union Army of the Civil War with the cavalry riding to the rescue on the frontier, the score becomes part of the process by which viewer sympathies are engaged on behalf of the Union. For listeners who know the lyrics, the point is even more emphatic: "The Union, forever, hurrah, boys, hurrah! / Down with the traitor and up with the star / We will rally round the flag, boys, rally round the flag / Shouting the battle-cry of freedom."

During the 1930s, a set of principles coalesced in Hollywood for the musical accompaniment to dramatic film. In this model, nondiegetic music was used to sustain narrative structure and coherence, to illustrate narrative content, and to control narrative connotation, and was placed in such a way that it was rendered unobtrusive, even inaudible. For the successful completion of these goals, the classical score depends upon its ability to harness music's expressivity by tapping into powerful musical signifiers encoding specific cultural meaning. Songs, because of their lyrics, function as a kind of shorthand of this process, quickly summoning up cultural associations. This can even be the case when lyrics are left unvoiced, but the audience may know them. Songs are also highly recognizable, however, and therein lies the rub: they increase the threshold of audibility and draw attention to themselves, potentially threatening a film's impression of reality. Hollywood therefore used song sparingly and carefully in the nondiegetic film score.

The score for *Stagecoach* is at odds with this model. In the Lordsburg section of the film, for instance, diegetic song and period music, some of it highly recognizable and some of it clearly positioned to be audible, are used to fulfill functions generally left to nondiegetic and largely unnoticed background scoring: sustaining narrative unity, illustrating narrative content, and controlling narrative connotation. The sequence begins as the first travelers arrive in Lordsburg. The diegetic piano music functions exactly as nondiegetic background scoring conventionally would, matching the mood of the music to events on screen: the spirited and upbeat "Little Joe the Wrangler" as the first wave of passengers arrive in Lordsburg (this song has been heard earlier on the streets of Tonto), the slower and highly sentimentalized "Gentle Annie" for the newly rehabilitated Dallas, complete with the newborn in her arms. What a coincidence—the pianist just happens to change numbers as she steps down with the baby.

In the saloon where Luke Plummer (Tom Tyler) learns of Ringo's return, piano arrangements of first "Joe Bowers" then "Rosa Lee" become increasingly jazzy, with the chromatic chordal progressions of ragtime. These musical signifiers embedded in jazz attach to Plummer and bring a dimension of Otherness to his villainy, reinforced when we meet his swarthy Mexican sidekick. Something interesting is going on here. An almost antiphonal relationship between Plummer and the piano player develops, where the diegetic piano music responds to Plummer's actions in the way nondiegetic music more typically would. When it is reported, for instance, that the "Ringo Kid's in town," the action stops while Luke glances around the room. The music is silenced here as well, the piano player hesitating while Luke digests the information. Later, the diegetic music dramatically stops when Luke cashes in his chips. There is a particularly nice example prior to Doc's entrance where Luke casts a sidelong glance at the piano player, who looks him straight in the eye and responds with a jazzy, chromatic progression. This use of diegetic music to respond specifically to narrative action is atypical of the conventional Hollywood film score; nondiegetic music usually performs this function.

Curley allows Ringo to settle his score with the Plummers, and before Ringo seeks them out, he accompanies Dallas home. Again, it is diegetic music that functions to characterize the geographic space they enter and telegraph to the audience the nature of the establishments they pass. The sequence begins with "Lilly Dale," heard in the background on a saloon piano. But when Dallas and Ringo reach the wrong side of town, the songs "Up in a Balloon" and "She's More to Be Pitied Than Censured" (an obvious comment on Dallas for those who recognize the tune) emanate from the open doors of the bordellos. Additionally, the instrumentation, a honky-tonk piano, and the spirited, upbeat melodies provide ironic accompaniment for Dallas and Ringo's stoic, purposeful walk.

Earlier in the film, the score even collapses the diegetic and nondiegetic. Just as Hatfield is about to shoot Mrs. Mallory, he is himself killed. Suddenly, she seems to be hearing what we had perceived as the nondiegetic score: "Can you hear it? It's the bugler sounding the charge!" At this point, the diegetic bugle call emerges from and then merges back into the dense nondiegetic score.

There are some quite conventional uses of nondiegetic music in the film too: the use of leitmotifs to identify and accompany the stagecoach and various characters (Mrs. Mallory and Hatfield; Dallas and Ringo); and the use of music to signal important information (like the "stinger" after the first mention of Geronimo), to bridge sequences and cover transitions, and to provide emotional resonance. The shootout in Lordsburg exploits several conventional scoring practices to create suspense: a rising musical line, tremolo strings, and even mickey mousing, the synchronization of musical to visual action. And the conclusion of the film relies upon standard conventions for musical endings, a privileged reiteration of the main leitmotif as Dallas and Ringo escape.

I'd like to take a theoretical turn here to flesh out more fully the ideological function of folk and period music in *Stagecoach* and its relationship to the creation of national identity and nationhood. Of all the elements in a filmic text, music has remained the most resistant to critical analysis, traceable both to the assumption that specific knowledge of musical analysis is necessary to understand a film score and to culturally potent discourses that establish music as the timeless and universal expression of individual genius, untouched by social and historical forces. The work of the Frankfurt School has deconstructed this network of cultural assumptions and exposed the ideological function of music. Yet music as an art form divorced from worldly influences and constraints remains "a highly pervasive fiction,"[32] with a remarkable resilience. Caryl Flinn argues that one of the most potent and persistent of the discourses attached to music has been that music "has the peculiar ability to ameliorate the social existence it allegedly overrides, and offers, in one form or another, the sense of something better. Music extends an impression of perfection and integrity in an otherwise imperfect, unintegrated world." Music's "utopian function" purportedly offers listeners a "fullness of experience . . . an ability to return . . . to better, allegedly more 'perfect' times and memories."[33] Film scores transport listeners from the technological, fragmented experience of a postindustrial mechanically reproduced art form to an idealized past of imagined plentitude and recaptured unity. Thus film music always carries with it a kind of nostalgia, which Hollywood has been particularly adept at exploiting.

Music's utopian function can be extremely helpful in coming to terms with the use of music in Ford westerns. Film music's power to return us to a general idealized past is transformed through folk and period song into a specific idealized past, the nineteenth-century American West, a mythic past that never actually existed. Bruno David Ussher, in his 1939 review of the film, recognized this power, noting that the American music makes *Stagecoach* "more of a correspondingly true portrayal of life as it was on the middle-border half a century ago."[34] Folk and period songs not only make the imagined past real, however, they create nostalgia for it, harnessing the pleasures and plentitudes of film music, its ability to offer a utopic alternative to experiential reality (more integrated, harmonic, and aesthetically pleasing), to Ford's particular vision of a moment in America's past. The use of folk and period song is a critical component in Ford's seductive vision and provides more than just a tapestry of westernness. Song not only convinces us that Ford's vision of the American past is authentic, it wraps that vision in nostalgia. We long for that vision and what is attached to it: a particular way of thinking about what makes America a nation.

In Ford's vision, America's national character was forged on the frontier, and what it means to be American emerged from the process of settling the West. *The Iron Horse* and *3 Bad Men* concern themselves with Manifest Destiny and the epic processes that carved out the space for western expansion. *Stagecoach* is more intimate, focusing on the experience of life in that space and the place of community in facing it. Ford described *Stagecoach* as "a simple, intimate little thing. . . . It isn't even colossal in a small way."[35] The film follows a group of passengers journeying by stagecoach from Tonto to Lordsburg, with Geronimo on the warpath somewhere in between. The assembled travelers embody a spectrum of social classes and occupations in American society, a representative frontier community: the sheriff, the banker, the salesman, the soldier's eastern wife, the doctor, the driver, the southern gambler, the prostitute, and the outlaw. They are the forward guard of settlement on the frontier, and they are threatened from forces both outside and inside the coach. The stagecoach itself becomes a forge in which the group is tested, and characters' fates will be determined, as they are in most Ford films, by their social function, by the extent of their ability to participate in and serve the community.

The aristocratic southerner Hatfield (John Carradine), who cannot move beyond his class privilege and embrace the more egalitarian ethos of the West, is killed. The banker Gatewood (Berton Churchill), who refuses to set aside his selfish goals, goes to jail. On the other hand, Mrs. Mallory (Louise Platt), who accepts the help of the socially outcast Doc Boone (Thomas Mitchell) and Dallas (Claire Trevor) and learns to respect them both, survives with her newborn to be reunited with her husband. The working-class prototypes Buck (Andy Devine) and Curley (George Bancroft), whose primary missions are to serve and protect the passengers, survive, as does Mr. Peacock (Donald Meek), meek though he may be, who is able to put his own physical needs behind those of the others, and who reminds all, "Let's have a little Christian charity one for the other." Drunken Doc Boone sobers up and does his duty. That leaves Dallas and Ringo (John Wayne). Despite the film's democratic ethos and its pointed attack on class elitism, *Stagecoach* is as much a film about fitting in as it is about freedom, as much about the necessity of exclusion as about the cost of inclusion. Gaylyn Studlar reads this disjunction at the film's ideological core in terms of "longstanding social contradictions inscribed in depictions (both fiction and nonfiction) of the frontier."[36]

Stagecoach would be neither the first nor the last western, filmic or otherwise, to grapple with what Doc calls the "blessings of civilization."

Dallas's fate—although accepted by the passengers, she is excluded from reintegration into the larger community—bears the traces of the dominant cultural ideologies about female sexuality. Despite her punishment and penance, she remains an outcast. And think of the ways the music participates in this process: Mrs. Mallory gets "Jeanie with the Light Brown Hair"; Dallas gets the bluesy "Careless Love" and, even after she helps with the delivery of the baby, the saloon songs "She's More to Be Pitied Than Censured" and "Up in a Balloon." When she is holding a baby, however, or when she is with Ringo, the music takes a more forgiving approach, with the aptly named "Gentle Annie" accompanying her relinquishing the baby and the almost beatific "I Love You" for her scenes with Ringo.

The case with Ringo, I think, is more complicated. As Tag Gallagher has argued, Ringo "seems the most community-minded." [37] His appearance, in his Union cavalry garb, the mark of his inclusion, as well as a subtle reminder of Hatfield's outsider Confederate status, marks him as a hero of the new American order. Yet, as Gallagher points out, "he gave vengeance priority over defense during the Indian chase." [38] It comes as a bit of a shock when Ringo announces, "I lied to you Curley. Got three left." It's a telling detail, and not only because it points to Ringo's willingness to put his vengeance first. Three bullets for three men presumes either an extraordinarily reckless ego or superlative marksmanship. When the latter option is confirmed in the shoot-out with the Plummer boys, it reminds us of just how dangerous Ringo is and points to a darker reading of his character than the innocent ranch boy persona he presents to the passengers. Hatfield is killed, Gatewood goes to jail, Ringo is allowed to escape, and Dallas decides to follow Ringo, but one way or another, they all have to leave.

The cement that binds the community together and protects it against outsiders is ritual. In Ford westerns, rituals are inherently musical: religious services, weddings and funerals, dances, marches, and singing. Much has already been written about the function of dance in creating and sustaining emergent frontier communities. Peter Stowell, for instance, describes dance as "Ford's ultimate expression of community cohesion . . . sealing civilization's compact," and Joseph Reed calls it "climactic community summary." [39] And while dance is an obvious signifier of the community and its power, song is equally revelatory of the power of music to bind the community together and identify those who belong to it.

In fact, so many moments of community cohesion are celebrated through song in Ford westerns that it comes as a bit of a surprise that the passengers in *Stagecoach* don't sing. But in an earlier version of the film, they did. In a sequence cut after previews, the assembled passengers sang "Ten Thousand Cattle." Apparently, it was assumed by the music department at Paramount that "Ten Thousand Cattle" was a folk song. In the 1930s, several anthologies of cowboy music reproduced the song without attribution, probably depending upon the venerable folklorist John Lomax, among the earliest collectors of frontier folk songs, who included it as a folk song in his 1938 edition of *Cowboy Songs and Other Frontier Ballads*.[40] "Ten Thousand Cattle," however, was actually under copyright to Owen Wister and was used for the stage adaptation of his novel *The Virginian* in 1904.[41] The song appears in a number of films, including the first sound *Virginian* (1929), starring Gary Cooper. Little wonder then that Paramount found itself at a very late date in the production using a copyrighted song it had thought was in the public domain.

According to Dudley Nichols's final revised script of November 11, 1938, the passengers were to sing "Ten Thousand Cattle," initiated by Doc Boone, after Ringo enters the coach, in an attempt to restore the fragile camaraderie among the passengers.[42] But both the preliminary undated cue sheet and the final music cue sheet of January 30, 1939, position the song differently. In these documents "Ten Thousand Cattle" is sung as the passengers await the birth of Mrs. Mallory's baby at Apache Wells, with a six-second snatch reprised by Doc Boone as the passengers leave. Since the cue sheets postdate the final revised script by over two months, they are more reliable evidence.

Additionally, placing the singing of "Ten Thousand Cattle" at Ringo's entrance is at odds with the narrative. The song is a slow ballad, with melancholy lyrics. Its content seems much more appropriate for the tense waiting scene at Apache Wells than for Ringo's initial appearance. Additionally, a publicity still from the production shows the cast, with a pianist, rehearsing a song, which would have to be "Ten Thousand Cattle." All the stagecoach passengers are in the photo, in costume, with the exception of Mrs. Mallory, another indication that it was meant to be sung in the waiting sequence, in which she would have been otherwise engaged. In either place, the song was positioned to bind the passengers together. And the song, with its cowboy lyrics and simple harmonies, so obviously connotes folk song that no one on the production thought otherwise.

Figure 7. Cover of "Ten Thousand Cattle Straying (Dead Broke)" depicting
Frank Campeau, who first sang the song on stage. He would later star in
Ford's *3 Bad Men*. Courtesy Archive of Popular American Music, UCLA.

TWO OUTCASTS AT TABLE (Part 2)

10		
:51	Leo Shuken	
	Irving Berlin, Inc.	inst. back
	no	no

TEN THOUSAND CATTLE

11		
:06	Owen Wister	partial
	Witmark	vocal vis. & inst. back
	YES	YES

PARTING OF COACH AND TROOPS

12		
:19½	John M. Leipold	
	Irving Berlin, Inc.	inst. back
	no	no

SNOW COUNTRY AND THIRSTY PASSENGERS

13		
:30	John M. Leipold	
	Irving Berlin, Inc.	inst. back
	no	no

APACHE WELLS ARRIVAL

eel 5		
14	John M. Leipold	
:51	Irving Berlin, Inc.	inst. back
	no	no

MRS. MALLORY FAINTS

15		
1:10	W. Franke Harling	
	Irving Berlin, Inc.	inst. back
	no	no

BIRTH OF A BABY

16		
:23	W. Franke Harling	
	Irving Berlin, Inc.	inst. back
	no	no

TEN THOUSAND CATTLE

17		
1:21	Owen Wister	partial
	Witmark	vocal vis. & inst. back
	YES	YES

THE BABY IS BORN

18		
1:10	W. Franke Harling	
	Irving Berlin, Inc.	inst. back
	no	no

THE KID PROPOSES

eel 6		
19	Leo Shuken	
3:29	Irving Berlin, Inc.	inst. back
	no	no

OUTCASTS IN KITCHEN

eel 7		
20	Leo Shuken	
1:58½	Irving Berlin, Inc.	inst. back
	no	no

APACHE FIRES AND LEE'S FERRY

21		
5:52	Gerard Carbonara	
	Irving Berlin, Inc.	inst. back
	no	no

GERONIMO THREATENS

eel 8		
22	Gerard Carbonara	
:55	Irving Berlin, Inc.	inst. back
	no	

Figure 8. Cue sheet, *Stagecoach*, Paramount Music Department. Note the appearance of "Ten Thousand Cattle," which was deleted from the final release version. Courtesy Paramount Music Department.

"Ten Thousand Cattle" never made it into the final cut. Matthew Bernstein contends that Ford cut the scene himself after preview audiences reacted negatively.[43] There may have been reticence about using "Ten Thousand Cattle" even before previews. It was assumed that "Ten Thousand Cattle" was in the public domain. Given the number of people at work on this film and the murky provenance of the song, it is not entirely surprising that the "Ten Thousand Cattle" sequence was filmed before it was discovered that the song was actually under copyright. "Ten Thousand Cattle" was hastily pencilled in on the preliminary cue sheets. Studio executives briefly considered reshooting the sequences with another song rather than pay what they felt to be an outrageous permission fee.[44] But time was running short. The problem was discovered in mid-January; the recording of the score was scheduled for January 24, 1939, and previews for February 2. So "Ten Thousand Cattle" remained in the film for the previews and was still listed on the final music cue sheet of January 30. When audiences reacted badly, the song was cut, and it seems possible that copyright problems figured in the decision to eliminate it.

Inside the coach, the passengers establish their fragile community without the help of song, but not without the help of music. The score is part of the apparatus by which the Anglo inhabitants of the coach are established as an American community, the rightful heirs to the vast "unpopulated" virgin wilderness of the West. The Indians, the native population in the West, are positioned as the Other, from whom the wilderness must be wrested. Music helps to draw these distinctions. The Anglo passengers are represented by what is perceived by most listeners as folk song. Because of the immense cultural investment in folk music as a distinctly American art form, especially in the 1930s, its use confers Americanness on whom it accompanies: the Anglo passengers inside the coach, the towns they emerge from and move to, and even the wilderness itself.

Music accompanying Indians, on the other hand, exploits powerful musical and cinematic codes to reinforce cultural stereotypes about Otherness. Music thus both defines the boundaries of the dominant white community and positions Indians outside it, indeed, outside the very definition of Americanness. The use of music to define ethnic and racial boundaries, what K. J. Donnelly describes as "expelling that which you disown and reconfiguring the outside to fit your fears,"[45] was a staple of classical Hollywood scoring. But it has a long history outside of Hollywood too.

Figure 9. Publicity still, *Stagecoach:* cast members rehearsing a song—probably "Ten Thousand Cattle"—at the piano; from the left, John Carradine (just barely visible), Andy Devine, Berton Churchill, George Bancroft, John Wayne, and Claire Trevor. Courtesy Academy of Motion Picture Arts and Sciences.

Indian music was derived from musical stereotypes for the representation of the West's Others—Turks, Chinese, and Arabs, in particular—that developed concurrently with western imperialism and exploded onto the musical scene in the nineteenth century: unusual, repetitive rhythms; modal melodies; short, descending motifs; a tendency to veer away from conventional major and minor tonalities and toward chromaticism; and a reliance upon unusual instrumentation, especially percussion. As Michael Pisani has documented, such musical stereotypes were ready at hand in the nineteenth century for composers and performers looking for ways to accompany Indians on the stage and in Wild West entertainments such as outdoor extravaganzas and pageants.[46] Extant music from Buffalo Bill's Wild West, for instance, includes clear examples of these stereotypes in compositions such as "On the Warpath" and "The Passing of the Red Man."

Pisani argues, as does Claudia Gorbman, that actual examples of Na-

tive American song, captured and preserved through ethnographic tran-
scription and recording, had far less impact on the musical representation of Indians than did popular culture.[47] In fact, Pisani makes a strong
case that even serious art composers, in both this and other countries,
such as Dvorak in his *New World Symphony,* based their musical representations of Indians on popular culture models.[48] Not surprisingly, these
stereotypes found their way into film. Gorbman points out that "stock
Indian music" was fully developed by the 1910s,[49] verifiable by even a
cursory glimpse into any of the several important musical encyclopedias
of the era. Hollywood developed a specific vocabulary for representing
Indians: a rhythmic figure of four equal beats with the accent falling on
the first beat often played by drums or low bass instruments; the use of
perfect fifths and fourths in the harmonic design; and the use of modal
melody.[50] These conventions for Indianness trailed with them connotations of the primitive, the exotic, and the savage. Indian music had become so generic that a composer like Max Steiner would recycle the same
cues for Indians from one film to another. In *Stagecoach,* the tom-tom
rhythmic structure, what Gorbman aptly describes as the "Indian-on-
the-warpath motif,"[51] and the use of parallel fourths in the harmonic design establish the Indians as wild, powerful, primitive, and exotic.

Music in *Stagecoach* not only establishes Indians as Other, it also establishes them as intruders on the frontier landscape. In one of the most
oft-quoted sequences in Ford, the stagecoach, in extreme long shot,
moves through the gigantic dimensions of Monument Valley followed by
a pan to a menacing group of Indians ready to attack it. The sequence is
so stunning that Ford repeats it. Musical stereotypes establish Indians as
savage and threatening. Up until this point in the film, shots of Monument Valley have been accompanied by the stagecoach's theme, the
folksy "Oh, Bury Me Not on the Lone Prairie," building a powerful connection between Americanness, white civilization, and the frontier. In
fact, immediately prior to the appearance of Indians, the majestic image
of the frontier is accompanied by the stagecoach theme. It is Indian
music that seems out of place in Monument Valley and Indians who do
not belong.

Music also codes Yakima (the uncredited Elvira Rios), the Apache
wife of the jovial stationmaster Chris (the uncredited Chris Pin Martin),
as the sexualized female Other. Although married to Chris, Yakima
clearly has divided loyalties and abandons him to return to Geronimo.
Is it Yakima who alerts Geronimo to the existence and whereabouts of
the stagecoach? Her sexuality is established in a variety of ways: the nar-

rative situation itself (she is surrounded by men, to whom she sings), the veiled comic reference to her sexuality ("She's a leetle bit savage, I theenk," Chris says), her sultry voice, and her song, seductive even if you don't understand Spanish and more provocative if you do. Yakima sings to three *vaqueros* outside the station house. She lets them know—in Spanish—that the coast is clear, and they steal the spare horses. But editing and cinematography sever the natural connections between them. Yakima is positioned as a spectacle of exoticism, sensuality, and Otherness, and her performance will find an interesting parallel in Chihuahua's songs in *My Darling Clementine*.

As Charles Ramirez Berg argues in his important essay on the multicultural dynamic in Ford westerns, "it is a mistake to dismiss Ford too hastily as one more racist filmmaker."[52] Similarly, J. P. Tellote, writing on racial representation in the film, points to *Stagecoach*'s many "small reminders" of the cultural integrity of Geronimo's people.[53] In Ford, the representation of the Other is generally and genuinely complicated. Song becomes part of that complication. It comes as no surprise that Indians are represented as Other in a film made in 1939. What is surprising is the way the Other is given a voice, literally, through the film's music. The narrative is suspended to allow Yakima to sing—a marker not without import in Ford. Song provides the context where, as Edward Buscombe points out, "the voice of the Other forces its way through,"[54] where something of an alternative experience of what white settlers term the "wilderness" is suggested. Her song, "Al pensar en ti," is a love song for her native land, a stunning example of the Other voicing a desire to return to her people: "When I think of you / Land where I was born / Nostalgia fills my heart. / This song / Brings relief and solace to my pain. / The sad notes of this song / Bring me memories of that love / When I think of him / Once again happiness / Is reborn in my sad heart."[55] Yakima willingly abandons the relative security of both the stagecoach station and her marriage to its stationmaster when she learns that Geronimo has jumped the reservation. She chooses to return to the land and to her tribe. Her song and its message function as a counterbalance to the stereotypical aspects of the Indians in the film. Still, when Yakima's disappearance is announced, there are some broad comic strokes at her expense, such as when her husband describes her disappearance and in the linguistic confusion she is mistaken for a horse. In the final continuity screenplay, it is clearer that Yakima engineers the taking of the spare horses and that she was married against her will. Says Chris: "I buy her for two horses. Of course she don't like me much. She

like big Apache buck, maybe."[56]But Yakima doesn't have the song. It
must have been added after the final version of the screenplay was complete. Was it Ford who inserted it?

I think the film's representation of the Mexicans is worth a closer
look, too. There are plenty of Mexican stereotypes here: the simple-
minded Mexican (Chris, the station master), the threatening greaser
(Luke Plummer's Spanish-speaking and clearly coded Mexican sidekick).
And when Yakima sings, it's in the Spanish of her adopted Mexican culture, not her native tongue, as if the Mexican and Apache cultures are
interchangeable. (Since Elvira Rios was a Mexican singer of some note,
casting contributes to this conflation.) But around the edges of the film,
there is also recognition of the cultural diversity of the historical West
and some attempt to move past negative stereotypes. Intermarriage between Indians and Mexicans (Chris and Yakima) and Anglos and Mexicans (Buck and Julietta) is an accepted and even routine part of the
world depicted in *Stagecoach*. Chris has no fear of the Apaches, because,
as he explains to Buck, he has an Apache wife. And Buck, an Anglo, who
complains about his Mexican wife, sounds like any henpecked husband
grousing about unappetizing cooking and ever-multiplying relatives. Intermarriage may be played for laughs in *Stagecoach*, but it is not represented as threatening or wrong. *Stagecoach* also includes Anglo-Mexican
friendship. Chris warns Ringo about the Plummer boys because Ringo's
father "was a good friend of mine." It's also interesting that Ringo is
bilingual, as are many Ford protagonists. Yakima, too, is fluent in Spanish, and her song, sung in Spanish, could also be seen as a form of cultural exchange, evidence of Berg's contention that Ford "regarded cultures not as autonomous, static, or fixed states, but rather as fluid,
evolving, and organic ones that were inextricably intertwined."[57]

Cultures blend on the frontier, and music plays an important, if subtle, part in this process. In *Stagecoach,* Yakima, an Apache, sings in Spanish to the accompaniment of guitars, in Hollywood scoring, a typical signifier of Mexico. Earlier, the stagecoach bearing its Anglo passengers
arrives at a former Apache watering hole, Apache Wells, now the
province of the Mexican stationmaster, to the accompaniment of music
also coded as Mexican. This time the musical cue borrows the instrumentation and harmonics of the mariachi band. Mexican music becomes the medium of exchange in the meetings between Anglos and Indians in *Fort Apache* and *She Wore a Yellow Ribbon,* the meeting
between Anglos and Mexicans in *Rio Grande,* and even Anglo courtship
rituals are negotiated through Mexican song in a scene cut from *Fort*

Apache. It is *Two Rode Together,* however, whose narrative features the story of a Mexican woman held captive by Indians, that offers the fullest development of the soundtrack as a medium of cultural exchange.

Stagecoach was immensely successful, and it charted new territory both for Ford and for Hollywood, but it would be a while before Ford returned to the western. The war intervened, and Ford was called into active service in the Navy in 1941. He was put in command of the Field Photographic Branch of the Office of Strategic Services (OSS), and in that capacity, he produced a number of films, including two Oscar-winning documentaries, *The Battle of Midway* and *December 7th* (1943). Ford was released from active duty in 1945 to film the wartime drama *They Were Expendable.* His first film after the war would be another western, *My Darling Clementine.*

CHAPTER 4

Two Fordian Film Scores

My Darling Clementine
and *The Man Who Shot Liberty Valance*

The Man Who Shot Liberty Valance and *My Darling Clementine* may seem an odd pairing.[1] The two films were made eighteen years apart, their visual designs are strikingly different, their narratives have little in common, with the exception of the classic generic confrontation between the lawful and the lawless, and they employ none of the same actors in either starring or supporting roles. But in terms of their music, they have more than a little in common. Cyril Mockridge is credited as the composer of both scores, but these films share more than just Mockridge's credit. *The Man Who Shot Liberty Valance* returns to Ford's roots in the early sound era and connects more profoundly to the musical design of *My Darling Clementine* than any other Ford western.

Ford envisioned the score for *My Darling Clementine* as virtually all diegetic, comprised of folk songs, period music, and a Protestant hymn, carefully chosen and sparsely orchestrated. It is the most Fordian of his western scores in my opinion. The film chronicles the establishment of law and order in the frontier town of Tombstone by a new marshal, Wyatt Earp (Henry Fonda), who is driven by revenge for the murder of his brother James (Don Garner) at the hands of the lawless Old Man Clanton (Walter Brennan) and his sons. The Clantons aren't the only force standing in Earp's way. Doc Holliday (Victor Mature), a gambler and gunslinger, is the town's corrupt power broker, and his girlfriend Chihuahua (Linda Darnell) is trouble. Wyatt and Doc become friends, although their relationship is strained, especially when Holliday's fiancée,

Clementine (Cathy Downs), arrives on the scene. The Clantons are vanquished, and Doc Holliday is killed, in the celebrated shoot-out at the OK Corral, and Clementine settles in to become the new schoolmarm, but Wyatt leaves Tombstone.

Like *Stagecoach, My Darling Clementine* is about civilization and its stabilizing effects on the American frontier. It is about the power of the dominant community to define a collective identity, exclude outsiders, and protect and sustain its citizens, through violence if necessary. Community becomes the mechanism by which the West is tamed, and that frontier community resonates as a prototype of the American nation itself. But, as in so many other Ford westerns, there is a deep ambivalence about the need for and consequences of civilizing the frontier.

Music in *My Darling Clementine* provides a wash of authenticity for the film's evocation of the historic past. The main title is an excellent example of the use of period music to do so. The sequence features three American songs, "My Darling Clementine," a period piece; "The Devil's Dream," an Anglo American folk song; and "Ten Thousand Cattle," which sounds like a folk song (but isn't). They are arranged for accordion, guitar, and violin; one, "The Devil's Dream," is instrumental, played on a country fiddle, and the other two are sung by a male chorus. The guitar is more usually a signifier of Mexico in Ford and it serves that purpose in *My Darling Clementine*. But here in the main title sequence (and in the end title), it connotes westernness. These uncomplicated arrangements of American music, with their focus on simple and characteristic western instrumentation, are a departure from the typical scoring practices of the era, but they are reassuring signs of the authenticity of the images.[2]

All three pieces of music have the patina of genuine folk song, despite the fact that two of them, "Ten Thousand Cattle" and "My Darling Clementine," date from after the time in which the film is set. The gunfight at the OK Corral occurred in 1881. "My Darling Clementine" is generally attributed to Percy Montrose, under whose name it was first published as "My Darling Clementine" in 1884, but Montrose borrowed the lyrics and changed the melody from an earlier song, "Down by the River Liv'd a Maiden," published in 1863 by H. S. Thompson, and probably intended for the minstrel stage. The song's lyrics are voiced in the main title, the famous chorus first—"You are lost and gone forever, dreadful sorry, Clementine"—followed by the verse—"In a cavern, in a canyon. . . ." Audiences today, however, may be unfamiliar with this touchstone of American music. "My Darling Clementine" tells the story of loss, of Clementine's death by drowning in a mining accident. Its blend of tragedy and melancholy—and remember that the lyrics are heard here—make the choice of "My Darling Clementine" to open the film a bold musical strategy for a major studio production. The song will come to represent the character of Clementine and serves as a reminder of the central position women occupy in Ford's frontier communities.

"My Darling Clementine" is one of seventeen separate pieces of period music used in the film. "Oh My Darling Clementine," "The Devil's Dream," and "Red River Valley" are traditional Anglo American songs. "Buffalo Gals" is a folk song, too, but it was a hit on the minstrel stage at one point in its history.[3] "Four Little White Doves," "El Sombrero Blanco," and "Carmela" are Spanish Californian folk songs. "I Dreamt I Dwelled in Marble Halls" is a sentimental English ballad by Michael Balfe. "Ten Thousand Cattle" was heard on Broadway in 1904. "Camptown Races," "Nelly Bly," and "Ring, Ring de Banjo," by Stephen Foster, "Oh! Dem Golden Slippers," by James A. Bland, "Little Brown Jug" by Joseph (Eastburn) Winner, "Shew! Fly Don't Bother Me!" by Frank Cambell and Billy Reeves, "The Quilting Party" by J. Fletcher, and "Old Dan Tucker," by Daniel Decautur Emmett are all minstrel songs. The Protestant hymn "Shall We Gather at the River?" makes its second appearance in a Ford western.

This wealth of period music in *My Darling Clementine* is at the expense of the nondiegetic score, which virtually disappears from the film. There is simply much less music in *My Darling Clementine* than in a typical studio film of the era or even a typical studio western. There are no musical transitions to bridge sequences and no use of the conventional practice of sneaking in or tailing out the musical cues. Climactic sequences are left unscored: Wyatt's chasing down of the stagecoach bearing Doc Holliday; Wyatt and Doc's ensuing gun battle; Chihuahua's shooting; Billy Clanton's escape and Virgil's chase. The gunfight at the OK Corral has no music, and even Wyatt and Clementine's farewell is silent, with music coming in only after their conversation. When music is needed, it is usually diegetic. Sometimes this music responds to the emotional content of the sequence: the conclusion of Chihuahua's operation, accompanied by sentimental minstrel ballads on the saloon's honky-tonk piano. Sometimes it doesn't: Wyatt and Doc's first, tense meeting with "Camptown Races" and "Shew! Fly Don't Bother Me," or Doc's private moment of self-loathing with "The Cuckoo Waltz" wafting up into his hotel room, or the start of Chihuahua's operation with "Ring, Ring de Banjo" on a honky-tonk piano. In fact, there might not have been a nondiegetic score at all had not fundamental changes been made to Ford's musical design.

Ford chose the music for the film, and he appears to have done so before Mockridge was assigned. By November 1945, when Ford was beginning work on an adaptation of Stuart Lake's *Wyatt Earp, Frontier Marshall,* he was already deciding on songs and had contacted Alfred Newman, head of Twentieth Century–Fox's Music Department, for copies of songs he was considering. That he contacted Newman, not Mockridge, is an indication that Mockridge was not involved at this stage. Newman sent sheet music over to Ford's house for his approval, phonograph records being difficult to come by just after the war. "Please let me know how you like, or if you like, any of them," Newman wrote.[4]

Twentieth Century–Fox's publicity capitalized on Ford's involvement with the music in the film's press book. "When the director could have called up the studio music department and said, 'Write me a couple of authentic tunes that could have been sung in Tombstone during the eighties,' Ford insisted that absolute authenticity be the byword, and the research department had a job on its hands," the press book boasts.[5] It sounds to me as though the publicity department had a job on its hands. Ford chose the songs heard in his films carefully, but authenticity was not paramount among his considerations, and I doubt whether he used any of the studio's so-called research. Moreover, the press book's description of the activities of the "research department" seems suspicious: "Poring over a stack of old Bird Cage Theatre programs of 1879, 1880, and 1881; Checking with old-time residents of Tombstone and Tucson; and searching copies of the Old Tombstone 'Nugget' and 'Epitaph,' the researchers came up with such numbers as "Ten Thousand Cattle Gone Astray" [interesting, because it wasn't written until 1904—but perhaps those old-timers in Tombstone remembered Chihuahua singing it] and 'Four White Doves.'"

Almost all of the songs in the film were in the public domain. Like Paramount before it, however, Twentieth Century–Fox initially assumed that this was the case with "Ten Thousand Cattle," as the final cue sheet shows. The problems that beset *Stagecoach* as a result of the belated realization that the song, which figures in *My Darling Clementine* in both instrumental and vocal arrangements, was still under copyright taught Ford to stick to the public domain whenever possible (a bit of wisdom that he specifically passed along to his grandson Dan).[6]

Using music in the public domain was obviously cost-efficient. For instance, on *Fort Apache,* a film loaded with music, the astoundingly low total for music clearance was $50. RKO, the film's distribution company, typically budgeted $3,000 per film for this line item. For *Cheyenne Autumn,* the cost would be zero.

The one other song still under copyright was "The Cuckoo Waltz." Listed as a folk tune on the cue sheet (and it is), the song created some last-minute confusion when it was determined that the arrangement was still under copyright to the Indiana Historical Society. Twentieth Century–Fox's legal department had cleared the copyright once before for *Young Mr. Lincoln.* They cleared it once again for *My Darling Clementine.*

Mockridge gets sole screen credit for "Music" and Edward Powell for "Orchestral Arrangements," but *My Darling Clementine* was a multi-authored score if ever there was one. David Bottolph and John N. Scott wrote the originally composed cues in the score, and, in addition to Mockridge and Powell, several arrangers contributed to the score, some substantially: Charles Henderson, Curt Barrett, John N. Scott, Arthur Morton, Herb Taylor, Urban Thielmann, and Ray S. Martinez. The score for the final release version was recorded on September 18, 1946, under the direction of Alfred Newman, who is credited with "Musical Direction."

My Darling Clementine focuses on the development of a frontier community, and the musical design of the film reflects its concerns. Tombstone is defined by a confluence of law, race, ethnicity, and a value system dominated by a Protestant work ethic. Its residents include the lawman Wyatt Earp, the future schoolteacher Clementine Carter, and various law-abiding white inhabitants. It excludes the Other. The music of this community, heard in the hotel, the church, and the theater, consists of folk tunes, such as "The Cuckoo Waltz"; period songs, such as "My Darling Clementine" and "I Dreamt I Dwelt in Marble Halls"; and hymnody: "Shall We Gather at the River?" in simple orchestrations.

The forces threatening this community include those defined as Other by their racial or ethnic difference: the entire Mexican and Indian populations, for instance. Especially revealing, or troublesome, as the case may be, is the extent to which the film conflates the two: "Indian" Charlie, the town troublemaker, speaks Spanish and is coded more as Mexican than as Indian; Chihuahua, whose very name bespeaks Mexican geography, is told to "get back on the reservation" by Earp. Also excluded are those who fail to adopt the Protestant value system: law breakers, the idle, and the drunk. Doc Holliday is triply disenfranchised: he operates outside the law; drink has rendered him unfit for honest work; and he has a girlfriend who is decidedly Other. The cattle-rustling and presumably shiftless Clanton clan, who are unable or unwilling to submit to authority; Chihuahua, a female Other of indeterminate racial/ethnic origin; and the drunken Shakespearean actor Thorndyke (Alan Mowbray) are also outsiders. Their music emanates from saloons and consists of minstrel tunes and Spanish Californian folk songs, often played on a honky-tonk piano, a signifier of the cheap and the tawdry. That the borders between the emergent community and what threatens it are not fully in place when the Earps arrive testifies to the struggle of the community to establish itself and its need for violence to do so.

The famous church dedication and celebratory dance demonstrate the linkage of Anglo American folk song and Protestant hymnody in the frontier community. Much has already been written about this sequence, and specifically about the function of dance in creating and sustaining the emergent community.[7] And while dance is the most obvious signifier of the community, song is equally, or perhaps even more, revelatory of the community's values. The sequence begins with a prologue in which Tombstone's citizenry gather at the site of the future church, a skeletal bell tower and wood plank floor, to sing "Shall We Gather at the River?" The choice of the hymn could hardly be more appropriate or telling. It was one of Ford's favorites. Lindsay Anderson, in one of the first book-length studies of Ford, argues that his films are not derived from Catholic roots (like Hitchcock's, for example) but from Protestant values, "a philosophy that finds virtue in activity [and] see[s] struggle as a necessary element in life."[8] Later critics would disagree with this assessment,[9] but musically speaking, it is difficult to avoid Anderson's conclusion. Although Ford retained his Irish Catholic identity and regularly attended mass, he gravitated to Protestant hymns for his films.

Like "Bringing in the Sheaves" and "Rock of Ages," "Shall We Gather at the River?" is commonly associated with the American frontier, and it functions as Ford's audible signature. But "Shall We Gather at the River?" was written by a Baptist minister, Robert Lowry, in 1862, for his Brooklyn, New York, congregation. In describing the genesis of the hymn, Lowry wrote that he had a vision of the apocalypse in which he saw the throne of God shining brightly next to the heavenly river, with saints gathering around it. Apparently, the hymn was popular with his congregation; it was first anthologized in 1865 and published separately as "Beautiful River" in 1866. It soon became known by its first line.

"Shall We Gather at the River?" is steeped in the notion of predestination. The river of the title is the river Jordan, the crossing denotes the

crossing to the afterlife, and the gathering refers to the community of
Christians who await their turn to cross.[10] Thus Ford's use of the hymn
is at its most appropriate as it is used in *The Searchers,* at funerals, although it was more commonly used on the frontier at baptisms. The
lyrics organize themselves around a question, "Shall we gather at the
river?" But the gentle invocation, "Shall we . . . ?" masks the power of
predestination and the role of the community in determining the chosen.
This is not an open invitation. (And think how different the hymn would
be if "Would you like to . . . ?" replaced "Shall we . . . ?") This is a community of the chosen coming together to take their rightful place, and it
is inclusion in the group that verifies chosen status. No wonder Ford
liked it: the lyrics resonate with the power of community. The ethos of
the hymn is played out in the sequence. The assemblage of the congregation is represented as an instance of social inclusion, but who are gathered (Wyatt and Clementine) and who are not (most conspicuously, Doc
and Chihuahua) reflects the principle of exclusion by which a community operates.

The church dedication is followed by a dance to the strains of "The
Cuckoo Waltz." Again, music connects Protestant values to the emergent
community. "The Cuckoo Waltz" has a long and interesting pedigree as
a kind of Protestant dance music known as play-party music, which
emerged during the colonial period and was used throughout the nineteenth century, surviving in some places into the twentieth. Many of the
Protestant sects populating the new nation, Quakers, Mennonites,
Methodists, Baptists, and Presbyterians, as well as fundamentalists of
many sects, viewed dance as a "wicked sport."[11] Playing games to the accompaniment of music, however, was another matter entirely. Play-party
music was generally homespun, created by settlers themselves, sometimes based on the folk songs of their native countries, sometimes originally composed, and mostly an improvisational mix of the two. Play-
party music was characterized by simple, repetitive rhyme structures and
would usually be sung without musical accompaniment. Intricate game
patterns enacted to the music were handed down from generation to generation and traded between communities.[12] "The Cuckoo Waltz" enjoyed a renaissance of sorts in the 1910s and 1920s, appearing in a collection of folk songs published by the Indiana Historical Society,
published as sheet music in 1921,[13] and appearing in the venerable Carl
Sandburg's *American Songbag* in 1927.

The genesis of "The Cuckoo Waltz" as Protestant dance music brings
an interesting subtext to the sequence. Although the tune is jaunty and

upbeat and may initially seem out of place at a religious gathering, "The Cuckoo Waltz" has a Protestant lineage and a clear religious function. "Shall We Gather at the River?" followed by "The Cuckoo Waltz" makes perfect sense for listeners who know the history of the song. Ford certainly did, since the book he turned to, not once but twice, for "The Cuckoo Waltz," *The Play-Party in Indiana,* contains a history of the form. There is a certain irony in its use in *My Darling Clementine,* however. Immediately before playing "The Cuckoo Waltz," John Simpson (Russell Simpson) announces: "I've read the good book . . . and I've nary found one word against dancing."

The town's two saloons, marked by lawlessness, bawdyness, ignorance, and the Other, become the locus of what opposes the establishment of community in Tombstone. The music here is a mixture of minstrel tunes, largely played on a honky-tonk piano, and Spanish Californian folk songs. "Buffalo Gals," a hit on the minstrel stage, can be heard first when "Indian" Charlie is apprehended and later in the saloon where Wyatt Earp plays cards. "Camptown Races" and "Shew! Fly Don't Bother Me" can be heard in the tense meeting between Doc and Wyatt, and "Little Brown Jug" during Thorndyke's entrance, a musical cue for his inebriation. Later, when Doc performs surgery on Chihuahua, the honky-tonk saloon piano plays two sentimental minstrel ballads, "Nelly Bly"[14] and "The Quilting Party." Two Spanish Californian folk songs "Four Little White Doves" and "El Sombrero Blanco," accompany Chihuahua's appearances, and when Chihuahua strums on the guitar, it is to the strains of another Spanish American folk song, "Carmela." Chihuahua sings "Ten Thousand Cattle," whose lyrics about lost cattle taunt Wyatt Earp, in the saloon.

In Ford films, group singing symbolizes the power of community and signals acceptance. Villains don't sing. As Shiloh Clegg remarks in *Wagon Master,* "Never did know a bad man who had any music in him." But often the dispossessed do sing, and it is interesting to note how many of the solo performances of song belong to them. For a variety of reasons, Ford generally gave solo performances of song to supporting characters (and Henry Fonda croaking out "Red River Valley" in *The Grapes of Wrath* might be one of them). Often their songs offer a window into the emotional terrain of dispossession: the street performer (Dennis O'Dea) in *The Informer* singing "The Minstrel Boy," a tune adopted by Irish rebels; Yakima singing "Al pensar en ti," a song of longing for her native land in *Stagecoach;* Connie Joad (Eddie Quillan) serenading the dispossessed migrants with "Going Down the Road Feeling

Bad" in *The Grapes of Wrath;* a Filipino nightclub singer (Pacita Tod-
Tod) crooning "My Country 'Tis of Thee," on a U.S. Navy base at the
onset of World War II in *They Were Expendable;* the Abilene Kid (Harry
Carey Jr.), singing "The Streets of Laredo" to the orphaned newborn in
3 Godfathers. Song provides a moment when the outsider is given a voice
and an opportunity to raise concerns that the films do not fully develop:
the tragedy of the British occupation of Northern Ireland; the psychic
and emotional cost to the Indians of white settlement on the frontier; the
assault on masculinity occasioned by the Great Depression; the anxiety
of a people whose nation and culture are facing assault; the morally ambiguous position of the young outlaw.

   Chihuahua's performance of "Ten Thousand Cattle" is another example. The song tells of "10,000 cattle straying," leaving their owner,
"dead broke" and with nothing to do but waste his time in gambling
halls. In the stage adaptation of Owen Wister's *The Virginian,* the song
very likely served to provide a musical respite from the violent proceed-
ings on stage, which included plenty of gunplay and a hanging. It was
sung by the character Trampas, played by Frank Campeau, who would
later play one of the protagonists in *3 Bad Men*. In *My Darling Clementine,* the reference to lost cattle clearly refers to the Earp brothers' rus-
tled cattle, but in a larger sense, the song is a reminder of the possibility
of failure on the frontier. In giving the song to Chihuahua to sing, the
film allows us to glimpse her experience of the frontier: not making it,
not fitting in, giving up. Of course, Chihuahua, like Yakima in *Stagecoach,* is made the object of spectacle while voicing this point of view,
filmed in ways that underscore her lack of social integration. When Chihuahua sings, the saloon is marked as a performance space, and Chihuahua remains unconnected to the card players she entertains through
both the narrative construction (they are paying little or no attention to
her) and her position in the mise-en-scène (she is behind them). Camer-
awork further isolates Chihuahua, specifically separating her from Earp.

   Wyatt moves between the two worlds of Tombstone. Initially positioned outside the community, Wyatt is gradually absorbed into it, and
his movement from one locus to the other is marked in musical terms;
the songs that accompany Wyatt chart his progress away from corruption and lawlessness and toward a social contract with the community.
The Earps' first experience in Tombstone, however, positions Wyatt and
his brothers as outsiders. As the Earps approach the town, the rousing
music of "The Devil's Dream" (the title foreshadowing narrative events
for those who recognize it) and "My Darling Clementine" rolls out from

the saloons. Initially almost unrecognizable because of the quick tempo at which it is played, "My Darling Clementine" is wrenched out of context here, like "Shall We Gather at the River?" in *Stagecoach,* a signal to the listener that something is wrong. The tempo so materially alters the tone and mood of the familiar song that most listeners fail to recognize it. The Clantons have told Wyatt that Tombstone is "a fine town." The arrangement of "My Darling Clementine" tells us otherwise.

A mix of the raucous and the folksy can be heard during Wyatt's visit to the barbershop, which features both minstrel music and genuine folk song. Offscreen but clearly diegetic piano music can be heard emanating from nearby saloons: "Oh! Dem Golden Slippers," a minstrel tune, concluding as Wyatt attempts to sit in the chair, followed by "Old Dan Tucker," another minstrel tune. But next we hear "Red River Valley," a folk song. The music's diegetic origin is demonstrated when the shooting starts and the music abruptly stops, the piano player presumably taking cover. Similar care is taken elsewhere in the film to establish the music as diegetic: listen to the music when Doc first enters the saloon and the music stops, the musicians afraid that Doc might turn on them, or when Clementine, standing on the porch of the hotel, turns her head in the direction of the music when the congregation begins singing "Shall We Gather at the River?" "Buffalo Gals" begins only after Wyatt apprehends "Indian" Charlie, as if the musicians had been hiding until Charlie was caught.

As the narrative advances, Wyatt finds himself more and more drawn to the community and especially to Clementine. That progression is marked by the music. The first time we hear "My Darling Clementine," Wyatt has just met Clementine in the hotel. Wyatt responds to Clementine's invitation to attend the church dedication and is foregrounded in his passage through town with her, accompanied by "Shall We Gather at the River?" At the celebration following the dedication, he dances with Clementine to "The Cuckoo Waltz," which mixes religious and folk elements. In scenes eliminated from the final release print, "Red River Valley" accompanied Wyatt both as he awaited the arrival of Clementine's stage and during his departure from Tombstone. "My Darling Clementine" accompanies his farewell to Clementine.

In fact, it is music and dance that establish Wyatt's status as the community's leader, and the choice of song deepens an understanding of his position. The congregation begin to dance to "The Cuckoo Waltz." Wyatt is soon singled out of the crowd when he attempts to dance with Clementine, and his privileged access to the dance floor is a mark of the

growing respect accorded him. "The Cuckoo Waltz" was used dramatically in Ford's *Young Mr. Lincoln* and in a situation similar to the one
here: at a dance where Lincoln, also played by Fonda, is pathetically (or
charmingly?) out of step. The reference to Abe Lincoln, via the casting
of Fonda, the similar dance steps, and recycling of "The Cuckoo Waltz"
connect Abe to Wyatt, both ennobling Wyatt and pointing to his equivocal position within the community: the heroic leader who never quite
fits in. The lyrics to "The Cuckoo Waltz," although we don't hear them
here, revolve around a story of loss and a cuckoo's call, evoked in the
melody, brings another dimension to the sequence. A cuckoo is a bird
who deposits its eggs in other bird's nests to be hatched and raised.
Cuckoos are born outsiders, always different from those around them.
Thus the use of the song suggests that both Abe and Wyatt are out of
place, something their dancing confirms. I think this is why "The Cuckoo
Waltz" is used briefly for Doc Holliday. He, too, is an outsider, the connotations of the cuckoo underscoring his displacement.

Despite the clear progression of the film toward the development of
law and order, necessary to maintain a community, the ending demonstrates the uneasy fit between the needs of social cohesion and the demands of individualism that characterizes the genre of the western as a
whole. This plays itself out in Wyatt's departure from the very community he has given so much to establish. In this way, *My Darling Clementine* mirrors *Stagecoach,* which ends with sympathy for the outsider and
nostalgia for the outside. In general, Ford films tend more to complication than resolution in their endings, and in the westerns, this tendency
displays itself in a tension between the ideals of the protagonists and the
demands of the communities they have served and often leave. Scott Simmon argues that the film "is so clearly set up . . . to end happily that it
cries out for dissonance."[15] Darryl F. Zanuck, head of Twentieth Century–Fox, may have inserted that kiss between Wyatt and Clementine
(Ford did not shoot that footage), but Ford supplied the dissonance. The
one line of lyrics to be heard ("I'll be loving you forever, oh, my darling
Clementine") and the lonely arrangement for accordion (a guitar comes
in at the very end) bespeak Wyatt's feelings for Clementine and underscore the missed opportunities and sense of loss that hangs over the end
of the film. Ford got the last word after all.

As was his usual practice, Ford worked on *My Darling Clementine* the
way he liked to, without studio interference, in both the preproduction
and production stages. But as the preceding description of the film's ending indicates, the studio did interfere, in the person of Darryl F. Zanuck.

Ford's rough cut, finished in late June 1946, included a musical score that was virtually diegetic, using extremely simple arrangements of Anglo American folk tunes, period songs, and Protestant hymnody. Previews apparently went badly. Zanuck attended a screening, and on June 25, he fired off a memo to Ford detailing what he perceived to be the film's many problems: "I recommend that you have a talk with Sam [Engel, the film's producer] and that you suggest that I be given the film to edit. You trusted me implicitly on *Grapes of Wrath* and *How Green Was My Valley*."[16] But this time Ford would have none of it. Ford left the production and Zanuck took control of the film, making changes without Ford's input or approval. Zanuck trimmed perhaps thirty minutes, generally tightening the dialogue, and cutting some comic bits but leaving the score intact.

A version of the film at this stage of its evolution, known as the preview print, was discovered in the UCLA film archives in the 1990s.[17] This print is not complete; at some point in its history, the first reel, approximately twenty minutes, was lost and replaced with the first reel of the final release print. What remains, however, is an interim version of *My Darling Clementine* much closer to Ford's rough cut of June 25 than the final release version. Zanuck continued making changes to this preview version, now more substantial. He ordered reshoots directed by Lloyd Bacon, including at least the graveside visit and the ending, trimmed even more footage, and made changes to the score, deleting some of the period songs and adding several nondiegetic orchestral cues. The critical consensus seems to be that Zanuck's changes did not damage the film. I feel differently about the changes Zanuck made to the music. The score for the preview print appears to have been a succession of simply arranged and orchestrated folk tunes, hymns, and period music, virtually all of it diegetic. They lend the film a stark, almost modernist, quality. Zanuck's cuts deleted some of the most recognizable folk tunes. The added nondiegetic orchestral musical cues that he authorized alter the musical design of the film.

The preview version of *My Darling Clementine* shows Ford's intentions vis-à-vis the music. The first reel of the preview version, however, is missing; only the final release print exists of the sequences of the Earp brothers arriving outside Tombstone with their cattle; the meeting between the Earps and the Clantons; the campsite camaraderie among the Earp brothers; the Earp brothers' trip to Tombstone; the Earps return and discovery of James's murder and the missing cattle; the return to Tombstone and confrontation with the Clanton clan; a short street se-

quence involving the Earps; and a significant part of the first saloon sequence featuring Chihuahua singing "Ten Thousand Cattle." Some of
these sequences bear the marks of Zanuck's interference and some do
not. The opening credits, for instance, simply and sparsely orchestrated
and dependent upon folk material, sound like Ford. So does the Earp's
first visit to Tombstone with its exclusively diegetic songs and what is left
of the first saloon sequence with Chihuahua's performance of "Ten
Thousand Cattle."

Other sequences do not sound like Ford. The first musical cue in the
diegetic portion of the film, entitled "The Prairie," is a fully orchestrated,
originally composed cue, which accompanies the opening scene of the
Earps with their cattle and includes an entirely conventional musical cue
connoting the sinister Clantons. This cue, and the one entitled "Elegy"
that accompanies the Earps' return to find James dead and their cattle
gone, were composed by David Bottolph. Neither of these cues is in
keeping with Ford's musical design. They were, I believe, added by
Zanuck.

I have my suspicions too about the music underscoring the campsite
sequence, where James displays the piece of jewelry he has bought for his
girlfriend, Corey Sue, and the graveyard farewell when Wyatt visits
James's grave. Both sequences use the sparse orchestrations characteristic of Ford's design—the campfire sequence uses guitars, harmonica, and
a few violins, and the graveside visit, a guitar. But the music here is highly
sentimentalized and distinctly nondiegetic. At least one of these sequences, the graveyard sequence, was reshot by Lloyd Bacon, and the
campsite sequence may have been reedited, perhaps even reshot. These
two musical cues may also have been added by Zanuck.

After the first reel, it is clear which musical cues Zanuck tampered
with. Several musical cues were cut when the sequences they accompanied were trimmed or eliminated: "Four White Doves," sung by Chihuahua before she begins spying on Wyatt's hand at the card game;
"Red River Valley" played on an accordion as Wyatt awaits the arrival
of the stagecoach bearing Clementine; "Oh, Susannah" played on the
banjo and accordion by members of the congregation arriving for the
church dedication; "Camptown Races" during Thorndyke's dramatic
farewell; and "Red River Valley" again, underscoring Wyatt's farewell
to Tombstone.

Several conventional nondiegetic orchestral cues were added: "The
Stagecoach," a lengthy cue marking the arrival of the stagecoach and
continuing through the conversation between Wyatt and the gambler he

kicks out of town and "A Woman Scorned," added as accompaniment
to Chihuahua's angry protest at Doc's leaving her behind. The version of
"My Darling Clementine" that accompanies Clementine's first appearance starts much earlier in the final release print, when Clementine exits
the stagecoach (not when she enters Doc's room, as in the preview print),
and the song is more fully orchestrated. The final reprise of "My Darling
Clementine" was moved earlier in the last sequence, entering immediately after Wyatt finishes his last line, instead of waiting for him to disappear into the distance.

To my mind, the most disruptive changes are the added nondiegetic
orchestral cues, "The Prairie," "Elegy," "Stagecoach," and particularly
"A Woman Scorned," and the biggest loss to the score's design are the
deletions of the two reiterations of "Red River Valley" and "Oh, Susannah." "Red River Valley" was to have accompanied both a sequence
of Wyatt waiting for the stage and his farewell to the town of Tombstone, and it could have functioned as a leitmotif for Wyatt, solidifying
his connection to folk song, and thus to the developing community of
Tombstone. "Red River Valley," of course, had special resonance for
Fonda. The song had been used to dramatic effect in *The Grapes of
Wrath,* a much acclaimed Ford film starring Fonda as Tom Joad. Offscreen, the song took on a life of its own for Ford's crew. It became
Danny Borzage's theme for Fonda, which he would play on his accor-
dion when Fonda arrived on the set. Losing this connection in *My Dar-
ling Clementine* severs a musical thread that connects Tom Joad to
Wyatt Earp in the same way that "The Cuckoo Waltz" connects young
Abe Lincoln to Wyatt.

The other folk song deleted from the film is "Oh! Susannah," played
diegetically on a banjo and an accordion. (Is that Danny Borzage
glimpsed briefly playing the accordion on the back of one of the wagons?) "Oh! Susannah" is often mistaken for folk song. Actually, it was
written by Stephen Foster for the Christy Minstrels. As I have argued earlier for *Stagecoach* and will later in more depth for *The Searchers,* minstrel music operates in a complex, multileveled way. For most listeners,
"Oh! Susannah" connotes folk song and western expansion. It was one
of the West's most popular songs, sung by pioneers on the Oregon Trail,
gold miners in California, and cowboys on the prairie. I believe that this
is how the song is meant to function in *My Darling Clementine,* as a
marker of westernness and authenticity. As a minstrel song, however,
"Oh! Susannah" also bears the traces of the history of African Americans in the nineteenth century and in the settling of the West, a story all

but elided in the Hollywood studio western. Ford himself would seek to redress the omission in *Sergeant Rutledge* (1960).

If *My Darling Clementine* is the most Fordian of the western film scores, *The Man Who Shot Liberty Valance* runs a close second. Characterized by sparse musical textures and a dependence upon source music, and full of the folk songs, hymnody, and period music that Ford loved to use, *The Man Who Shot Liberty Valance* represents a return to Ford's roots in the early sound period, even incorporating, at Ford's insistence, a melody recycled from the era's *Young Mr. Lincoln*. This nostalgic score complicates standard readings of *The Man Who Shot Liberty Valance* as a revisionist western, a critique of the western's past, imbued with cynicism, pessimism, and irony. While there are good reasons to interpret the film in this light, and many critics have done so,[18] there are also musical reasons that compel reconsideration. The film indeed looks backwards, but at least musically speaking, it is as much with nostalgia as with critique.

The Man Who Shot Liberty Valance revolves around a defining moment from the past retold from the perspective of the present. Senator Ranse Stoddard (James Stewart) and his wife, Hallie (Vera Miles), have returned to Shinbone, a western town, for the funeral of Tom Doniphon (John Wayne), a man they both knew and loved. Stoddard is asked by the local newspaper editor to recollect his past in Shinbone, and he tells the story of the man who shot Liberty Valance, an amoral gunslinger who ruled the town. Bullied by Valance, but repelled by violence, Stoddard finally confronts the gunman after being coached by Doniphon. In a tense shoot-out, Stoddard is wounded and Valance is killed. Stoddard's triumph over Valance sets off a chain of events that forever change the participants: Hallie chooses Stoddard over Doniphon, prompting the latter's attempted suicide, and Stoddard goes on to a brilliant career as a politician. It turns out, however, that the man who shot Liberty Valance was Doniphon, lurking in the shadows, not Stoddard, a fact that Stoddard learned soon afterwards. Back in the present, Stoddard attempts to unburden himself of a lifetime of guilt and confesses the truth to the reporter, only to be told that his admission is not news. For those who know and love Ford's westerns, it is an unforgettable film.

As they are in *Stagecoach* and *My Darling Clementine*, songs are central to *The Man Who Shot Liberty Valance*. Song in Ford westerns generally works on a number of levels, but one of its most important functions in *The Man Who Shot Liberty Valance* is to lend versimilitude to the film's portrayal of the historical West. Critics of the film have generally interpreted its cheesy production values in one of two ways: the film is either a deliberate comment by Ford on the genre of the western, a reflection of "Ford's ambivalence about civilization's 'progress,'" and a "statement of Ford's loss of faith in the ideal of the American frontier,"[19] or it is a result of Ford's boredom and "lack of concern."[20] "[V]isually it's among the most ordinary of his movies," Scott Eyman writes.[21] For whatever reason, the film lacks a distinctive Fordian look. The iconic awe-inspiring vistas of Monument Valley have been replaced by essentially flat images, largely shot on Paramount's back lot and soundstages. To evoke and authorize its vision of the past, *The Man Who Shot Liberty Valance* depends more upon the score than usual. Diegetic music is closer to the threshold of recognition than nondiegetic music, and it thus functions on a more conscious level for the audience. And when those songs are familiar, they have increased power to catch the audience's attention. The recognizable songs in *The Man Who Shot Liberty Valance* help to establish authenticity in a film whose image track can be less than convincing. Given that the film's representation of the West turns out to be false, music also becomes imbricated in the thorny issues of history and representation with which the film grapples.

The Man Who Shot Liberty Valance looks to the past in a variety of ways, but none more pointed than the way in which its musical score connects with earlier Ford films, particularly *My Darling Clementine* and *Young Mr. Lincoln*. It is tightly connected to these films in a number of musical ways.[22] Cyril Mockridge, who composed the score of *The Man Who Shot Liberty Valance*, also scored *My Darling Clementine*.[23] A distinctive leitmotif from *Young Mr. Lincoln*, a theme for the character Ann Rutledge, composed by Mockridge's boss at Twentieth Century–Fox, Alfred Newman, is recycled in *The Man Who Shot Liberty Valance*. Like *My Darling Clementine*, *The Man Who Shot Liberty Valance* is dependent upon source music and contains very little nondiegetic music.

Much of the period music heard in *The Man Who Shot Liberty Valance* is recycled from other Ford films: "Hail, Hail, the Gang's All Here" from *Steamboat Round the Bend*, *The Sun Shines Bright*, and *The Last Hurrah* (1958); "Sweet Genevieve" from *Hellbent*, *The Sun Shines Bright*, and *Fort Apache*; "Oh, Dem Golden Slippers," from *Fort Apache* and *My Darling Clementine*; and "My Darling Clementine," Camptown Races," "Four Little White Doves," "Carmela," "Little Brown Jug," and "Ring, Ring, de Banjo," from *My Darling Clementine*. "(There'll Be a) Hot Time in the Old Town Tonight," "Polly Wolly Doodle," "Home on the Range," and the Mexican songs "La Barca de Oro," "Fumare,"

"Marianina," and "Jarabe Tapatío" (aka "The Mexican Hat Dance") round out the playlist for and make their first appearances in a Ford western. But other musical moments harken back to past practices. Danny Borzage's accordion playing can be heard in the film (listen for Borzage playing Ann Rutledge's theme when Hallie returns to Doniphon's ranch and during Doniphon's flashback). As in so many other Ford westerns, good men are associated with music in *The Man Who Shot Liberty Valance* (Tom Doniphon makes his entrance to the strains of "Sweet Genevieve") and villains interrupt it, always a sign of trouble in Ford. *The Man Who Shot Liberty Valance* thus has an interesting edge, produced by the combination of its contemporary focus on the history and mythology of the West and an "old-fashioned" score recycling a 1930s leitmotif and exploiting a musical aesthetic Ford forged in the early years of sound film: a dependence upon period music and especially American folk tunes, sparingly orchestrated and largely used diegetically.

The film's musical descent from *My Darling Clementine* is pronounced. The original musical design of *My Darling Clementine* was dependent upon diegetic period music. *The Man Who Shot Liberty Valance* is similarly dependent upon diegetic period music, produced in Shinbone's saloons, restaurant, and Mexican cantina and at the territorial convention. The nondiegetic music heard in *The Man Who Shot Liberty Valance* is largely comprised of leitmotifs for Tom Doniphon and Hallie, an original motif for Doniphon, and the recycled Ann Rutledge theme for Hallie. (The score does use some conventional scoring techniques in Doniphon's flashback—stingers, tremolo strings, and a vibraphone.) There are also many other convergences in the musical designs of these films: in *My Darling Clementine,* Wyatt and Clementine walk through Tombstone to the Sunday morning church dedication accompanied by church bells; *The Man Who Shot Liberty Valance* opens with characters walking down the street of a western town to similar accompaniment. In *My Darling Clementine,* most sequences lack any musical accompaniment, diegetic or otherwise, including the shoot-out at the OK Corral; in *The Man Who Shot Liberty Valance,* the most dramatic sequence in the film, the climactic shoot-out between Valance and Stoddard and Doniphon, is unscored, as is the confrontation afterwards between Doniphon's and Valance's sidekicks.[24] There is no music during the shooting lesson Doniphon gives to Stoddard, the beating of Dutton Peabody (Edmund O'Brien) by Valance, Nora and Peter Ericson's desperate attempts to persuade Stoddard to leave town, Stoddard's discovery of Peabody, the celebration following Liberty Valance's death, or Doniphon's suicidal burning of his ranch.

The period songs in *The Man Who Shot Liberty Valance* work not only to authorize the film's historical credentials, and thus to verify the image track, but more conventionally to establish the setting, develop the characters, and control narrative connotations. Many of the period songs heard in the saloon, restaurant, and cantina, for instance, function in a fairly standard way to signal the nature of these establishments (Spanish American and Mexican folk song for the cantina, Anglo American period music for the saloon). In several sequences, there is some interesting use of diegetic period music to supply dramatic underscoring but, as is typical in Ford's work, it often does not synchronize with the action or match the mood of the sequence: the minstrel song "Ring, Ring de Banjo" during Doniphon's and Stoddard's dramatic confrontation after the latter's humiliation by Valance; the upbeat "Fumare" emanating from the Mexican cantina and underscoring Dutton Peabody's rant about politics and publishing; "Carmela" sung diegetically during Peabody's conversation with Applegate; the flippant "Mexican Hat Dance" as Peabody lurches drunkenly down the street quoting Shakespeare and later when Valance destroys the newspaper office; "My Darling Clementine" during Valance's last card game; and "Fumare" again as Doniphon walks dejectedly from the restaurant after seeing Hallie and Stoddard together after the shoot-out.

The music heard at the territorial convention represents slightly different terrain for a Ford western, the political arena, and here the songs deftly comment on Ranse Stoddard's character. The convention marks the beginning of Stoddard's political career and represents a physical space—the convention hall—and public place—politics—that become uniquely his. Doniphon, asked to assume a political role, has refused. Thus the music used to accompany the convention comes to stand for Stoddard. Three songs form the aural backdrop: "(There'll Be a) Hot Time in the Old Town Tonight," "Hail, Hail, the Gang's All Here," and "Home on the Range." The first two songs have clear associations with politics, and one of them, "(There'll Be a) Hot Time in the Old Town Tonight," has had quite a checkered history. The last song, "Home on the Range," is one of those nostalgic western songs popular in the 1930s.[25] Taken together, they signal that Stoddard is an imposter and an opportunist. The film ultimately sides with Doniphon, the archetypal westerner, and the music is part of the reason.

"The Gang's All Here" functioned in the 1950s as a kind of universal campaign music in Ford: it appears accompanying political campaigns in both *The Sun Shines Bright,* a remake of *Judge Priest,* and *The Last Hurrah.* It had appeared earlier, in *Steamboat Round the Bend* in a similar capacity, accompanying the appearance of some political bigwigs. "The Gang's All Here" was published and popularized during World War I, and it was probably due to its connection with the war effort that the song took on its political dimensions.[26]

"(There'll Be a) Hot Time in the Old Town Tonight," however, has a more interesting story. Composed in 1886 as a bawdy minstrel song, with lyrics by Joe Hayden, it was later sanitized and became a hit during the Spanish-American War, adopted by Teddy Roosevelt's Rough Riders as their anthem. It later became Roosevelt's presidential campaign song, hence its link to political campaigns. It was supposed to have originated in a brothel, and its original lyrics do seem to evoke that context: "There'll be girls for ev'rybody in that good, good old town / For there's Miss Consola Davis and there's Miss Gondolia Brown / And there's Miss Johanna Beasly she am dressed all in red / I just hugged her and I kissed her and to me then she said / Please oh please, oh do not let me fall / You're all mine and I love you best of all / And you must be my man or I'll have no man at all / There'll be a hot time in the old town tonight, my baby."

Revised versions of the song are not nearly so interesting. Still, there is an edge, however blunted, to its title. With its original lyrics, it was a favorite of jazz artists in the 1920s: Jelly Roll Morton liked to perform it, and Bessie Smith recorded it. Bernard Herrmann exploited both the song's original bawdy meaning as well as its political dimensions when he used it to accompany the publisher's party in *Citizen Kane* (1941), where political discussions about the Spanish-American war are intercut with Kane's dancing with chorus girls. Ford clearly knew the song's bawdy past. He initially used it as one of a trio of songs played on a honky-tonk piano. On the Paramount cue sheet, it is identified as "saloon music," and it accompanies beer drinking and rowdy behavior. It is heard a second time in the saloon, prompted by a drunken Doniphon, and functions to foreshadow the suicidal burning of his ranch that follows. Thus when "(There'll Be a) Hot Time in the Old Town Tonight" returns at the territorial convention, it trails with it tawdry associations of the saloon, cheapening both the new source of power in the West—politics—and the new westerner who inherits that power—Ranse Stoddard.

The last song at the political convention is "Home on the Range," heard in accompaniment to Buck Langhorne's nomination. "Home on the Range" rode the mid-twentieth-century wave of interest in country-and-western music, and like other discourses that shaped national consciousness about the West, it did so in accordance with a highly romanticized notion of the frontier. "Home on the Range" epitomizes this sentimentalizing of the frontier past when the prairie was vast and unpopulated, teeming with wildlife, a virgin territory to be tamed by the cowboy and settled by the pioneer. Even in a genre marked by sentimentality, this song is sappy: deer and antelope play, buffaloes roam, and the sun always shines. The frontier becomes a place of positive thinking: discouraging words are banished, and self-determination is realized. In subsequent verses, the air is pure, the zephyrs free, the heavens are bright with glittering stars, wild flowers bloom, flocks graze, streams flow, and swans glide. The "red man" makes a token appearance but is benign and gentle. Women are absent, as are any marks of encroaching civilization. This nostalgic reconstruction of the frontier masked several historical realities, the most obvious being the virtual disappearance of the buffalo as early as the 1870s and the systematic annihilation of the Indians. The cowboy song guise of "Home on the Range" also masked the fact that it had been written by Brewster Higley, an Ohio minister, and Dan Kelley, a Rhode Islander, in 1873.[27] Although John Lomax included it in his anthology of genuine cowboy music published in 1910, it was largely unknown until the emergence of country-and-western music in the 1920s, when it was published by at least ten different publishers and recorded by the cowboy singers Vernon Dalhart, Jules Verne Allen, and Ken Maynard. During the Great Depression, "Home of the Range" became one of the most popular tunes in America. President Franklin Delano Roosevelt called it his favorite song, and Admiral Richard Byrd claimed to have listened to it for six months in Antarctica. It is still included in innumerable anthologies of western folk song and remains a staple of school music collections.[28]

Ford utilized dozens of period songs in his westerns, and recycled many of them from film to film. But "Home on the Range" appears in no other western of his. It is an awfully sentimental and unsophisticated song. I suspect that Ford recognized it as an imitation cowboy ballad and used it as a marker for fakery. Career politicians tend to come off poorly in Ford films, and Ranse Stoddard in *The Man Who Shot Liberty Valance* is no exception. The music is part of the apparatus that signals his political opportunism.

The Man Who Shot Liberty Valance is often referred to as an old man's film, and both the songs and nondiegetic score harken back to the past on a number of levels. Musical references to the Fordian past give the film an emotional resonance that most viewers perceive as emanating from the music, even if they can't identify the source. For those listeners who do recognize the specific musical references, and there may have been quite a few at the film's initial release, the music not only raises the film's emotional ante but participates in a complex intertextual process in which one Ford film speaks to another.

The promotion of songs specifically composed for a film was a hallmark of 1960s film marketing, and music associated with *The Man Who Shot Liberty Valance* became highly visible in this way, or perhaps I should say audible. Hal David and Burt Bacharach wrote the words and music for a song, "The Man Who Shot Liberty Valance," that was a hit for Gene Pitney in 1962. Although the song did not appear in the film, its lyrics were customized to the film's narrative, and it was published and recorded to coincide with the release of the film. More interesting is the publication of "Ann Rutledge's Theme" as sheet music with clear tie-ins on the cover to *The Man Who Shot Liberty Valance*. Released simultaneously with the Hal David–Burt Bacharach song, "Ann Rutledge's Theme" appears not to have succeeded to the degree that the song "The Man Who Shot Liberty Valance" did, but it was nonetheless promoted in connection with the film and prompted at least some listeners in the audience to recognize Ann Rutledge's theme in the film.

Aggressive marketing of songs and soundtracks was not the only way in which Hollywood was changing. Ford was growing uncomfortable with both the increased emphasis on the bottom line that accompanied the breakup of the studio system and with the growing pressure to use a new generation of stars. For *The Man Who Shot Liberty Valance*, he stuck with his stock company—John Wayne, James Stewart, Woody Strode, Andy Devine, John Qualen, Vera Miles, John Carradine. Trying to get *The Man Who Shot Liberty Valance* off the ground drained Ford of energy. He watched John Wayne and James Stewart negotiate what must have seemed like astronomical salaries,[29] he fought with Paramount over his desire to shoot in black and white (Ford insisted that the climactic shoot-out wouldn't work without it); and he waited, endlessly it seemed, for the go-ahead from executives who were taking his picture "under consideration." According to Dan Ford, Ford "was fed up with *Liberty Valance* even before he began it."[30]

Ford took an active hand in choosing the music, however, and the decision to reuse Ann Rutledge's theme was his. "I love it—one of my favourite tunes—one I can hum," he told Peter Bogdanovich.[31] It works powerfully in *The Man Who Shot Liberty Valance* on at least two levels. The first is musical: here the music itself encodes longing, with the soaring notes of the melody followed by a downward melodic trajectory, delayed in its completion by haunting chromaticism. The second is contextual: the tune originally appeared as a love theme for the young Lincoln and his lost love, Ann Rutledge. It reappears after Ann's death as an elegy for her, and as the film progresses, it accompanies a series of losses that Lincoln suffers. Ultimately, Ann Rutledge's theme comes to represent the past and the ways in which the past determines the future. It is among the most beautiful pieces of original music written for Ford's films, and I would venture the single most recognizable moment of originally composed nondiegetic music in the Ford oeuvre.

As it is used in *The Man Who Shot Liberty Valance*, Ann Rutledge's theme fleshes out the failed love affair between Hallie and Tom Doniphon, the growing love between Hallie and Ranse Stoddard, and the traumatic loss experienced by Hallie over her choice of one over the other, none of which is clearly articulated by dialogue. As it does in *Rio Grande*, music manifests emotions that characters neither voice nor recognize. In *The Man Who Shot Liberty Valance*, Ann Rutledge's theme functions as the expression of repressed desire, bringing to the surface of the film what is barely realized in the image track.

The first use of Ann Rutledge's theme comes early in the film, when Hallie, having returned to Shinbone with her husband, "drives out desert way" without him to visit Tom Doniphon's ranch. Her leaving her husband behind to visit a man's house is our only clue at this point in the film that there are deep and complex emotions pulling Hallie toward Tom. At the ranch, Hallie looks around her, with Link Applegate (Andy Devine) her only companion. Ann Rutledge's theme begins to play, alerting listeners to the depth of Hallie and Doniphon's love and its tragic outcome. Like Lincoln, who could not express his feelings to Ann Rutledge or even to himself, Hallie does not and cannot put into words what she is feeling. The music does it for her.

Ann Rutledge's theme also fleshes out Hallie's growing feelings of attachment to Stoddard in the sequence in which he offers to teach her to read, and Stoddard's reaction to Doniphon's gift of a cactus rose. Like Hallie, Stoddard does not understand what he is feeling for Hallie, and, given his friendship with Doniphon, he does not want to know. His sly observation upon seeing Hallie's obvious pleasure in the cactus, "Ever see a real rose?" is accompanied by Ann Rutledge's theme, through which we are asked to understand his remark as a measure of his affection for Hallie. Ann Rutledge's theme can be heard during the school-room sequence when Stoddard teaches Hallie to read, and after the shoot-out, when Hallie tends Stoddard's wound, indicating how far Hallie has moved away from Doniphon. The latter scene is witnessed by Doniphon, whose appearance interrupts Ann Rutledge's theme, which is replaced by Doniphon's chromatic leitmotif, played with martial overtones by the brasses.

If joining into singing indicates acceptance into the community in Ford, interrupting music-making indicates a character's unsuitability for communal life: Thunder Flint, in *Straight Shooting*, who interrupts the playing of a phonograph recording; Doc Holliday, who silences the saloon band with his entrance in *My Darling Clementine*; Colonel Owen Thursday, who interrupts a dance not once but twice in *Fort Apache*; the Clegg clan, who stop the dance in *Wagon Master*; Ethan Edwards, who disrupts the singing of "Shall We Gather at the River?" in *The Searchers*; and Liberty Valance, who interrupts "Camptown Races." Characters who interrupt music in Ford westerns do so at their peril—their fate is expulsion or death. Sometimes the interruption of music signals pure villainy, as in the case of the terrifyingly lawless Liberty Valance or the inexplicably evil Cleggs. More often, however, the men who interrupt music are not traditional villains but deeply complex characters with disturbing antisocial tendencies.

I would place Tom Doniphon in this last group—a powerful loner unable, ultimately, to sacrifice individual expression to the greater needs of social order. Although the interruption here is on the nondiegetic level, Doniphon's theme interrupts Ann Rutledge's, and the consequences couldn't be clearer. Doniphon is excluded from Shinbone and its society, although in Doniphon's case, it is a voluntary exodus. From the moment his leitmotif interrupts Ann Rutledge's theme, Doniphon will abandon his romantic quest for Hallie. He burns down part of his ranch house (foreshadowed by "[There'll Be a] Hot Time in the Old Town Tonight") and attempts to take his own life. He will seclude himself on his ranch with his devoted companion Pompey (Woody Strode) for the rest of his life.[32]

The cost to Hallie is not articulated with such clarity: it is rendered musically and symbolically through Ann Rutledge's theme and the cactus rose. These displacements of Hallie's desire converge in Hallie's placing the cactus on Doniphon's coffin. Ann Rutledge's theme can be heard when Stoddard enters the room and sees Hallie weeping. Her regret over rejecting Doniphon and her love for him are made palpable at this moment through the music. Ranse has entered the room belatedly and has not seen who placed the rose on the coffin. On the train out of town, he asks her who put it there. She answers, unhesitatingly, "I did." Her confession is accompanied by Ann Rutledge's theme for the final time, reminding listeners of the price that Hallie has paid for choosing Stoddard.

One last thing about the music. In the most oft-quoted line from the film, the newspaper editor pronounces: "This is the West, sir. When the legend becomes fact, print the legend." But as many commentators have noted, beginning with Peter Bogdanovich, "Ford prints the fact."[33] I wouldn't disagree with this assessment, although I would point out that of the music for *The Man Who Shot Liberty Valance* muddies the waters a bit. On the surface, the score appears utterly simple: limited musical cues, a modest number of leitmotifs (one for Tom and one for Hallie), and a dependence upon source music, much of it recycled from earlier Ford films. This apparent simplicity, however, belies the score's rich, dense tapestry of references and intertextual connections, which work to romanticize the very past that the film interrogates. How can we disregard the power of a song like "Camptown Races," perceived by most listeners as an authentic historical reference, or the rich and emotional orchestration of Ann Rutledge's theme and its connection to Lincoln? The score for *The Man Who Shot Liberty Valance* taps into a powerful musical mythology, which is put to use idealizing the past. "When the legend becomes fact, print the legend." If only it were that simple. An analysis of the film's music reminds us that history and mythology, legend and fact, are sometimes inextricably linked. And as I read the film, it is as much nostalgia for what is lost as disillusion for what remains that characterizes Ford here.

My Darling Clementine helped establish John Ford as the premier director of westerns, a reputation he cemented with five westerns he made between 1948 and 1950, produced for his own Argosy Pictures: *Fort Apache, 3 Godfathers, She Wore a Yellow Ribbon, Wagon Master,* and *Rio Grande.* Their musical scores depart in some significant ways from the scores of *My Darling Clementine* and *The Man Who Shot Liberty Valance.* While all of Ford's westerns employ period music, the postwar Argosy westerns are characterized by more conventional musical scores, with more symphonic orchestration, and more nondiegetic music. There were some quite practical reasons for this shift in musical directions, which are explored in the next chapter.

CHAPTER 5

"Western as Hell"

3 Godfathers and *Wagon Master*

With its wall-to-wall symphonic music, heavily dependent upon original composition, *3 Godfathers* could scarcely sound much more different from *Stagecoach, My Darling Clementine,* or *The Man Who Shot Liberty Valance*. *Wagon Master* also departs significantly from Ford's earlier westerns: the characteristic folk and period music is largely replaced by originally composed songs performed by Sons of the Pioneers. Of course, *3 Godfathers* and *Wagon Master* have privileged performances of song in common with earlier Ford westerns. And like all of Ford's westerns, *3 Godfathers* and *Wagon Master* do indeed sound "western as hell,"[1] Ford's evocative description of what he wanted for the music of *Wagon Master*. But the scores for *3 Godfathers* and *Wagon Master* represent a turn away from those of *Stagecoach* and especially *My Darling Clementine*. *3 Godfathers* is much more in tune with the conventions of classical Hollywood scoring, and *Wagon Master* more tapped into contemporary popular music, a phenomenon that was beginning to figure importantly in the genre of the Hollywood western.

Part and parcel of understanding Ford's work after the war is Argosy Pictures, incorporated by Ford and the producer Merian C. Cooper in large part to escape the strictures of the studio system. Argosy is technically credited as the production company on *The Long Voyage Home*, but it was not until after the war that Argosy was fully capitalized and functioned as an independent production company. Argosy's first independently produced film, *The Fugitive* (1947), an arty adaptation of a

controversial Graham Greene novel, was a commercial and critical dis-
aster and almost sank the fledgling company. Ford and Cooper then
turned to a proven moneymaker, the Ford western, and churned out *Fort
Apache, 3 Godfathers, She Wore a Yellow Ribbon, Wagon Master,* and
Rio Grande in the space of three years.[2]

In some ways, independent production proved even more inhospitable than the studio system, and Argosy Pictures did not turn out to
be the haven from Hollywood's commercial pressures that Ford had
imagined it would be. A dependence upon a reliable genre, the move to
color, and the presence of a more conventional film score, including contemporary popular music, all developments in keeping with what the
moviegoing public had come to expect, are part of Argosy's imprint on
Ford's work. In spite of these constraints, Ford produced some of the best
and most beloved work of his career with Argosy and the scores for the
westerns, although they stray from the pattern of *Stagecoach* and *My
Darling Clementine,* embody certain Fordian core principles: music to
both mark and bind the community, the privileging of song, and the inclusion of Anglo American folk song, period music, and Protestant
hymnody.

Both *3 Godfathers* and *Wagon Master* were scored by the composer
whose name is most indelibly connected to Ford's, Richard Hageman,
who would score six Ford films and collaborate on a seventh, four of
them Argosy westerns. He was one of the composing team for *Stagecoach,* and he also scored *The Long Voyage Home,* but his preeminent
status as a member of Ford's stock company was established with his
score for *The Fugitive.* In 1946, with the war over and travel across the
Atlantic again a possibility, Hageman was determined to sail to Europe,
North Africa, and uncharted territory. He claimed to be ready to "free
myself from very lucrative Hollywood." As he wrote to Ford, "The only
thing that might tempt me to postpone my . . . sailing would be doing a
score for you."[3]

At work on James Edward Grant's *Angel and the Badman* at the time,
Hageman had probably heard that Ford was about to realize his longtime dream of an independent production company and was starting
work on what would become *The Fugitive.* He advised Ford to get "a
good free lance man" and avoid "one of those shop worn factory jobs
as turned out by most music departments"; if Ford chose not to hire him,
Hageman suggested, he should contact "the next best man . . . Louis
Gruenberg." Gruenberg, he said, was "so good . . . that the studio musicians are afraid of him. He does not depend on Hollywood for his

bread and butter, having pretty much of a world reputation."[4] That
world reputation was not turning out to count for much in Hollywood,
however, and Gruenberg was finding film work more and more difficult
to come by.[5] Hageman in fact found himself similarly underutilized.
Gruenberg did not get the job scoring Ford's first independent production; Hageman did. Hageman would describe his work on *The Fugitive*
as "that happy, immeasurably satisfactory experience that prevailed in
Mexico," adding that it "was really making music in ideal surroundings,
and I never enjoyed any picture work more." Although he once complained to Ford: "I shall not write another Western score with nothing
much to underscore except cattle!"[6] (a reference presumably to *Angel
and the Badman*), he was happy to work on the score of *3 Godfathers*.
He also appears as the piano player in the saloon in New Jerusalem. Initially, Argosy considered the possibility of having Hageman compose an
original song, with lyrics by Laurence Stallings, but by the time Hageman's contract was drawn up, there was no mention of songwriting, and
no original songs appear in the film.[7] Lucien Cailliet conducted the score,
and Jester Hairston was the choral director.

Jester Hairston is a musician with a fascinating story that deserves
some attention. Hairston, one of Hollywood's premiere choral arrangers
and directors of the studio era, was African American. A member of the
famous all-black Hall Johnson Choir of Harlem, Hairston performed
with the group on Broadway in *Green Pastures* and traveled with them
to Hollywood in 1935 for its filming. Hairston eventually formed a
group of his own, the well-regarded Jester Hairston Singers. Befriended
and championed by the composer Dimitri Tiomkin, Hairston would
arrange and direct the choral work in all of Tiomkin's scores. But it was
not without a fight. Tiomkin wanted the Jester Hairston Singers for
Frank Capra's *Lost Horizon* (1937), but he ran into what Hairston described as "the backstage color bar," and the producers refused to hire
Hairston.[8] Tiomkin, in turn, refused to work without him. Hairston
would go on to work with Tiomkin for the next twenty years. In an era
when few African Americans found work in studio music departments,
Hairston created the first integrated studio choir.[9] He did the choral
work for Howard Hawks's *Red River* in 1948, and perhaps this was
what brought him to Ford's attention. Hairston would work with Ford
on *3 Godfathers* and *She Wore A Yellow Ribbon*. The studio wanted
Mitch Miller and his singers to record the title song in *Sergeant Rutledge,*
but Ford saw to it that the Jester Hairston Singers, under the direction
of Hairston's wife, Margaret, got the job.[10] At Harry Carey's funeral,

Figure 10. Publicity still, *Friendly Persuasion* (William Wyler, 1956): from the left, William Wyler, Gary Cooper, Dmitri Tiomkin at the piano, Walter Catlett, and Jester Hairston, foreground right. Hairston and Tiomkin collaborated on a number of films, both before and after Hairston worked for Ford. Courtesy Cinema-Television Library, USC.

staged by Ford, the Jester Hairston Singers sang spirituals as Carey's casket left the chapel at the Field Photo Farm.

3 Godfathers tells the story of three outlaws, the Abilene Kid (Harry Carey Jr.), Bob Hightower (John Wayne), and Pedro Roca Fuerte (Pedro Armendáriz), cattle rustlers and bank robbers, who rob the town bank in Welcome, Arizona, and flee into the desert. Giving chase is Welcome's marshal, Perley Sweet (Ward Bond), who matches wits with Hightower. Out of water and horses, the three come upon a pregnant woman (Mildred Natwick) in a broken-down covered wagon, who gives birth and dies, but not before exacting from the outlaws a promise to care for the newborn. The Kid and Pedro die in the desert, and only Hightower is left to save the baby. The godfathers have read in a Bible that Jesus, when he was about to enter Jerusalem (and they are headed for New Jerusalem), told his disciples: "Go into the village . . . and . . . ye shall find an ass tied, and a colt with her: loose them, and bring them unto me" (Matt. 21:2). In what Hightower interprets as divine intervention, and the film does not explain, a burro and a colt appear. Hightower and the baby are saved, although Hightower must do penance for the robbery—one year in prison. He is given a rousing send-off by the town, including Marshal Sweet, grateful for Hightower's selflessness in saving the baby. Hightower will presumably return to Welcome and take up his role as father to the baby boy, Robert William Pedro Hightower.

The classical Hollywood film score is characterized by a set of conventions to help tell the film's story and to engage the audience. Hageman's score for 3 Godfathers exemplifies this. From the symphonic main title to the lush orchestral arrangement of "Shall We Gather at the River?" that brings the film to a close, music saturates it. It is there to elide transitions between sequences (music actually begins before the titles to sweep us into the world of the film); to accompany the characters' movements and even gestures (the three godfathers riding into town to rob the bank and hightailing it out of town to make their escape, the way the music imitates the upward sweep of Hightower's arm as he lights a cigarette); to simulate natural and mechanical phenomena (dripping water, the wind, a sandstorm, but also a train and its whistle); to draw attention to narrative developments (such as the dramatic musical cue heard when Perley Sweet dons his marshal's badge; the stingers accompanying the first gunshot in the bank robbery; the horn fanfare when the Kid is shot; or the use of the tri-tone, a disturbing interval in western music, at the mother's death); to create suspense (the series of rising musical phrases preceding the bank robbery); and to provide emotional resonance (for the death of the mother in the desert). Dialogue is often underscored, cues can be lengthy (the robbery, chase, and escape into the desert is continuously scored for close to seven minutes); and music enters and exits the film surreptitiously through typical techniques of sneaking in and tailing out.[11] The score depends upon melody, and its idiom is romantic, although there are some interesting modernist-inflected cues as the men wander in the desert. The sandstorm, in particular, is orchestrated quite uniquely. (Hageman had intended to use an alternation of male and female voices singing the syllable "Ah," against trombones, woodwinds, strings, horns, and a harp, but Ford didn't use the cue.)[12]

Hageman's musical background was in art music and specifically opera. He was a conductor and coach at the Amsterdam Royal Opera and later conducted at the Metropolitan Opera in New York and for opera companies in Chicago and Los Angeles. He served for a time as the head of the Opera Department at the Curtis Institute of Music in Philadelphia. His own opera, *Caponsacchi,* had its American premiere at the Met in 1935, after a world premiere in Freiberg, Germany. I think that you can hear that operatic background in *3 Godfathers*—in its massive orchestral resources, in its referencing of specific operas, and in the way that Hageman scores emotional sequences as if he were composing for the operatic stage.

The mother's death provides a good example. Hageman has composed a melody for her that is played in the strings, very simply orchestrated, and memorably as a violin solo at one point. I would not call this cue a leitmotif for the dying mother. It's more like a set piece from an opera, an aria without words. The melody is highly reminiscent of the "Meditation" from Massenet's opera *Thais,* the plot of which revolves around the conversion to Christianity of an Egyptian courtesan. Massenet's "Meditation" showcases a memorable violin solo. Was Hageman thinking along these lines when he composed the scene in which the three outlaws experience a religious conversion of their own? Did Hageman's operatic background seep through in the creative process?

Something similar happens when Hightower finds his salvation through the discovery of the burro and colt. Again, Hageman creates another operatic moment, each repetition of the melody growing in the orchestra until a spectacular and fully orchestrated musical finale ends the sequence. In its use of the resources of the symphony orchestra, in its increasingly lush arrangements of the melody, and in the melody itself, the music is highly reminiscent of another operatic moment, Hansel and Gretel's "Evening Prayer," or "Now I Lay Me Down to Sleep," the English translation of the most famous musical moment from the Engelbert Humperdinck classic *Hänsel und Gretel.* The children are lost in the woods and they fear for their lives as they pray to God to watch over and guard them. In Peter B. Kyne's source novel, Bill Kearney recites the very prayer that Humperdinck set to music: "Now I lay me down to Sleep / I pray the Lord my soul to keep / If I should die before I wake / I pray the Lord my soul to take."[13] Was Hageman prompted by Kyne's cue on some level?

As it does in all Ford westerns, song figures prominently in the score of *3 Godfathers.* Heard in the film are the western ballads "The Streets of Laredo" and "Oh, Bury Me Not on the Lone Prairie" (heard briefly as the stagecoach enters town), the Protestant hymns "Shall We Gather

at the River?" and "Bringing in the Sheaves," the Christmas carols
"Hark! The Herald Angels Sing" and "Silent Night," and the Victorian
sacred ballad "The Holy City." Early in the production, several other
songs were considered, including signature tunes for each of the three
godfathers: "Little Joe, the Wrangler," for the Abilene Kid, "Git Along
Little Dogies," for Pedro, and "The Last Roundup" for Hightower. At
one point, Ford considered opening the film with a cowboy orchestra
and singers performing either "Shall We Gather at the River?" or "The
Yellow Rose of Texas."[14] "Whoopee Ti Yi Yo (Get Along Little Dogies)"
was considered for the Abilene Kid to sing to the newborn, as were
"Empty Saddles" and "The Last Roundup." Ultimately, it was Ford who
came up with "The Streets of Laredo."

As they do in all Ford westerns, songs function in *3 Godfathers* in part
to lend verisimilitude to the images on the screen. Period songs, especially
those perceived as genuine folk songs ("Oh, Bury Me Not on the Lone
Prairie"; "The Streets of Laredo") or authentic hymns ("Shall We Gather
at the River?"; "Bringing in the Sheaves"), make the film's representation
of the West seem authentic. When on-screen characters sing what we recognize as folk song and period music, the images are more compelling.
Of course, each song also carries its own unique meaning, often derived
from the lyrics, but sometimes created by more general cultural associations attached to it. Although these individual meanings may not be
available to all listeners, they are an important operant in the film's
meaning system. Finally, songs can also affect listeners on a less than
conscious level, manipulating response without the listener's conscious
attention.

"The Streets of Laredo" operates on all these levels. It is sung a cappella by the Abilene Kid as a lullaby to the newborn, and later, very
briefly, by Robert Hightower. In Kyne's source novel, the wounded Bill
Kearney[15] tries to sing a lullaby to calm the newborn, but "his voice
broke in the second line of the chorus."[16] The Bob Hightower character
sings "The Yellow Rose of Texas" instead.[17] "The Streets of Laredo" was
Ford's choice, and he sprang it on Carey, who luckily knew the words,
having learned them from Burl Ives. "The Streets of Laredo" is woven
throughout the score from the main title through the end of the film, but
it is sung most memorably by Carey.

As is true of most folk songs, this one's history is murky. "The Streets
of Laredo" is derived from Anglo Irish folk sources, specifically "The
Unfortunate Rake," a song about venereal disease and the price one
young soldier pays for his dissipation. The song existed in a number of

variants in different geographic locations, including Appalachia, the South, and the Midwest, before settling down as a cowboy ballad. The folklorist Jim Hoy has traced the origins of the song, originally entitled "The Cowboy's Lament," to one Francis Henry Maynard, who, in 1876, created lyrics reflecting cowboy life in Texas "to fit the tune of an old song that used to be sung by the cowboys."[18] According to Hoy, the song was popular as a night herding song in the 1870s under the title "The Whore's Lament," and cowboys knew exactly what were they singing about.[19] The Anglo Irish origins of "The Streets of Laredo" are evident in language and imagery not particularly resonant with cowboy life, such as the reference to a military funeral, "Bang the drum slowly and play the fife lowly."

Cowboy songs and the singing cowboys who recorded them had a large audience in the 1930s and 1940s, and recognizing the tune and recalling the lyrics of "The Streets of Laredo" may have been fairly easy for a large segment of the moviegoing audience in 1948. It was recorded by the singing cowboys Gene Autry and Ken Maynard, as well as by folk singers like Burl Ives, and it appeared in several westerns in the late 1940s including *Pursued* (Raoul Walsh, 1947) and *Red River* (Howard Hawks, 1948) both of which featured Carey. In *3 Godfathers,* the first and last verses are sung by Carey. It is a song of death, a funereal dirge for a fallen cowboy, wrapped in his shroud of white linen, awaiting burial. The melancholy of the song is encoded not only in its lyrics but also in its insistently downward melodic design. Although the song functions in the film as a lullaby, it clearly foreshadows the Abilene Kid's own death.

As Carey tells the story, Ford came up with the idea of using "The Streets of Laredo" on location. It's not too difficult to figure out where Ford got the idea. Ford liked to think that he had discovered Harry Carey Jr. (he certainly set him on the road to stardom), but Carey had appeared in several films before *3 Godfathers,* including *Pursued* and *Red River.* In *Pursued,* Jeb Rand (Robert Mitchum) sings "The Streets of Laredo," and later the song can be heard on a saloon piano when the character played by Carey is killed. As the cow herder Dan Lattimer in *Red River,* Carey sings some lines from the traditional herding song "I Ride an Old Paint" to quiet the cattle and is killed moments later in a stampede. When Dan's body is found, "The Streets of Laredo" can be heard in the score. Carey had no idea, however, that he was supposed to sing in *3 Godfathers,* and although he had sung in *Red River,* he was still "scared to sing in front of people."[20] Out on location at the end of a day's shooting, and with no warning, Ford asked Carey to sing "The Streets of Laredo." Ford called Danny Borzage over to provide accompaniment on the accordion. The rehearsal went well. The actual process of capturing Carey's a cappella performance on film proved much more difficult. Ford demanded take after take; Carey's singing got lower and lower and more and more muffled, until he sounded "like a record winding down." Carey would later write that the scene was "painful" for him to watch.[21] But Carey's exhausted voice brings pathos to what is already a melancholy song. Ford was attracted to the outsiders, and they are often the ones who sing in his films. The Kid, still wet behind the ears and in over his head in the botched robbery, will pay with his life for his brief detour into crime. "The Streets of Laredo" ennobles him and turns him into the cowboy that he wanted to be.

3 Godfathers employs some heavy religious symbolism, which figures into the score. Hageman marked the main title "allegro religioso," and a number of Christmas carols, sacred songs, and hymns can be heard.[22] With the exception of "Silent Night," the hymns are Protestant:[23] The hymns "Bringing in the Sheaves" and "Shall We Gather at the River?" are used diegetically to end the film. "Shall We Gather at the River?" is also heard at the mother's burial, first sung diegetically by the Abilene Kid, then crossing over into the nondiegetic score. "Hark! The Herald Angels Sing," credited to Felix Mendelssohn and Charles Wesley, is used nondiegetically during Robert Hightower's delusional moments before his salvation in the desert.[24] "Silent Night" is played on the saloon piano in New Jerusalem by Richard Hageman himself (that's Danny Borzage with his accordion just barely visible in the shot). Also heard in the saloon is the chorus from "The Holy City," a Victorian sacred ballad, sung diegetically by a congregation of townspeople.

"The Holy City" makes an appearance in the source novel, when the Hightower character "reeled into New Jerusalem."[25] An extremely popular genre in Victorian England, the sacred song used many of the conventions of popular music for a sacred subject. "The Holy City," published in 1892, was one of the most popular sacred songs of the nineteenth century, in both England and America, and its legacy can be heard in some surprising places.[26] (Listen to the opening of Duke Ellington's "Black and Tan Fantasy," which quotes from it.)[27] The song's lyrics center on reaching the city of Jerusalem, an allegory for Christians reaching heaven itself, and clearly the content of the song refers to Hightower. Here is the verse, not heard in the film, that precedes the chorus: "And once again the scene was chang'd; / New earth there seemed to be; / I

Figure 11. Publicity still, *3 Godfathers:* Richard Hageman at the piano with Ruth Clifford at far left and Danny Borzage on the accordion. Courtesy Lilly Library, Indiana University, Bloomington, IN.

saw the Holy City / Beside the tireless sea; / The light of God was on the streets, / The gates were open wide, / And all who would might enter, / And no one was denied. / No need of moon or stars by night, / Or sun to shine by day; / It was the New Jerusalem / That would not pass away."[28] A reference in the film to "the old Mormon trail" places the action of *3 Godfathers* long enough after the Mormons arrived in Utah in 1846 for the Mormon trail to have become "old."[29] Using a song first published in 1892 seems a bit of a stretch from the standpoint of historical verisimilitude. It would be neither the first time nor the last that period songs would be used for their meaning without regard for historical accuracy in one of Ford's films.

"Bringing in the Sheaves" was one of the most popular Protestant hymns sung on the frontier, along with "Rock of Ages" and "Shall We Gather at the River?" "Rock of Ages" appears to have held little fascination for Ford, at least in the westerns.[30] The Protestant hymn "Bringing in the Sheaves," composed by George Minor in 1880 to lyrics by the "singing Evangelist" Knowles Shaw, can be heard at the end of *3 God-fathers* when the townspeople bid farewell to Hightower. It is a harvest song and frequently used for Thanksgiving, based on Ecclesiastes 11:6 and Psalm 126:6, both of which revolve around the sowing of seeds, although it is the psalm in which the sheaves are mentioned: "He who goes out to weeping, carrying seed to sow, will return with songs of joy, carrying sheaves with him." In the late nineteenth century, a significant portion of the American population still lived on farms, but when Shaw penned the lyrics in 1874, mechanical harvesters had already replaced hand scything and bundling. Perhaps it was nostalgia for the old ways that drew people to the hymn. Minor struck gold, and the hymn became extremely popular, especially on the frontier. Its structure probably had something to do with it. More jubilant and spirited than "Shall We Gather at the River?" or "Rock of Ages," "Bringing in the Sheaves" is structured like a popular song, with a series of verses, followed by the chorus. It would serve as Ford's entrance music when he arrived on the set each day, played on the accordion by Danny Borzage. In *3 Godfathers,* the hymn reinforces the general celebration that greets Hightower as he is about to board the train taking him to prison and functions as a general reminder that you reap what you sow. In sacrificing his escape for the sake of the newborn child, Hightower has ensured his own salvation.

The film ends with "Shall We Gather at the River?" and now even Marshal Perley Sweet and his wife join in. Ford uses "Shall We Gather at the River?" at moments when the community comes together, whether it's the three godfathers uniting to save the baby or the entire town of Welcome embracing Hightower at the end of the film. Although Hightower is sent off to prison, he has been "gathered" into the congregation of Welcome; his godson will be tended to in his absence and a new wife is waiting for him in the wings. None of this is overtly stated: a few simple farewells are spoken and Hightower's concern for little Robert William Pedro is expressed. Nothing needs to be said about forgiveness, acceptance, and salvation. "Shall We Gather at the River?" says it all.

In the original source novel *Three Godfathers,* none of the characters are Mexican. Ford rewrote the part of Tom Gibbons as Pedro Roca Fuerte for the Mexican actor Pedro Armendáriz, who had worked with him on *Fort Apache.* Like Chris, the station master in *Stagecoach,* Pedro has an Indian wife. Moreover, Pedro's ethnic background makes Hightower uncomfortable. He prefers to call his friend "Pete" and insists that he not speak Spanish in front of the newborn: "Cut out the Mex lingo around the kid, will ya, Pete? First thing you know he'll be talking it. We got to raise him with good old American habla, like his Mom." At the end of the film, however, Hightower says farewell to his adopted son in Spanish! Given that this exchange takes place during the singing of "Shall We Gather at the River?" the musical symbol in Ford of the power of community, Hightower's embrace of the language is clearly endorsed by the film.

The film *3 Godfathers* is dedicated to Harry Carey Sr., with an inscription penned by Ford himself: "Bright star of the early western sky." The credits open against a backlit long shot of a cowboy (Cliff Lyons) astride Sunny, Carey's favorite horse. Carey had recently died, and Ford, no doubt, was experiencing regret over the loss and feeling guilty about the long-standing feud, apparently of Ford's making, that had effectively ended their friendship. Ford owed his early film career to Carey, who had starred as Cheyenne Harry in a series of successful westerns establishing Ford's reputation in Hollywood, including *Marked Men* (1919, now lost), the film Ford remade as *3 Godfathers*. "Harry Carey tutored me in the early years, sort of brought me along, . . . the only thing I always had was an eye for composition," he would tell Peter Bogdanovich.[31] Near the end of his life, the senior Carey explained to his son that Ford would never put their friendship right while he was alive, but that after his death, Ford would make it up to his son. Ford purportedly decided on hiring Harry Carey Jr. the day of Carey's wake.[32]

The shot memorializing Carey is accompanied by a quotation from the traditional western song "Good-bye, Old Paint," about a cowboy saying good-bye to an old horse. The chorus, "Good-bye, Old Paint / I'm leaving Cheyenne," is an unmistakable reference to Carey's Cheyenne Harry character. "Good-bye, Old Paint" is written in waltz tempo and as a result, was a popular dance tune on the frontier, frequently the last dance of the evening. Although "Good-bye, Old Paint" now seems the perfect memorial to Carey, several other western songs were considered first, including "Cheyenne, Cheyenne, Hop on My Pony" and "Empty Saddles in the Old Corral."

Although *3 Godfathers* was a successful film, it did not match the profits of the first Argosy western, *Fort Apache*. After the financial and critical debacle of *The Fugitive*, Argosy needed a few blockbusters. For months, *3 Godfathers* languished mere thousands of dollars beneath the contractual payout point with MGM, the film's distribution company, which would have given Argosy a much-needed influx of cash. Loans came due; Argosy stalled and was eventually paid. "Argosy was living a hand-to-mouth existence," Scott Eyman observes.[33] The healthy profits

of *She Wore a Yellow Ribbon,* made for RKO in 1949, helped the financial situation at Argosy, and a directing stint for Ford at Twentieth
Century–Fox, which resulted in *When Willie Comes Marching Home*
(1950), brought Ford some needed cash.

These financial constraints were pressing, and this could not have
been an easy time for Ford. His next film for Argosy would be *Wagon
Master,* a deeply personal western about the Mormons, with a minimal
budget and no stars. RKO, for which Argosy had made *The Fugitive,
Fort Apache,* and *She Wore a Yellow Ribbon,* had its doubts. Its new
agreement with Argosy no longer included Ford's right to the final cut,
which he had had on the earlier RKO films, and even had with MGM
for *3 Godfathers.* The budget for *Wagon Master* was measly, just under
$1 million. However, it gave Ford supporting players like Ward Bond,
Harry Carey Jr., and Ben Johnson their first chances at starring roles. The
film was shot in about a month: nineteen days on location around Moab,
Utah, and the remainder in the studio and at the RKO ranch in Encino.
Wagon Master would prove another modest success, like *3 Godfathers.*
Ford always liked the film, describing it as one of those "closest to what
I had hoped to achieve."[34]

With *Wagon Master,* Ford began a collaboration with the songwriter
Stan Jones and the country-and-western singing group Sons of the Pioneers that would extend through three films. As much as Ford knew
about music, he didn't keep current with contemporary popular music
and had never heard of Stan Jones, who had a huge country-and-western
hit with "Ghost Riders in the Sky," or Sons of the Pioneers, who were
acclaimed recording artists. Fred Zinnemann was concurrently working
on *High Noon,* the film that would bring the commercial potential of
songs by contemporary recording artists to Hollywood's attention. By all
accounts, Ford wasn't thinking of marketability; he simply liked Stan
Jones and his music, and he enjoyed the singing of Sons of the Pioneers.
But having America's reigning country-and-western singing group performing songs by a composer who had just graced the cover of *Time*
couldn't have hurt the film.

Jones turned out to be Ford's kind of man, a park ranger with a connection to the West and the outdoors, a modern-day frontiersman with
a guitar. Better yet, given that Ford often used military experience as a
barometer of character, Jones had served on a submarine during the war.
Their first meeting, however, was anything but promising. During the
filming of *3 Godfathers,* Jones was "the man who had the audacity to tell
John Ford that you couldn't squeeze water out of a cactus."[35] Jones was

a friend of the actor George O'Brien, with whom Ford had recently reconciled after years of icy relations.[36] It was O'Brien who brought Jones to Ford's office at RKO to sing. Harry Carey Jr., who was present, said Jones's performance, accompanied only by his guitar, "made the hair stand up on the back of my neck. I thought the walls were going to tumble down when he got to the end."[37] Then Jones sang "Rollin' Dust," and Ford hired him on the spot, asking for "Rollin' Dust" and three other new songs for *Wagon Master:* "You've got a hell of a start with that 'Rollin' Dust' thing. Make the others in the same vein. You know, western as hell. About a wagon train."[38] At that first meeting, Jones called Ford's attention to Sons of the Pioneers. Initially, the score was going to be performed exclusively, both vocally and instrumentally, by Sons of the Pioneers, but at some point, Ford decided to augment their vocals and use RKO studio musicians for the instrumentals.[39]

The genesis of Sons of the Pioneers parallels the birth and development of country-and-western music itself.[40] Country music began to hit the air waves in the 1920s, but it was in the 1930s that country-and-western music evolved from folk and traditional music, bluegrass, jazz, and big band swing. Sons of the Pioneers were an important part of that genesis, bringing distinctive and elaborate vocal harmonies and virtuoso instrumentals to the form. Sons of the Pioneers proved to be an evolving group of performers over the years, but several individuals left their mark on the group, notably the founder, Leonard Slye (later Roy Rogers), the singer-songwriters Tim Spencer and Bob Nolan, the instrumentalists Hugh Farr and his brother Karl, the vocalist Ken Curtis, and the comic Pat Brady.

A fascinating part of Sons of the Pioneers' career trajectory is how soon they were discovered by filmmakers. They made their first commercial recordings for Decca in 1934 and appeared in their first film, *The Old Homestead,* in 1935. Eventually, they would write songs for Roy Rogers, Gene Autry, Dick Foran, Tex Ritter, Rex Allen, Edie Dean, Johnny Bond, and Jimmy Wakely, and would perform in over a hundred series westerns themselves. By the late 1930s, their distinctive music was reaching a wider audience. Sons of the Pioneers spent the early war years entertaining troops on military bases, and several members of the group left for military service. After the war, Sons of the Pioneers regrouped and found their prewar popularity had been sustained by their numerous recordings and movie appearances.

When Stan Jones sent them his song "Ghost Riders of the Sky" in 1948, they passed on it.[41] By the late 1940s, there had been numerous personnel changes, including the retirement of two original members, Tim Spencer and Bob Nolan. In stepped Ken Curtis, a young baritone with a big band background, as well as Lloyd Perryman and Tommy Doss, who would lead Sons of the Pioneers into the age of rock 'n' roll. When they appeared in *Wagon Master,* the group consisted of Hugh Farr, Karl Farr, Lloyd Perryman, Shug Fisher, Ken Curtis, and Tommy Doss. They had a new recording contract with RCA, had begun appearing on Rex Allen's radio program, and would shortly spin off their own radio and later television program, *Lucky U Ranch.* They recorded with Perry Como, Vaughn Monroe, and Ezio Pinza. A Carnegie Hall concert awaited them in 1951. Sons of the Pioneers brought *Wagon Master* a distinctly country-and-western sound, a large and varied fan base, and an enthusiasm for publicizing the film. The group released its own recordings of the four songs it performed for *Wagon Master* and toured the southwestern United States promoting them.

Wagon Master chronicles the exodus of Mormon settlers, under the leadership of Elder Wiggs (Ward Bond), to the promised land, the fertile San Juan Valley. Their wagon train must find its way to their new home, and they hire a duo of seasoned cowhands, Sandy Owens (Harry Carey Jr.) and Travis Blue (Ben Johnson), to guide them. Absorbing a troupe of traveling entertainers as they go, as well as the Clanton-esque Cleggs, the group eventually reach their goal, but not without a life-and-death quest for water, a terrifying ride over a steep precipice, and a confrontation with Uncle Shiloh Clegg (Charles Kemper) and his four nephews, who must be killed if the Mormons are to survive. It is implied that both Sandy and Travis will remain with the Mormons, settling down to a peaceful life in their midst.

Although *Wagon Master* takes place in the Mormon community, it is not far removed from *Stagecoach* and *My Darling Clementine.* Like the passengers of *Stagecoach,* the Mormon settlers bind themselves into a community enfolding some unlikely members: the prostitute Denver (JoAnne Dru—are all prostitutes in Ford westerns named after cities?) and two feisty cowhands. And as in *My Darling Clementine,* the irony of needing violence in order to live peacefully underscores the plot. Ford was always interested in community on the frontier and the values that held them together. Given the Mormons' emphasis on hard work and piety, and their belief in the spiritual power of music, it is surprising that Ford didn't discover them sooner! After working with Mormon extras on *She Wore a Yellow Ribbon,* Ford began to generate ideas for a film about the pioneer Mormons of a century earlier. Ford came up with the story line for the film, but his son Patrick wrote the screenplay with

Frank Nugent. As usual, Ford took a direct hand in the musical score, not only hiring Jones to write songs, and Sons of the Pioneers to perform them, but approving Jones's songs and song lyrics.[42]

Richard Hageman returned to Argosy to compose the incidental music, and three RKO staff arrangers worked on the orchestrations: Leonid Raab, Gilbert Grau, and L. D. Gordon. Many of Hageman's cues borrow from and recycle the melodies from the Jones songs, and the score itself is an eclectic mix of Hageman's cues, folk songs, a Protestant and a Mormon hymn, and four contemporary country-and-western songs created for the film. This results in some extremely odd effects. In a dance sequence sung by Sons of the Pioneers, on-screen musicians (among them Danny Borzage) appear to play instruments but no one on screen is singing. Honky-tonk piano music heard during an early street scene seems to be emanating from an unseen saloons, but the volume of the piano modulates erratically and it stops too suddenly to be diegetic. Documentary realism reminiscent of *The Grapes of Wrath,* particularly in the shots of exhausted, tense pioneers in their wagons, is juxtaposed with the contemporary-sounding "Shadows in the Dust," performed by Sons of the Pioneers. Classic music cues for Indians accompany the Cleggs' bank robbery. "Red River Valley" is used as a leitmotif for the prostitute Denver (and this in a film with *The Grapes of Wrath* alums Jane Darwell and Russell Simpson). Finally, at the end of the journey, a hymn is "sung" by a group of Mormons who are not moving their lips.

Tag Gallagher, one the very few critics to treat the film, and the only one to address the music in any depth, argues that the "blatant artificiality" of the Stan Jones songs "apotheosizes the you-are-there authenticity of the images, underlines the stuff of legends." I would argue rather that the blatant artificiality of Sons of the Pioneers singing contemporary country-and-western songs undercuts the authenticity of the images. Gallagher is closer to the mark when he observes that "the Sons of the Pioneers, and their unmistakably 1949 sound disturbingly distances the movie's pictorial action."[43] The western genre had yet to embrace popular music, which it eventually did as a result of the extraordinary success of Tex Ritter's interpolated song "Do Not Forsake Me, Oh, My Darling," in *High Noon* (Fred Zinnemann, 1952). By the time of *The Searchers* in 1955, audiences were used to hearing pop songs and current recording artists in western films. But in 1950, the effect must have been a bit jarring for listeners who were conscious of the music. I find it a bit jarring myself. To a certain extent, the film's realist aesthetic covers over the incongruous contemporary songs and, of course, the folk songs ever present in a Ford western lend their aura of authenticity. Contemporary songs would never entirely replace folk and period music in Ford's westerns, but in the three films on which Stan Jones and Sons of the Pioneers worked, *Wagon Master, Rio Grande,* and *The Searchers,* popular song plays an important role.

There are four of them in *Wagon Master,* and they have specific functions: "Shadows of the Dust" (aka "Rollin' Dust," the song Jones sang in Ford's office); "The Song of the Wagon Master" ("I left my gal in West Virgin-ny"); "Chuckawalla Swing," a traditional square dance tune; and "Wagons West." Lyrics can be an effective way to anchor images to precise meanings. In the main title sequence, wagons roll through a frontier landscape, but it is the song that grounds the image in a particular historical time. "Wagons West" begins: "A hundred years have come and gone / But the ghostly wagons rollin' west and ever brought to mind." The date doesn't exactly work—the film was made in 1949 (released 1950), so if a "hundred years have come and gone" since Mormon wagons rolled west, that makes the great Mormon exodus from Illinois transpire in 1849 or 1850, when in fact it took place in 1847. Perhaps 1849 rhymed with "mind," sort of.

Songs function as a contemporary gloss on the action, with the voices of Sons of the Pioneers, clearly credited in the titles, positioning us in the present and beckoning us, through the lyrics, to interpret the film as historically accurate. As shots of pioneer wagons fill the screen, Sons of the Pioneers sing of the "ghostly wagons rollin' west," as if what we are seeing on the screen is the literal embodiment of the past. In "Shadows in the Dust," the lyrics speak of shadows of the past, long since turned to dust, which haunt the present, "loping through the dust . . . grim and silent 'cause for them all time has died." The call to history is even more pointed in this lyric: "You'll see them in the hist'ry books or in a cloudy sky. / Their fame will live forever, their ghosts will never die."

Historical accuracy was never Ford's strong suit—drama and action were. But Ford wanted his westerns to seem authentic, even if they did not always follow history, going so far as to throw dirt on his actors' costumes to make them appear realistic. The songs in Ford are generally period songs, which not only immerse audiences in the historical era in which the film takes place but work powerfully on the subconscious level to convince them that the images are authentic. The contemporary songs in *Wagon Master* work in a different way. Both the lyrics and the performers distance the audience from the historical era of the film, and while the lyrics may exhort the audience to accept the images as historically accurate, these contemporary songs lack the power that period songs have to impart authenticity. Perhaps the lyrics in the Stan Jones songs so insistently address the past in an attempt to compensate for this.

Not all the songs in *Wagon Master,* however, are contemporary. There are several folk and period songs: "Oh! Susanna" by Stephen Foster, heard as the show folk depart the wagon train; the traditional "Red River Valley," used as a leitmotif for Denver; "Shall We Gather at the River?" heard after the wagons have negotiated the last, treacherous part of the journey; and the Mormon hymn, "Come, Come Ye Saints," heard twice, first as the Mormons pause to dedicate their journey, and next, near the end of the film when the wagon train has reached the San Juan Valley. Several other songs were considered, and Harry Carey Jr. even received copies of three minstrel songs that Ford asked him to learn, "Noah's Ark," "Oh, Dem Golden Slippers," and "Jump Jim Crow,"[44] none of which appear in the film. Joseph Breen, director of the Production Code, objected to the lyrics of both "Noah's Ark" and "Jim Crow" *[sic],* and his complaints may have had something to do with the disappearance of these songs.[45]

"Oh! Susanna," played on the banjo, seems entirely appropriate here, a minstrel song for the show folk, who remind Elder Wiggs of a "hootchy-kootchy show." The "hootchy-kootchy" show is generally thought to have had its genesis in the belly dancing of Little Egypt at the Columbian Exposition in Chicago in 1893. "Hootchy-kootchy" was an Orientalist fantasy, but also an extremely popular and influential dance form around the turn of the century. "Hootchy-kootchy" shows featured female dancers in risqué costumes exposing large portions of their torsos, and the form fairly quickly degenerated into burlesque. Wiggs's reference to the traveling players in *Wagon Master* as a "hootchy-kootchy show" is historically inaccurate, but evocative nonetheless of burlesque, and attaches a certain element of transgressive sexuality to the medicine show. That sexuality is attached to Denver and is part of how the audience comes to understand her profession.

Denver's leitmotif is "Red River Valley," one of a handful of folk songs that have a clear legacy in Ford, both inside and outside the westerns. Although it is associated in the popular imagination with cowboys and the frontier, it is a folk song of contested origins, the Red River of the title being located in any number of places, from the Mohawk Valley in New York to Manitoba, Canada, to Texas and Louisiana and a lot of places in between, not to mention the many Anglo sources for the song. "Red River Valley" appears in John Lomax's first edition of *Cowboy Ballads and Frontier Songs* in 1910 as a Texas folk song, and it is treated as such in any number of similar anthologies, although cowboys singing lines like "do not hasten to bid me adieu" seems pretty fishy to

Example 2. Musical sketch, "Come, Come Ye Saints," the Mormon hymn, arranged by Richard Hageman from *Wagon Master* (RKO, 1950). Used by permission of Warner Bros. Entertainment. Arranged by Richard Hageman. Courtesy Arts Special Collections, UCLA.

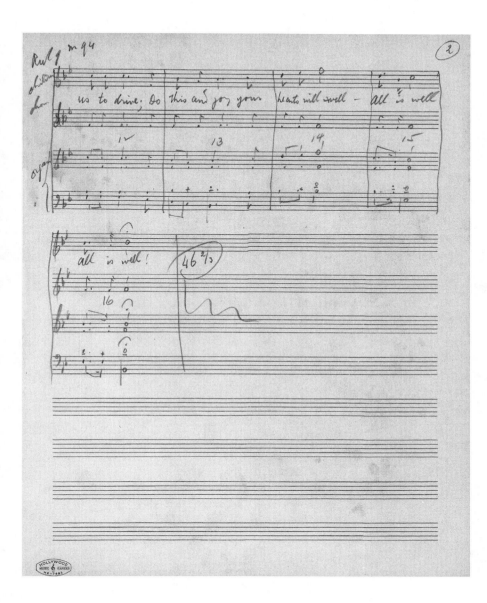

me. "Red River Valley" is heard most memorably in *The Grapes of Wrath,* where its melancholic lyrics about the loss of one's home function as a leitmotif for the Joad family. That association spins out in a number of other Ford films. It can be heard, briefly, in *My Darling Clementine* in the barbershop as Wyatt Earp, played by Henry Fonda, who earlier played Tom Joad, is being shaved, and was cut from later sequences featuring Wyatt. "Red River Valley" can also be heard in *They Were Expendable,* accompanying the character played by Russell Simpson, who had appeared as Pa Joad. Both Russell Simpson and Jane Darwell, Ma Joad, appear in *Wagon Master.* But "Red River Valley" becomes the leitmotif for Denver. The effect of "Red River Valley" is to soften Denver's character, suggesting her sorry past and making her more sympathetic. In one instance, Denver actually plays "Red River Valley" on the guitar, in Ford westerns usually the instrument of Otherness.

Two important religious hymns are used in the film: "Shall We Gather at the River?" functioning here as a song of celebration, and "Come, Come Ye Saints," a Mormon hymn, which functions as both a song of dedication when the journey begins and a song of celebration when it ends. Music was a key element in Mormon religious practice, "an expression of deepest faith and spirituality,"[46] and *Wagon Master* marks the importance of music in the Mormon lifestyle through the communal rituals of singing and dancing. "Come, Come Ye Saints" was published in 1851 by William Clayton, its melody based on an old English folk tune popular with pioneers, its lyrics penned by Clayton to celebrate the birth of his son, reportedly, while on the Mormon exodus from Nauvoo, Illinois, to Utah. Sometimes dubbed the "Mormon Marseillaise," the hymn is an evocation of tempered joy. "All is well, all is well," its opening verse, of which only the last two lines are sung in the film, allegorizes the Mormon exodus across the West as a spiritual journey to God: "Come, come, ye saints, no toil nor labor fear; / But with joy, wend your way. / Though hard to you this journey may appear, / Grace shall be as your day. / 'Tis better far for us to strive / Our useless cares from us to drive; / Do this, and joy your hearts will swell; / All is well! All is well!"

There are several additional musical moments worth pointing out: the bonding of Travis and Sandy as friends, and later with Elder Wiggs through singing, music and masculinity never being constructed as antithetical in Ford westerns; the association of the traditionally masculine hunting horn with a female character, Sister Ledyard (Jane Darwell), another example of Ford's disruption of cultural stereotypes about gender and music; the use of music to mark the inclusion of the show folk in the Mormon community; the villainy of the Cleggs, signified by their interruption of dance; and the rare glimpse into Navajo tribal life, a squaw dance, which parallels the Mormon dance and marks their tribe as a community.

It is hard to imagine that Ford's famous comment regarding what he hated about film music was directed at any film other than 3 *Godfathers:* "I don't like to see a man alone in the desert, dying of thirst, with the Philadelphia Orchestra behind him."[47] Yet its composer, Richard Hageman, was handpicked by Ford and would go on to score two more Argosy westerns. Ford was an enigma: quixotic, tyrannical, insightful, artistic, contradictory. He could be involved in every phase of a film's production, and he could be intensely critical. But he got great work out of the people he worked with, and often those he was hardest on produced the best work of their careers. One of those was Richard Hageman, the Philadelphia Orchestra notwithstanding.

CHAPTER 6

"The Girl I Left Behind Me"

Men, Women, and Ireland
in the Cavalry Trilogy

John Ford did not intend *Fort Apache, She Wore a Yellow Ribbon,* and *Rio Grande* as a cavalry trilogy. He made other cavalry films, *The Horse Soldiers, Sergeant Rutledge,* and the Civil War segment of *How the West Was Won,* and the films dubbed "the cavalry trilogy" don't entirely hang together as such.[1] But they have been treated as a group almost since they were produced, and there is a certain logic in doing so, at least from a musical standpoint, because several period songs traverse all three films: "(Round Her Neck) She Wore a Yellow Ribbon," "The Girl I Left Behind Me," "Garry Owen," and "You're in the Army Now." Men and music have a long history in Ford westerns, but it is in the cavalry trilogy where the nuances of this pairing are played out most fully against conventional cultural stereotypes of masculinity and femininity.

"The Girl I Left Behind Me" not only testifies to the condition in which most men found themselves on the frontier but also serves as a reminder of the need for women. With its roots in Irish song, it also points to another story being told in the cavalry trilogy: the place of the Irish immigrant in America. Although Ford once described *Fort Apache* as his "pro-Irish film," he had a deeply conflicted relationship to his Irish ethnicity. Even more than the films actually set in Ireland, the cavalry trilogy films give Ford the opportunity to work out that conflict. Ford instilled Irishness into the scores of these films through his choice of songs, some popularly associated with Ireland, others fairly obscure but with pointed political overtones.

Filmic meaning in the cavalry trilogy is structured by the placement of songs. Ford's use of "Battle Hymn of the Republic" at the end of *Fort Apache,* for instance, complicates standard readings of the film that interpret the ending as a cynical interrogation of history. *Fort Apache* is often compared to *The Man Who Shot Liberty Valance* on this basis as a film in which history is exposed as artifice, the past is defined falsely by the present, and fact turns out to be fiction. As I argue in chapter 4, however, this standard interpretation of *Liberty Valance* has not taken the music into account. The same is true of *Fort Apache*. To read its ending as a foreshadowing of *The Man Who Shot Liberty Valance* is to ignore the music.

One of Ford's biographers, Tag Gallagher, compares a Ford film to "a trailer for a musical,"[2] and listening to the cavalry trilogy, it's hard to disagree. Rituals are the formalized patterns that reaffirm common values, beliefs, and practices, and in Ford's films, they have always played an important role in binding the community together. In Ford, rituals always involve music, some performance of singing or dancing or both, and those who gather around become participants in a social contract. In Ford's idealized version of the military community, on an isolated post, amid a hostile land and inhabitants, the need for ritual escalates. Perhaps this is why there is so much song and dance in the cavalry films and why these rituals have such import. Research notes for *Fort Apache* describe the effects of the regimental ball: "next day . . . the men will have a dignity they lacked the night before; and the women, as the picture unfolds, will gain stature."[3] Typically in Ford, those who disrupt singing and dancing pay a price. Thus, when Colonel Thursday (Henry Fonda) interrupts a dance at the post not once but twice, his fate is sealed. Doing so marks him as a disruptive outsider, who must either leave or die if the community is to survive.

Fort Apache tells the story of the Seventh Cavalry stationed on the frontier in the 1870s during the Indian wars. Colonel Owen Thursday, newly assigned to what he feels is a backwater post, is determined to make a name for himself and get out. A martinet, despite his proclamation otherwise, he manages to turn his officers and his men against him. Refusing to treat the Indians who have fled the reservation as anything other than renegade savages, he rides to his death with his troop, killed to the last man, in a misguided bid for personal glory. The comparison to General George Armstrong Custer and the massacre at the Little Bighorn is irresistible.[4] In a coda, several years afterwards, Colonel Kirby York (John Wayne), who was Thursday's second in command, is being interviewed by a group of newspaper reporters. York eulogizes his former commander and proclaims the

Example 3. "The Girl I Left Behind Me" from the conductor copy of *Fort Apache* (RKO, 1948). Used by permission of Warner Bros. Entertainment. Arranged by Richard Hageman. Courtesy Cinema-Television Library, University of Southern California.

massacre a supreme sacrifice, knowing full well that the events proved otherwise. In sacrificing truth to the greater needs of myth, York has made a hero out of Thursday, a violation of historical veracity, but, as the film implies, a necessary element for the continued legacy of the cavalry.

Richard Hageman composed the score for *Fort Apache* with Lucien Cailliet, formerly of the Ballet Russe, the arranger and conductor. Hageman tends to saturate a film with music. He seems a bit more restrained here than in, say, *3 Godfathers;* in *Fort Apache,* he leaves some major action scenes unscored, including the massacre itself. Hageman does manage to include a variation on the signature tune, "Oh, Bury Me Not on the Lone Prairie," in accompaniment to the stagecoach bearing Thursday and his daughter, Philadelphia (Shirley Temple). He also depends upon some of the same conventional musical stereotypes for Indians that can be heard in *Stagecoach,* a film he worked on. In *Stagecoach,* the camera pans left from the stagecoach to the Indians positioned menacingly on the bluff above them. In *Fort Apache,* the pan works in reverse, panning right to reveal the Indians, but the musical cue is basically the same: a downward second, harmonized in parallel fourths, played in the brass section with an accent on the first beat of the measure.

Despite the fact that the depiction of the Apaches in the film offers a surprisingly sympathetic treatment of Indians for a film of this era, Hageman employs stereotypical Indian music, first heard in the main title, where it alternates with bugle calls and cavalry songs. The structuring of this cue foreshadows the confrontation between the Seventh Cavalry and the Indians. The triumphant cavalry fanfare at the end of the main title is, however, decidedly at odds with the film's outcome.

At times, the score does attempt to break through these musical stereotypes. The dramatic confrontation between Thursday and Cochise (Miguel Inclan), for instance, is negotiated in Spanish and accompanied by Mexican music. While the use of Mexican music promotes the slippage between Indians and Mexicans, as does the casting of the noted Mexican actor Miguel Inclan as Cochise, neither the first time nor the last that such conflation occurs in Ford, it also works to position the sequence as a kind of hybrid cultural exchange. The Spanish language and Mexican music become a lingua franca through which Anglos and Others are able to communicate.

Sometimes what is not present in a film score is more revealing than what is. In *Fort Apache,* the climactic massacre is unscored. Heroic cavalry charge music begins the fated assault, but soon the bugler is killed and the diegetic music stops. Soon the nondiegetic music stops, too. The rest of the sequence is unaccompanied, casting into aural relief the shouts, grunts, and groans of the doomed soldiers. "Stripped of the magisterial signs of superiority, the horse soldiers yip and yelp just as the Native Americans do," Charles Ramirez Berg observes. "By demonstrating that high-pitched war cries are not culturally specific to Native Americans, but simply the sounds made by warriors rousing themselves to enter battle, Ford dismantles a core stereotypical sign of Otherness in the Western, one that even he had used in *Stagecoach*."[5]

The most Fordian musical moments in the score, however, are the production numbers, the diegetic performances of song and dance that employ period music. Heard in *Fort Apache* are "Fiddlers' Green," "She Wore a Yellow Ribbon," "The Regular Army O!" "You're in the Army Now," "Garry Owen," "The Girl I left Behind Me," "Beautiful Dreamer," "All Praise to St. Patrick," "Oh, Dem Golden Slippers," "Home, Sweet Home," "Goodnight, Ladies," "Sweet Genevieve," and "Battle Hymn of the Republic," all of which, with the exception of "Fiddlers' Green," heard in the main title, and "Battle Hymn of the Republic," are diegetic, danced to or sung. Here Ford, as usual, was in control, inserting songs into the plot,[6] writing and arranging song lyrics, and selecting the songs: some recognizable, some obscure, many of them Anglo-Irish, and all of them affecting the meaning of the film.

Ford was an avid student of American history, and his interest in the U.S. cavalry, sparked perhaps by his own recent military experience, seems to have been the catalyst for the film. For the first time, he used historical consultants: Katharine "Tatty" Spaatz and Katherine Cliffton. Using both primary and secondary sources, extensive research was done on military history, procedures, personages, and even uniforms, much of it highly technical detail.[7] Ford's priority, however, was always a good story. According to the screenwriter Frank Nugent, Ford forwarded him the voluminous research, and when Nugent had finished going over it, told him: "Now just forget everything you've read and we'll start writing a movie."[8]

The music was thoroughly researched as well. Ford described the noncommissioned officers' ball in *Fort Apache* as "typical of the period. . . . I try to make it true to life,"[9] and the research submitted by Spaatz and Cliffton bears him out. Even books on and recordings of nineteenth-century bugle calls found their way to Ford. A significant portion of the musical research was devoted to identifying typical cavalry songs and popular music of the period. Ford eventually settled on thirteen titles from a longer

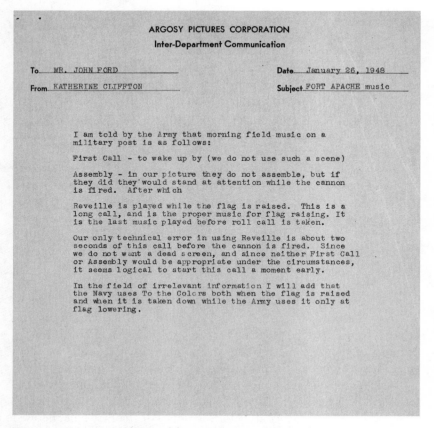

ARGOSY PICTURES CORPORATION

Inter-Department Communication

To   MR. JOHN FORD   Date January 26, 1948

From KATHERINE CLIFFTON   Subject FORT APACHE music

I am told by the Army that morning field music on a
military post is as follows:

First Call - to wake up by (we do not use such a scene)

Assembly - in our picture they do not assemble, but if
they did they would stand at attention while the cannon
is fired. After which

Reveille is played while the flag is raised. This is a
long call, and is the proper music for flag raising. It
is the last music played before roll call is taken.

Our only technical error in using Reveille is about two
seconds of this call before the cannon is fired. Since
we do not want a dead screen, and since neither First Call
or Assembly would be appropriate under the circumstances,
it seems logical to start this call a moment early.

In the field of irrelevant information I will add that
the Navy uses To the Colors both when the flag is raised
and when it is taken down while the Army uses it only at
flag lowering.

Figure 12. Memo to John Ford from Katherine Cliffton of the research staff.
Note the detailed information on bugle calls relayed to Ford, who concerned
himself with matters large and small relating to the music. Courtesy Harold B.
Lee Library, Brigham Young University.

list submitted to him.[10] All lyrics were subject to the Production Code, of
course, and MPAA chief Joseph Breen personally scanned the lyrics of the
eight songs ultimately submitted. Breen expressed concern over the use of
the word "hell" in "Fiddlers' Green" and "For Her Lover Who Was Far Far
Away," aka "(Round Her Neck) She Wore A Yellow Ribbon."[11] As a result, "Fiddlers' Green" would be used in an instrumental arrangement only,
and Ford himself rewrote the lyrics of "For Her Lover Who Was Far Far
Away,"[12] deleting the offending word and customizing them for the cavalry. The song was renamed "(Round Her Neck) She Wore a Yellow Ribbon" and was subsequently published and recorded under that title.

James Warner Bellah's source stories make no reference to troop song or music, but for cavalry troops on the frontier in the nineteenth century, music was an essential part of military routine, from reveille at dawn to taps for lights out. There were bugle calls for assembly, inspection, dress parade, drills, mounting and dismounting horses, meals, various emergencies, and more. Regimental bands accompanied troops leaving the post, and buglers accompanied troops into battle, sounding the charge and recall.[13] Soldiers would often sing; it helped to keep up morale. The regular soldier's work was dangerous and grueling. Mosquitoes and sun-blindness were persistent problems; conditions could be blisteringly hot, dusty, soaking wet, or freezing cold—in a word, miserable. Troops sang to divert themselves. As Colonel Yorke (John Wayne) commands his troops on patrol in *Rio Grande:* "Singers, sing. Make you forget your thirst."

Music was also a lively part of off-duty hours as well. John D. Billings writes: "There was probably not a regiment that did not boast of at least one violinist, one banjoist, and a bone player in its ranks—not to mention other instruments generally found associated with these—and one or all of them could be heard in operation, either inside or in a company street, most any pleasant evening." [14] H. H. McConnell comments upon the many regimental and citizen balls and notes the frequent singing of such songs as "Garry Owen," "The Girl I Left Behind Me," and "Captain Jinks [of the Horse Marines]."[15] Elizabeth Custer remembered weekly dances in the Seventh Cavalry.[16] "It was a surprise to strangers [to hear] . . . such good music," she writes.[17] They shouldn't have been surprised. Custer induced a professional musician, Felix Vinatieri, to accept a commission in the army and serve as his chief musician. Vinatieri presumably knew all the standard cavalry fare, but as the regimental band leader, he also composed original music for Custer. He and the regimental band would accompany Custer as far as the Powder River on the fateful day of the battle of the Little Bighorn.[18]

Many of the period songs in *Fort Apache* are military songs of one kind or another. The first is "Fiddlers' Green," heard instrumentally in the main title immediately after the opening bugle call.[19] Although the origins of "Fiddlers' Green" as a cavalry song remain cloudy, the general content of the song, as well as the term "Fiddlers' Green," are almost certainly borrowed from a traditional sea chantey of that name, very possibly of Irish origins.[20] "Fiddlers' Green" was a sailor's term for paradise in the afterlife. In the cavalry version, "Fiddlers' Green" refers to the cavalry soldier's final resting place, "halfway down the trail to hell."[21] It was traditionally sung by the Sixth and Seventh Cavalry. The lyrics were deleted when Breen indicated that he would not approve the script with its lyrics. The song is used again in *She Wore a Yellow Ribbon,* where it figures importantly in the characterization of Nathan Brittles (John Wayne).

A second military song used in the film, "You're in the Army Now," was typically sung by new recruits in basic training. The song became popular outside the military with the World War I–era version by Ole Oleson and Isham Jones in 1917. "You're in the Army Now" was used memorably in King Vidor's World War I epic *The Big Parade* (1925), and it seems possible that Ford recalled the prominent use Vidor's film made of the song when making *Fort Apache.*

The third military song is "The Regular Army O!" Written for the New York music hall stage in 1874 by the songwriting team of Edward "Ned" Harrington and David Braham, it was tremendously popular in its day and caught on with soldiers themselves, making the rounds from one military outfit to another, including the cavalry during the Indian wars of the 1870s and 1880s. In fact, it is a terrific marching song, with its march tempo, innumerable verses, and catchy chorus. "The Regular Army O!" remained in active publication through the 1930s and then dropped out of sight. Ford resurrected it for *Fort Apache.*[22]

"The Regular Army O!" offers a window into the history of Irish assimilation into American life. In the nineteenth century, the Irish faced harsh discrimination in their attempt to settle in America. Like many immigrant groups, they were largely unwanted ("No Irish Need Apply"). As if starvation, miserable living conditions, and fierce competition for jobs weren't enough, the Irish also had to contend with pernicious stereotypes that depicted them as drunks, violent brawlers, and mental deficients. Stereotypes are a powerful force to control difference, a tool of the dominant culture to retain its dominance in the face of change. Much stereotyping takes place in popular culture, where stereotypes are freely circulated, reinforced, and sometimes negotiated.

Ethnic comedy, which traded in conventional stereotypes, was extremely popular after the Civil War in urban centers such as New York, and a song such as "The Regular Army O!" reflects the changing position and growing power of Irish Americans in American cultural life. Unable to destroy the stereotype of themselves as hard-drinking, hard-fighting, and slow-witted, Irish and Irish American entertainers, songsmiths, and playwrights in the late nineteenth century (and filmmakers in the twentieth) began to redefine the stereotype, turning negative attributes into positives: hard drinking, for instance, became a sign of joie de vivre; pugnacious became principled; slow-witted became irascible or even charming. Harrington and Braham, who specialized in Irish comedies, constructed their sketches in a more sophisticated way than their competition, with plots, songs, and recurring characters. Those characters, such as Dan and Cordelia Mulligan, were the product of familiar Irish stereotypes, a necessary ingredient for commercial success, but negotiated through a sympathy for the disenfranchised that produced, if not a redefinition of the stereotype, at least some ambiguity about its use. Dan Mulligan was a veteran of the Civil War and a natural politician. He liked to fight, but his honesty, generosity, and loyalty got him into those fights; he was often drunk, but a charmer. Although many of Harrington's Irish sketches contained the stereotypical drunken brawl, the Irish took great pride in Harrington's plays and attended in droves.[23]

Harrington and Braham's song "The Regular Army O!" was originally part of an early music hall sketch of the same name that satirized a group of inept Irish recruits in New York City. With the Civil War over and conscription ended, the Grand Army of the Republic became, at least in the public consciousness, something a little less than grand. This postwar all-volunteer army depended upon immigrants (not unlike the U.S. military today), who saw the army as an upwardly mobile alternative to life in an immigrant ghetto. A significant portion of recruits were Irish.[24] "The Regular Army O!" was clearly designed to tap into a general cultural discomfort with a largely immigrant army and to satirize Irish recruits as inept. The cover of the sheet music, with its collection of unkempt misfits, gives a general indication of how the song may have been presented on the stage. The lyrics, however, tell a different story, representing those same recruits as generally affable, uncomplaining, hardworking, and above all, patriotic: "There was a sergeant John McCaffrey and Captain Donohue / They made us march and toe the mark in gallant company Q / Oh the drums would roll, upon my soul, / This is the style we would go / Forty miles a day on beans and hay / In the regular army O!" Many of Harrington and Braham's songs and theatrical entertainments sought to evoke the same kind of cultural frisson, pulling familiar stereotypes out of context and producing new and sometimes unexpected responses. I think this is precisely how Irish stereotypes work in the cavalry trilogy.

Ford has a complex relationship to his own ethnicity and to its representation in film.[25] It is useless to deny the existence of Irish stereotypes

Figure 13. Cover of the sheet music of "The Regular Army O!" by Edward Harrigan and David Braham. The cover illustration gives some indication of the way the song might have been performed—by a group of Irish immigrant misfits. Courtesy Brown University Library.

in Ford's films, and Ford has come under attack for exploiting them. Here is Jack Morgan on the Irish in the cavalry trilogy: "It is ironic then that this Irish Catholic auteur/director should be . . . the source of what are arguably some of the most disparaging stereotypes. . . . Ford's films often evidence a kind of vestigal colonialist mindset, a trace of racial self-contempt going oddly hand-in-hand with a maudlin Irish boosterism."[26] I read Ford differently. Like Harrington and Braham, Ford doesn't just use Irish stereotypes, he embraces them and, in doing so, destabilizes their functioning and drains them of at least some of their potency. Ford's Irish drunks come right out of the nineteenth-century ethnic the-atricals typified by Harrington and Braham. Convivial and comic, and never ashamed of their behavior, they act, Charles Ramirez Berg notes, "as if to say: We are Irish and proud of it, this is how we choose to act, and what are you going to do about it?"[27] Fighting, it seems to me, works the same way. The characters played by Victor McLaglen (English by birth, South African by upbringing) spend entire films itching for a fight.

When they get one, it's played for laughs, not violence, comic moments that deflate the stereotype. In *She Wore a Yellow Ribbon,* the character played by McLaglen, is actually stopped in mid-brawl by the commander's wife, Mrs. Allshard (Mildred Natwick), who simply tells him to behave and marches him to the guardhouse.

Ford's West is multiethnic, peopled by Germans, Jews, Italians, Swedes, Slavs, and Irish, all of whose ethnic origins are identifiable. They remain largely unhomogenized. Ford positions such ethnicity positively, as an invigorating influence on America's national character. As Paul Giles points out, the Irish in Ford "always operate as a threat to the pretentiousness . . . of those who believe in their own elective superiority."[28] In the cavalry trilogy, the Irish stand in for the ethnic margin, and are set up against the dominant majority, whose joyless conformity they oppose. In *Fort Apache,* we are presented, on the one hand, with the WASP mainstream in the shape of the New Englander Owen Thursday, as cold and humorless a character as Ford ever created, and, on the other, with a quartet of exuberant Irishmen, Sergeant Major O'Rourke (the ever-likeable Ward Bond), Lieutenant Michael O'Rourke (the handsome newcomer John Agar), Sergeant Mulcahy (the hulking but lovable Victor McLaglen), and Sergeant Quincannon (the sweet-voiced Dick Foran), full of the joy of life, not to mention liquor. In fact, part of the audience's antipathy toward Thursday is his prejudice against the Irish in his new command. Thursday cannot remember the Irish surname of a new lieutenant, he forbids his daughter to see that lieutenant, Michael O'Rourke, and he has trouble believing that O'Rourke's father has a Medal of Honor. All of the Irish characters in the cavalry trilogy are the work of Ford, who changed the names from the Bellah source story and invented Irish immigrant characters. In his story notes, Ford wrote of "*my* idea of [an] old Irish Sergeant . . . with a West Point son."[29]

Ethnomusicologists have long argued that music is a "means by which ethnicities and identities are constructed and mobilized."[30] Music is not simply a reflection of powerful cultural dynamics but a means by which such dynamics are negotiated. In a memo to Joseph Breen, Ford described *Fort Apache* as a patriotic and pro-Irish film.[31] The use of song is a key component in Ford's agenda. Irish music in the cavalry trilogy serves both as a marker of the historical assimilation of the Irish into American cultural life and a reminder of the positive contributions of ethnicity to America itself. The lyrics of "The Regular Army O!" function as an audible reminder of the general affability of the Irish, their work ethic, and their dedication to their adopted country, and many songs operate the same way. One might even argue that Ford's most Irish films are those that make up the cavalry trilogy.[32]

The song "Garry Owen" has Ireland written all over it. Its title consists of two Gaelic words: "garrai" (meaning garden)," and "Eoin" (often pronounced Owen, meaning John), and it refers to the area around King John's Castle in the environs of Limerick called "Garry-owen." It is an old Irish song, known by many names and with various lyrics, including "The Daughters of Erin," a version penned by Thomas Moore. Historically, Irish recruits in the U.S. Army sang it as a drinking song, and it became the unofficial marching song of George Armstrong Custer's Seventh Cavalry. Legend has it that Custer first heard the song at Fort Riley, Kansas, and learned it from Miles Keogh, who was born a short distance from Limerick.[33] Custer writes in his memoirs of the battle of Washita that he directed the regimental band to play "Garry Owen" moments before giving the command to attack. "At once the rollicking notes of that familiar marching and fighting air sounded forth through the valley, and in a moment were re-echoed back from the opposite sides by the loud and continued cheers of the men of the other detachments, who, true to their orders, were there and in readiness to pounce upon the Indians the moment the attack began."[34] The regimental band played "Garry Owen" again when the troops left them at Powder River for the Little Bighorn. The connection between "Garry Owen" and Custer's Seventh Cavalry was cemented by the popularity of Raoul Walsh's romanticized Custer biopic, *They Died with Their Boots On* (Raoul Walsh, 1941) complete with a Max Steiner score prominently featuring "Garry Owen."

"Garry Owen" was a drinking song, but its lyrics are not heard in any of the cavalry trilogy films: "Let Bacchus' sons be not dismayed / But join with me each jovial blade / Come drink and sing and lend you aid / To help me with the chorus." Its rousing chorus continues the drinking motif: "Instead of spa, will drink brown ale / And pay the reckoning on the nail; / No man for debt shall go to jail / From Garryowen in glory." And on it goes for numerous verses. Lyrics that omitted reference to drinking were later created for the Seventh Cavalry, but under Custer's command, "Garry Owen" proclaimed the delights of imbibing loud and clear. Breen warned Ford about the necessity of keeping drinking to "an *absolute minimum*,"[35] and this may be part of the reason why "Garry Owen" is heard in *Fort Apache* and *She Wore a Yellow Ribbon* in instrumental arrangements only.

An interesting aspect of the history of "Garry Owen" is its identification with the Irish movement for independence. This was not the first time Ford had used an Irish song that was politically contentious or used Irish song for political purposes. "The Minstrel Boy," composed by Thomas Moore, with a clear message about the oppression of Ireland at the hands of the British, can be heard in *The Informer*. The quintessentially Irish tune "Londonderry Air" can be heard in *Four Men and a Prayer* (1938), a film about four aristocratic British brothers trying to remove the stain of their father's military dishonor.[36] British pride was not a subject dear to Ford's heart, so when one of the brothers sits down at the piano in the family's baronial manse, he plunks out "Londonderry Air." The title of the song is an audible reminder of the British colonization of Ireland when the name of Derry, a town in northern Ireland, was changed to "Londonderry" by the British colonizers in 1613. Irish republicans continued to refer to the town as Derry and thus a simple tune becomes politically contentious. Irish Americans in the audience would have gotten the point.

Another Irish rebel song, "Down by the Glenside," more commonly known as "The Bold Fenian Men," which can be heard in *Rio Grande*, is decidedly more controversial. Composed in 1916 by Peadar Kearney, in the midst of a rebellion against Britain, "The Bold Fenian Men" commemorates an earlier, failed rebellion, the Fenian movement for Irish independence in the 1860s, when the Fenians, in order to effect the release of one of their members, bombed Clerkenwell prison in London, killing several people and injuring dozens more.[37] "The Bold Fenian Men" would have been a potentially incendiary song for British audiences of the 1950s: "Glory, O, Glory O to the bold Fenian men."[38] Ford didn't care. Like his father before him, he embraced republican sentiments and funneled cash to the IRA through relatives.[39] Inserting songs associated with the Irish movement for independence into the cavalry trilogy, even when they are historically inaccurate, and wrapping these songs in sympathy, may well be Ford's most subtle form of political action.[40]

Also worth noting is the fact that the music that opens the noncommissioned officers' regimental ball is an Irish Catholic hymn, "All Praise to St. Patrick," taken out of its usual context (it was and continues to be sung in mass on St. Patrick's Day). Although "All Praise to St. Patrick" is not a typical dance tune, it would have been well known in Irish communities in the nineteenth century, and, as it is written in $\frac{6}{8}$ meter, it works nicely as the Grand March. It is one of the few times that Ford used Catholic music. For listeners who recognized the tune, "All Praise to St. Patrick" points directly to Irish Catholicism and underscores the

class divide in the nineteenth-century military that Ford critiques. The
noncommissioned officers, those who rose through the ranks without the
benefit of a West Point education and a commission, dance to an Irish
Catholic hymn, followed by a song coded as unrefined and thus lower-
class, "Oh, Dem Golden Slippers" (in fact, a minstrel song).[41] On the
other hand, at the officer's ball for George Washington's birthday, cou-
ples waltz, with attendant connotations of class privilege, to music
coded as refined and upper-class: an original composition by Richard
Hageman[42] and a sentimental parlor ballad by Stephen Foster, "Beautiful Dreamer."[43] It is the elitist Thursday who cannot cross this divide, noticeably discomforted by having to dance with the wife of one of his Irish
(yikes!) noncommissioned officers. Ford is not content to leave these
matters without a comment: Mrs. O'Rourke contends that the noncommissioned officers' ball is clearly more fun than the other. And with the
punch spiked by Sergeant Mulcahy, there is every reason to believe her.

There are two military songs that appear in all of the cavalry trilogy
films: "You're in the Army Now" and the "The Girl I Left Behind Me."
The latter was a cherished song of the Seventh Cavalry and served as
their regimental march. Known in America for centuries and popular
during both the Revolutionary and Civil Wars, it is an adaptation of a
British military song, "Brighton Camp," which has a traditional Irish
melody. The lyrics were adapted by American soldiers and sung throughout the nineteenth century. (Custer's Seventh Cavalry had their own set
of lyrics.) The version sung in Ford's cavalry trilogy uses the lyrics of
"Brighton Camp," but is derived from Edward Dolph's collection *Sound
Off! Soldier Songs from the Revolution to World War II* (1942).[44] Elizabeth Custer distinctly remembered her husband's troops singing "The
Girl I Left Behind Me" as they left the fort for the last time before the
battle of the Little Bighorn.[45] The Seventh Cavalry in *Fort Apache* do the
same as they leave for their fate.

In *Fort Apache,* "the girl" left behind refers literally to the wives and
mothers of the soldiers, assembled on the rooftop watching the men
leave the fort. The women are anxious and tense, desperately seeking one
last glimpse of the men, and a profound sadness accompanies Mrs.
Collingwood's (Anna Lee) pronouncement: "I can't see him anymore. All
I can see is the flags." The women stay behind in the fort, a space clearly
domesticated by their presence, by the rituals, like the regimental dances,
that their presence makes possible; and by their organization and deco-
ration of the quarters they share with their husbands and families.
What's interesting is how effortlessly most men move through this do-

mestic space: Captain Collingwood (George O'Brien) clearly enjoys the elegant dinner party in his quarters; Sergeant Major O'Rourke and Lieutenant O'Rourke, father and son, are reunited, after years apart, in the family parlor. It is Colonel Thursday who cannot negotiate the domesticated space of *Fort Apache*. His possessions have yet to arrive, so the ladies of the fort provide him with what he needs. At first delighted, he soon falls through a chair and lands on the floor, trapped and unable to move. He is a destructive force who cannot accommodate himself to domestic space.

The title of the song "The Girl I Left Behind Me" encapsulates the condition that most men found themselves in on the frontier, but its lyrics express the longing for something else: for women, for family, and for community. Ford's version of the settling of the West always had a place for women, and men who cannot accommodate them are suspect. Gaylyn Studlar, among the first to offer a sustained argument about the representation of women in Ford, contends that "the sound Westerns of John Ford often focus, with unexpected 'poetic' intensity, on women and on 'femininity' in ways that run counter both to recent assertions and to more long-standing critical expectations for the Western as a cinematic and literary form."[46] Studlar notes that "some of his films go so far as to break down gender polarities to suggest the accommodation of masculinity to feminine values.[47] This is the argument that I intend to trace out for the music.

Traditionally, the performance of song and dance complicated the representation of masculinity in Hollywood film, especially in the genre of the musical. As Steven Cohan has argued compellingly of Fred Astaire, and, among others, of Gene Kelly,[48] musical performance threatened to compromise male stars' masculinity, as both Astaire and Kelly were well aware. In response, the studio publicity machine publicized their more conventionally masculine offscreen lives to emphasize their masculinity. In Ford westerns, men performing to music does not have the same effect.

Ford did not envision masculinity and music as antithetical. He was connecting men and music as early as *Straight Shooting* (1917), where cowboys relax to phonograph music, *Bucking Broadway* (1917), in which a cowboy strums a mandolin in the bunkhouse and the cowboys sing "Home, Sweet Home" around a piano, and *Hellbent* (1918), where the protagonist and his buddy sing "Sweet Genevieve." Musical performance is what makes Dan O'Malley of *3 Bad Men* sexually attractive to women. John Wayne sang as the Ringo Kid in a scene deleted from

Stagecoach and sings as Robert Hightower in *3 Godfathers*. Henry Fonda sings as Tom Joad in *The Grapes of Wrath*. Ben Johnson and Harry Carey Jr., as best friends in *Wagon Master,* at one point sing their conversation to each other. And Tom Doniphon rides into town in *The Man Who Shot Liberty Valance* to the strains of "Sweet Genevieve" emanating from Shinbone's restaurant. None of these characters compromise their masculinity through their proximity to song. This is possible partly because of the genre's hyperbolic masculinity that could sustain deviation from the norm, partly because of the series westerns that exploited country-and-western music through the figure of the singing cowboy (like Dick Foran, recruited by Ford for *Fort Apache*), and partly because of the resistance to gender stereotyping in Ford westerns.

Music has traditionally been associated in Western civilization with subjectivity and emotion, and for this reason, it has been thought to represent and appeal to the feminine side of human nature, as opposed to the supposedly masculine realms of objectivity and logic. The musicologist Susan McClary has pointed out that charges of effeminacy leveled against musicians and music lovers go "back as far as recorded documentation about music." Song carries especially powerful connotations of the feminine because, as a form, it is a condensation of subjective feeling: its performer is literally *in tune* with his or her emotions. Gender stereotyping has had a persistent effect in the twentieth century and beyond, and as McClary has demonstrated, it leaves "the whole enterprise of musical activity . . . fraught with gender-related anxieties."[49]

Oddly enough, Ford westerns resist gender stereotypes by actually embracing them. Male performances of song and dance *are* manifestations of the feminine in Ford. It's just that in his westerns, the embrace of the feminine is not a negative attribute. Ford's westerns redefine masculinity to accommodate traditionally defined feminine values. Ford's most sympathetic male protagonists and supporting characters have always had room for the feminine in their masculinity, the very femininity that is positioned elsewhere in the genre as oppositional to masculinity: Wyatt Earp, who smells like honeysuckle, Nathan Brittles, who tends the plants near the graves of his family (and who accepts a gift of flowers), Colonel Allshard (George O'Brien), who trades handkerchiefs with Miss Dandridge (JoAnne Dru) to dry his tears at Nathan's retirement, Kirby Yorke, who numbers among his possessions a music box. Inversely, the male protagonists who are the least sympathetic are those with an excess of masculinity, like Pa Clanton, Owen Thursday, Uncle Shiloh Clegg, or Ethan Edwards. It is not as if these characters cannot accommodate women in the films; they cannot accommodate the feminine in themselves, and this is seen as part of their failure.

This manipulation of gender stereotyping is reflected in the scores themselves. In the cavalry trilogy, men dominate the diegetic musical performances. In fact, the only woman who sings at all is Mrs. Allshard, drunkenly crooning a few lines of "The Girl I Left Behind Me" in *She Wore a Yellow Ribbon.* Men also dominate the nondiegetic background score; in the cavalry trilogy, music is just as likely to accompany the men as the women. In *Fort Apache,* the sentimental favorite "Home, Sweet Home," wafting in from the regimental ball, accompanies the reunion of Lieutenant Michael O'Rourke both with his father and (only afterwards) with his mother. In *She Wore a Yellow Ribbon,* a musical cue coded for sentimentality (violins, downward melodic trajectory) accompanies Nathan Brittles when he visits his family's grave. In *Rio Grande,* song lyrics externalize Kirby Yorke's repressed emotions.

Music also provides the very vocabulary through which men and women interact, whether it is "Good Night Ladies," which provides the unspoken context between Lieutenant O'Rourke and Philadelphia as they dance in the dark, or the serenading of Philadelphia by Sergeant Quincannon and members of the troop with "Sweet Genevieve," a popular love song of the nineteenth century.[50] In an early version of the screenplay, Mexican music serves as a form of communication between Anglo lovers. O'Rourke brings a mariachi band to serenade Philadelphia on her balcony with the song "Yo Va Me Voy" (I Am Already Leaving). It is sung in Spanish and O'Rourke translates its lyrics, the song literally speaking for him. "I'm sorry that I can't sing . . . but he's saying it for me," O'Rourke says,[51] another example of how Mexico, its culture, and its language become an expressive medium of exchange. In the exception that proves the rule, Kirby Yorke, in *Rio Grande,* disavows the song the regimental singers perform for his wife, "I'll Take You Home Again, Kathleen": "This song is not of my choosing." Yet the lyrics encapsulate exactly what he is thinking. Kirby's renunciation both signals and furthers his estrangement from his wife. Her answer, "I wish it had been," reinforces the blunder of his denial. In the cavalry trilogy, song and dance constitute an incorporation of the feminine that works, ironically, not to challenge masculinity, but to incorporate the feminine as a valid form of masculine expression.

Much has been written about the ending of *Fort Apache* and whether or not the film critiques the notion of history itself.[52] Certainly, York's valorization of Thursday is intended as ironic. The audience knows that

York is lying, because his retelling of events to the Eastern reporters does not coincide with what has gone before, and Wayne's acting here is noticeably stiff, a deliberate attempt to telegraph York's discomfort. As York delivers his moving speech about the immortality of soldiers killed in action ("They're not forgotten because they haven't died . . . "), an instrumental version of the Union anthem "Battle Hymn of the Republic" can be heard. Ford had used "Battle Hymn of the Republic" before and would use it again later as a distillation of patriotism. He never used it ironically: it accompanies the dying visage of the assassinated Abraham Lincoln in *The Prisoner of Shark Island* and the final glimpse of him in *Young Mr. Lincoln,* which foreshadows his greatness. Ford used it in the World War II combat drama *They Were Expendable* to accompany both the dramatic appearance of General Douglas MacArthur (Robert Barrat) and the uplifting ending, with MacArthur's famous promise "I Shall Return" superimposed on the screen. "Battle Hymn of the Republic" can be heard twice in *She Wore a Yellow Ribbon* at emotional highpoints: as Nathan Brittles rides to inspection for the last time as an officer in the cavalry and when he reads the telegram appointing him chief of scouts, and thus ending the uncertainty about his future. On location for *Cheyenne Autumn,* Ford had Harry Carey Jr. sing "Battle Hymn of the Republic" after John F. Kennedy's assassination was announced. "Battle Hymn of the Republic" was played one last time for Ford as his casket was carried out of church after his funeral mass. The use of the hymn in *Fort Apache* makes an unmistakable appeal to emotion, its patriotic connotations covering over any skepticism and irony, both York's and the audience's. For those who can summon up the lyrics, the final line of the chorus, "His truth goes marching on," clearly resonates with the film's conclusion. York may be covering up Thursday's failure, but the use of the "Battle Hymn of the Republic" makes it clear that the heroic history of the cavalry is not being called into question. When York rides off with his troop, we hear "The Girl I Left Behind Me," the song that dispatched Thursday to the massacre. The music enfolds failure into triumph, tragedy into heroism, Thursday into York, the past into the future. Myth may be a necessary part of history, but whatever cynicism may be tied up in that recognition is elided by the use of "Battle Hymn of the Republic."

The other period song of note in *Fort Apache* is "(Round Her Neck) She Wore A Yellow Ribbon," a song that is more fully developed in the second film of the cavalry trilogy, which bears its name. *She Wore a Yellow Ribbon* focuses on Captain Nathan Brittles, who is about to retire from the military. The film chronicles his last patrol from the fort into hostile Indian territory. Strapped by the women he has been asked to escort, his commanding officer's wife and niece, he is not able to save a suttler's outpost, capture the renegade Indians, or deliver his charges. When he returns to the fort, he pronounces his mission a failure and is prepared to retire in disgrace. It is left to his two lieutenants, Lieutenant Cohill (John Agar) and Lieutenant Pennell (Harry Carey Jr.), at war themselves over the niece, to finish the job and defeat the renegades, albeit with a little help from Brittles, who averts an all-out war by driving off the Indians' horses. As he rides away into the sunset, Brittles receives a telegram (unlike the one in *Fort Apache*, this one arrives in time) appointing him head of the Army scouts. He will not retire after all. "Old soldiers . . . hate to grow old," Brittles says earlier in the film.

The song "(Round Her Neck) She Wore a Yellow Ribbon" refers to the practice of a woman wearing a yellow ribbon to signal her affection for a particular soldier. Some historians believe that the custom dated back to the Civil War, when women wore yellow ribbons (mimicking the yellow stripes on the Union cavalry uniform) while they waited for their soldiers to return.[53] This appears to be a point of some contention, however.[54] Gerald E. Parsons of the Library of Congress writes that "although it is perfectly plausible that the families of Union army troops did adopt such a token, prudent historiography would demand evidence. . . . So far, no such evidence has come to our attention, and we must keep open to the possibility that the distant recollections of the Civil War have been grafted onto the symbolism of a much later popular motion picture [*She Wore a Yellow Ribbon*]."[55] The venerable Civil War historian Shelby Foote "could not recall any reference to the practice of wearing yellow ribbons."[56] More recently, Tad Tuleja has argued that practice of wearing yellow ribbons existed but with a very different meaning: "When U.S. cavalrymen's sweethearts wore ribbons around their necks in the nineteenth century, the symbolic signal was not simply one of affection. The yellow band also served as a combined property tag and off-limits sign—a signal to other service branches that the girl was 'cavalry goods' and also possibly infectious (yellow being the color of the quarantine flag)."[57] This is clearly not the meaning that the film intended.

The song that commemorates this disputed practice has its own murky history. "(Round Her Neck) She Wore a Yellow Ribbon" was first copyrighted in 1917 by George A. Norton (who would later pen "My Melancholy Baby"), but copyright is not always an accurate indicator of a song's genesis, and in this case, it is misleading. The minstrel song "All

Round My Hat," which appeared in 1838, is generally regarded as the ancestor of the 1917 version: "All round my hat / I vear a green villow / All round my hat, for a twelvemonth and a day / If hanyone should hax, the reason vy I vears it, / Tell them that my true love is far, far away." This minstrel version is built upon a popular English dance tune of the same name, which itself derived from a folk source perhaps hundreds of years old. According to Dolph's generally reliable anthology of military music, a version of the song was sung in the nineteenth-century cavalry, minus the minstrel dialect.[58]

This is the version of the song that composer Richard Hageman claims to have used.[59] Ford provided the lyrics, deleting an offensive word in the original and customizing the song for the cavalry trilogy.[60] Regent Music published the sheet music in connection with the film's release as "(Round Her Neck) She Wore a Yellow Ribbon," but with new lyrics, which eliminate the cavalry references. "(Round Her Neck) She Wore a Yellow Ribbon" was a best seller as sheet music and a hit for the Andrews Sisters, among others. Mitch Miller both recorded it and published it in one of his songbooks as late as the 1960s. However, unbeknown to anyone at RKO or Argosy, Norton still held the copyright (the song was in active publication through the 1930s), and his publishing company, Jerry Vogel Music, intended to file suit against Argosy Pictures, RKO, and Regent Music for copyright infringement.[61] As it turned out, Dolph proved to be an unreliable source,[62] and Argosy scrambled to dig up an earlier published version to prove that the song was in the public domain. The song, with slightly altered lyrics, had been popular in the 1920s and 1930s as a college song. Ford suggested looking at Williams College, where indeed a copy of the song predating the Norton publication was found ("She wore it for her Williams man who's far, far away"). Apparently, this version satisfied Jerry Vogel Music, because no further mention of the litigation turns up in the Argosy files.

Regardless of the dubious history of the yellow ribbon as an authentic military symbol in the nineteenth century and the checkered history of the song that immortalizes it, both the symbol and the song point to the heart of Ford's film and its concern with the past, with honoring loved ones, and with the perpetuation of memory. Before we are introduced to Nathan Brittles, we are shown a close-up of photographs of his wife and daughters, who, we come to understand, are dead. Nathan's visit to their grave and his conversations with his dead wife, Mary, mirror other graveside scenes in Ford, particularly Lincoln visiting Ann Rutledge in *Young Mr. Lincoln* and Wyatt Earp visiting his brother James in

Figure 14. Cover of the sheet music of "(Round Her Neck) She Wore a Yellow Ribbon." Its publication triggered a lawsuit and Argosy lawyers had to do some fancy footwork to prove that the song was in the public domain. Courtesy Archive of Popular American Music, UCLA.

My Darling Clementine. For Nathan, as it is for these other Fordian characters, the past is still alive. Nathan talks to his wife in the present tense, as if she were there listening to him. When he returns at the end of the film to find a dance in his honor, he excuses himself first to make his report—he must go and tell Mary what has happened. The past lives in the present, the present will live in the future. It is a mythos that mitigates the ravages of time. Period music works nicely to support these effects. Songs such as "Garry Owen," "The Girl I Left Behind Me," and "(Round Her Neck) She Wore a Yellow Ribbon" not only authenticate the version of the past presented by the film but carry traces of the past into the present.

Richard Hageman was again at the composerly helm for *She Wore a Yellow Ribbon.* Lucien Cailliet was the arranger, and Constantin Bakaleinikoff, music director at RKO, conducted. Jester Hairston, who had first worked with Ford on *3 Godfathers,* did the choral work. The score has all the marks of Ford: the incorporation of Anglo Irish folk tunes adopted by the cavalry ("The Son of a Gambolier," "The Girl I Left Behind Me," "Garry Owen," and "Fiddlers' Green"); an Irish Catholic hymn ("All Praise to St. Patrick"); period music ("She Wore a Yellow Ribbon," "You're in the Army Now," "Battle Hymn of the Republic," and "Dixie"); an American folk tune ("Oh, Bury Me Not on the Lone Prairie"); and historically accurate bugle calls. With the exception of "The Son of a Gambolier" and "Dixie," all this was recycled from *Fort Apache.* The same authentic nineteenth-century bugle call, "Assembly of the Guard," which opens the main title of *Fort Apache,* accompanies the appearance of John Ford's name in *Rio Grande.* It was heard around eight in the morning, when guard details were posted for the day.

The nondiegetic score of *She Wore a Yellow Ribbon* is vintage Hageman. There are numerous examples of stereotypical Indian music, including a musical motif Hageman had used before, the descending minor second, when Indians ominously appear. Also audible is the stereotypical Indian tom-tom drumbeat—four beats with the accent on the first. A rather arresting cue built upon open fourths and fifths lends several sequences featuring Indians something of the pageantry of ancient Rome. A distinctive element of the score are its many diegetic and historically accurate bugle calls, and Hageman uses some of these to inaugurate some striking brass fanfares. One can be heard early in the film, when the patrol dismount to walk their horses and a diegetic bugle call morphs into an impressive nondiegetic fugue for brass instruments. The fording of the river provides another opportunity when an extremely dense musical cue played by a complement of brass instruments is separated into choirs (the trumpets seem to take on the other brasses) in an antiphonal sequence where one choir of brass instruments, in effect, presents a challenge and the other responds, each in a different meter. Given that the cavalry is fording the river, the tension created by the antiphonal structure of the music cannot be coincidental. The result is stunning.

It is the song "(Round Her Neck) She Wore a Yellow Ribbon," however, that provides the framework of the score. In a sense, it becomes the troop's regimental song and functions much the way "The Girl I Left Behind Me" does for the Seventh Cavalry in *Fort Apache*. It appears numerous times diegetically and is woven into the nondiegetic score throughout. I particularly like the arrangement that accompanies the return of the troop after its failed mission. Here an accompanying counter melody grows increasingly dissonant, competing with the familiar melody and transmitting the troopers' disappointment and dejection.

Three other songs used in the film as part of the nondiegetic score should be noted. The first is "The Son of the Gambolier," a traditional Irish drinking song, which can be heard "slow and tired," according to Hageman's score, when the patrol dismount to walk their horses.[63] The song is somewhat out of context here: it is a kind of rake's progress, a gambolier being a worthless tippler of dubious morals. The lyrics detail both the desire for a drink ("I take my whiskey clear") and its consequences ("every girl turns up her nose"), with poverty both the cause and effect of drinking. In some versions of the song, the son of the gambolier is forced by poverty to become a soldier. The song became a favorite among college students in the nineteenth century and is immortalized in Georgia Tech's fight song, "I'm a Ramblin' Wreck from Georgia Tech." *She Wore a Yellow Ribbon* downplays the drinking context—the lyrics are not used. Still, the song has an obvious connection to the Irish sergeant, Quincannon (Victor McLaglen), always on the lookout for his next drink, and is part of the general Irish ambience that infuses the cavalry trilogy.

"Fiddlers' Green" is another traditional cavalry song heard in *Fort Apache* and recycled more audibly here. It is first heard in accompaniment to Nathan Brittle's morning walk to inspect his troops, and it functions, for those who recognize the tune, to enrich his characterization. The song's military history and general content (and lyrics, for those listeners able to summon them up) provide yet another example of the care with which Ford chose the songs. Brittles, who is anticipating his retirement and nearing the end of his life (even his name connotes age), is associated with a song describing the place where old cavalry soldiers go after death, a far superior resting place than that of other soldiers: "Marching past, straight through to Hell, / The Infantry are seen, / Accompanied by the Engineers, / Artillery and Marine, / For none but the shades of Cavalrymen / Dismount at Fiddlers' Green."[64]

Two songs of note are used nondiegetically at the discovery of the Indians' savagery. "Oh, Bury Me Not on the Lone Prairie" can be heard as the bodies of the suttlers are discovered, and "Dixie" can be heard during Trooper Smith's death and burial. Smith (Rudy Bowman) is an elderly soldier, a lowly trooper. But his past is revealed at his death, and he is honored by the patrol with burial as an officer of the Confederacy. "Dixie" is one of a group of traditional American songs, growing smaller with each succeeding generation, that remains recognizable by a large portion of the audience. Although it was the unofficial anthem of the Confederacy and enjoyed immense popularity in the South, "Dixie" originated as a minstrel song, composed by a northerner, Daniel Decautur Emmett. In *She Wore a Yellow Ribbon,* the association of Trooper Smith with "Dixie" functions both as a kind of aural shorthand to identify "Smith's" past quickly and reliably and a way to generate sympathy for him. In this way, "Dixie" is similar to the use of "Jeanie with the Light Brown Hair" in *Stagecoach* as a leitmotif for Hatfield, a southerner and former soldier of the Confederacy. "Dixie" also figures prominently in *Rio Grande,* where it serves as a condensation of both the southern background and rebellious nature of Kathleen Yorke (Maureen O'Hara).

Rio Grande has not been a favorite of Ford scholars.[65] It has been overshadowed by both *Fort Apache,* the critics' darling among the cavalry films, and *The Quiet Man,* the blockbuster that followed it, featuring the same stars, John Wayne and Maureen O'Hara. *Rio Grande* marked the inauguration of a new partnership for Argosy Pictures with Republic. Created as a dry run for *The Quiet Man,* the Irish film Ford had wanted to make for well over a decade, *Rio Grande* was designed to make enough money to offset what Republic's production chief, Herbert Yates, was sure would be the financial losses of *The Quiet Man* (1952).[66] Unlike *Fort Apache* and *She Wore a Yellow Ribbon,* shot in Monument Valley, *Rio Grande* was shot in less isolated locations near Moab, Utah, where *Wagon Master* was also shot and production costs were lower. It was shot in black and white. But it seems to me that if *Rio Grande* is a rehearsal for anything, it is *The Searchers,* with the dark and bitter Colonel Kirby Yorke foreshadowing Ethan Edwards. Edwards proves beyond redemption, but there is still hope for Yorke. He may be "a man trapped in a man's world," as Barton Palmer puts it,[67] but there is, after all, his attachment to that music box.

Kirby Yorke commands Fort Starke in Texas, to which his wayward young son, Jeff (Claude Jarman Jr.), has been assigned. Jeff has flunked out of West Point and enlisted in the cavalry. His mother, Kathleen, has been separated from Kirby for fifteen years, a result of his torching of her family plantation, under orders, during the Civil War. She has never forgiven Kirby but finds herself confronting him once again when she travels west to reclaim Jeff and buy him out of the army. Hostile Indians kidnap the fort's children, and Jeff must prove his mettle under fire. The children are retrieved safely. Kirby and Kathleen reconcile. None other than General Phil Sheridan (J. Carrol Naish) has the regimental band play "Dixie" in her honor at the ceremony rewarding the bravery of several troopers, including Jeff.

In *Fort Apache,* Ford probed the history of the cavalry, focusing on the nature of command, the definition and requirements of heroism, the essential duty that defines the military. In *Rio Grande,* Ford focuses on the cost of that duty, not to life itself, as does *Fort Apache,* but to personal fulfillment and psychic health. Kirby's estrangement from his wife has been precipitated by his allegiance to military duty over family loyalty. Not that the film questions his choice to obey orders and burn Bridesdale, his wife's plantation, during the Civil War. It's just that the film makes clear the consequences of doing one's duty. As Kathleen tells Kirby in no uncertain terms, his commitment to duty "destroyed two beautiful things: Bridesdale and us." Kirby learns to live without his wife and son, but repressing his desire has made him hard and bitter. Robert D. Leighninger describes the film as "an expression of the anguish of men caught in gender contradictions" and compares its "understanding of men in such binds" to the analysis of women's social roles in the melodramas of Douglas Sirk and Vincente Minelli.[68] More than one critic has referred to the film as male melodrama.

The first scene between Kirby and his son demonstrates the toll that duty has taken on Kirby. When he greets the new recruits, Jeff among them, Kirby seems especially mean-spirited, and in his first meeting with Jeff in fifteen years, he is cold and distant. If it weren't for a private moment of obvious delight in his son after their meeting (Kirby can't resist secretly measuring his height against Jeff's), Kirby would come off unsympathetically, even though played by John Wayne. In the source story by James Warner Bellah, "Mission with No Record," the character is de-

Example 4. From the conductor copy of *She Wore a Yellow Ribbon*. Note the annotations, "Garry Owen" and "O Bury Me Not on the Lone Prairie." Used by permission of Warner Bros. Entertainment. Arranged by Richard Hageman. Courtesy Arts Special Collections, UCLA.

scribed as "a frigid shadow of a man . . . alone and friendless."[69] Jeff
asks his mother, "What kind of man is he . . . ?" She answers in terms
of his emotional state: "He's a lonely man." Jeff continues: "They say
he's a great soldier," and Kathleen's rejoinder encapsulates the central
crux of the film: "What makes soldiers great is hateful to me."

The film is concerned with the demands of duty and the divided loyalties that are inevitably a soldier's lot. Kirby must learn to respect the
needs of his family. He does so when he assigns Jeff to what he thinks
will be a safe assignment, essentially putting him out of harm's way. His
decision runs counter to his better military judgment, but it demonstrates
Kirby's new willingness to compromise. Wounded in the final Indian
skirmish, Kirby will depend upon his wife to nurse him back to health.
And is it a coincidence that Kirby is shot through the chest near his heart?
If there ever was an allegorical wound in Ford, this is it.[70] Kathleen, for
her part, must learn to forgive Kirby and, given that this is a Ford film,
she must also learn to give up her class privilege, "special privilege for
the special born," as Kirby describes it. Leighninger suggests that class
bias is made the linchpin of the separation because it's an easier problem
to resolve than others, such as political differences, the pressures of frontier life on the family, or Kathleen's separation from her family and way
of life.[71] All it takes is Kathleen's willingness to get her hands wet,
metaphorically joining the working class by doing laundry along with
the other women, to ensure her redemption. The resolution of class differences cannot disguise another story being told here, however. It's discomforting to watch Kathleen's happy embrace of traditional wifely duties, preceded by her high-strung responses, emotional vulnerability, and
physical weaknesses. Even Kirby is dismayed by her lack of fortitude, an
indicator that she has strayed outside the boundaries of a Ford frontier
heroine, and Kirby makes a point of telling her so: "We can't have the
commander's lady fainting at the first sign of trouble." He seems perfectly content with her laundering abilities, however.

The film ends where it began: with the troop returning home after a
mission, with the women and families of the fort looking anxiously for
their loved ones. The final sequence shows Kirby and Kathleen reconciled,
but the preceding close-ups of the women's frightened faces and Kathleen's
own grim determination when she finds the wounded Kirby, borne on a
travois, remind us of the costs of duty. Still there is a happy ending, with
a patched-up Kirby and a radiant Kathleen, clearly reconciled, watching
a medals ceremony on the parade grounds and listening to "Dixie."

The score of *Rio Grande* was composed by Victor Young, with Leo Shuken and Sid Cutner arranging and orchestrating. It was the first of three scores Young composed for Ford. A contemporary of Max Steiner, Erich Wolfgang Korngold, and Alfred Newman, Young brought a song-writer's ear to film music. He had been born in Chicago but moved to Warsaw, Poland, after his mother died and his father abandoned him and his sister. Trained as a concert violinist, Young toured Europe and then America, where he was repatriated at the outbreak of World War I. He gradually moved into popular music, radio, and motion picture work, starting as the concertmaster in a silent film orchestra in Los Angeles and taking over the helm of the orchestras at the Chicago and the State and Lake theaters. Young added song composing to his resume when he started his own dance orchestra. With the lyricist Ned Washington, he composed dozens of hit songs, including "Stella by Starlight" and "My Foolish Heart." Many of these songs were composed for films. Before he was done, Young had worked on over 350 film scores. For most of his film music career, he worked in Paramount's Music Department, but he also wrote scores for Columbia and Republic. One of his last was for Mike Todd's *Around the World in Eighty Days*. It was at Republic that his path crossed with John Ford's on *Rio Grande*. Young also scored *The Quiet Man* and the largely forgotten *The Sun Shines Bright* for Ford, both at Republic. He died suddenly in 1956 at the age of fifty-six.

Young was a good match for Ford. Like all of Ford's westerns, *Rio Grande* incorporates many songs into its score, including several sung by Sons of the Pioneers. The original theme Young composed for the film, heard initially in the main title, was also constructed along the lines of a popular song, with a standard four-part structure. Richard Hageman could be operatic, and he knew how to marshal the resources of a symphony orchestra, but Young knew how to write a song and deliver a memorable tune. The main title for *Rio Grande,* in my opinion, provides as beautiful an original melody as Ford ever got from any of his composers.[72]

Young knew the tricks of the trade. He composed a memorable leitmotif for father and son; he used "I'll Take You Home Again, Kathleen" as a leitmotif for Kathleen, and did the same with "Aha! San Antone" for the three trooper buddies Travis Tyree (Ben Johnson), Jeff Yorke, and Daniel "Sandy" Boone (Harry Carey Jr.). Young uses mickey mousing to underline key moments in the image track, such as the harp glissando when Kirby bends backwards precipitously to check

his height against Jeff's, the stinger at Kirby's unexpected arrival at the
soldier's fight, and Quincannon throwing a bucket of water. He pulls
out all the stops for a lush string orchestration of "I'll Take You Home
Again, Kathleen" the first time Kathleen and Kirby see each other and
provides a peppy arrangement of "Dixie" for the film's conclusion.
Young uses the Mexican song "La Cucaracha" in the cavalry patrol's
meeting with Mexican officers and mostly stereotypical Indian music
for the Indians. Despite the fact that he scored Ford's most successful
Irish picture, Young was not particularly well versed in Irish music. His
record collection consisted of nineteenth-century art music, opera, Russian folk music, American popular music, and some jazz.[73] His lack of
firsthand knowledge of Irish music did not prove a limitation, however:
he had Ford to help him there. Two Irish tunes are quoted in *Rio
Grande*: "The Irish Washerwoman," and "Oh, the Days of the Kerry
Dancing," both associated with Kathleen and heard while she is wash-
ing clothes.

Irishness works into way into *Rio Grande*'s score, however, in a number of ways. Much of the music in the cavalry trilogy connotes Irishness
explicitly: through song titles like "The Irish Washerwoman" or through
songs identified with the Irish such as "Oh, the Days of the Kerry Dancing." But cultural identity can also be transmitted through potent musical signifiers for ethnicity that operate on something less than a conscious
level. Hollywood was quick to adopt stereotypical musical tropes for
Irishness—pentatonic melodies, lively rhythms associated with dance
forms such as the reel and the jig, and specific harmonic patterns. Victor
Young is particularly fluent in this kind of "Hollywood Irish." Listen, for
instance, to the original cue he composed for Kathleen's first appearance
as she descends the covered wagon or even the "Rio Grande" theme that
forms the main title, although the Irish signifiers here are a bit more subtle. With a central character delineated as Irish, the use of Irish signifiers
in the main title is not without narrative justification. What's interesting
is that the ethnic coding is pronounced enough to actually compete with
musical signifiers of westernness, and may even win. This cultural logic
may account for the fact that many listeners do not immediately identify
the "Rio Grande" theme as western at all.

There is also, however, an attempt in *Rio Grande* to deliver something
authentic in the way of Indian music. Twice in the film, the Indians sing,
the first during their incarceration at Fort Starke and second, a vengeance
song and dance performed in celebration of their apparent victory over

the cavalry. Of course, it should be noted that such music was not au-
thentic in the way the film presents it to be. Ford liked to use the Navajo,
a tribe he had befriended when he first came to Monument Valley to film
Stagecoach, as Indian extras. The Navajo dubbed him "Natani Nez,"
Tall Leader. *Rio Grande* was not shot in Monument Valley, but in
Moab, Utah. Nonetheless, it was Ford's practice to import Navajo to his
other locations, such as Moab for *Wagon Master* and the Wasatch
Mountains, also in Utah, the stand-in for the Mohawk Valley in *Drums
Along the Mohawk.*[74] Generally, Ford left it to the Navajo to provide the
dialogue, as well as song and dance in their native tongue and with their
native custom, no matter what tribe they were supposed to portray. Thus
the Apaches and Comanches in his films all speak and sing in Navajo.[75]
So to the extent that the Apaches in *Rio Grande* are singing and chanting in Navajo, the Indian music is not authentic. But the Navajo songs
and tribal chants heard in *Rio Grande* are traditional Navajo songs and
chants provided by the Navajo themselves. This would be the case for all
of Ford's westerns that feature diegetic Indian chanting, with the exception of *Cheyenne Autumn.* I'm not quite sure how you reconcile these extended musical numbers, which lend the Apache a kind of dignity, with
their representation in the film as savage killers who kidnap children.
Perhaps you can't.[76]

   As usual, the film is loaded with songs: the traditional songs "You're in
the Army Now," "Erie Canal," "Down by the Glenside" (aka "The Bold
Fenian Men"), and "The Girl I Left Behind Me"; period music, "I'll Take
You Home Again, Kathleen"; and several original songs: "My Gal Is Purple," "Footsore Cavalry," and "Yellow Stripes," all by Stan Jones. The score
also includes two country-and-western hits of the recent past: Tex Owens's
"Cattle Call," written in 1934, but revived by Eddy Arnold in 1943, and
"Aha! San Antone" by Dale Evans, written and recorded as a solo number
by Evans in 1946.[77] Sons of the Pioneers, whom Ford had used on *Wagon
Master* earlier in the year, were on the payroll again. Ford was always enthusiastic about Sons of the Pioneers; he genuinely liked their music. But it
was Herbert Yates who wanted them to appear in the film, having built Republic on the backs of singing cowboys. According to Patrick Ford, his father was none too happy about using them. "He thought they cheapened the
picture artistically."[78] But Ford put them into cavalry uniforms and inserted
them into the picture. That's Ken Curtis, Ford's future son-in-law, singing
lead. Sons of the Pioneers perform "You're in the Army Now," "I'll Take
You Home Again, Kathleen," "Down by the Glenside," "My Gal Is Pur-

ple," "Footsore Cavalry," "Cattle Call," and "Yellow Stripes." "Aha! San Antone" is sung by Ben Johnson, Harry Carey Jr., and Claude Jarman Jr.

Lyrics are one obvious way that a song can control music's connotation and affect the meaning of a film. More than any of the other cavalry films, *Rio Grande* displays the closest connection between the song lyrics and the narrative itself. For instance, when we hear "You're in the Army Now" ("You're not behind the plow") in *Rio Grande,* it is sung by seasoned veterans to taunt the new recruits filing past them. Songs also reinforce the tension the film explores between allegiance to duty and individual happiness. But the most interesting and complex way in which song lyrics work is through the dimension they add to the relationship between Kirby and Kathleen Yorke.

John Wayne does not generally play the romantic lead in Ford westerns; the love stories, typically, are played out among a younger generation, especially in the cavalry films. But *Rio Grande* is about sexual desire, and John Wayne, for once, is at the center of it. Debra Thomas, who has written provocatively about Wayne's body, argues that *Rio Grande* "offers one of the most convincingly eroticised images of John Wayne's body in all of his films."[79] She is referring to the sequence of Kathleen's first night at the fort. Kirby gallantly offers Kathleen his quarters for the night and removes himself to a Conestoga wagon, where he begins to undress. The sequence is remarkable in its focus on Wayne's body as both object and subject of erotic desire. Shortly afterwards, when Quincannon (Victor McLaglen) beckons Kathleen out of Kirby's tent, we think that he will lead her to Kirby. He takes her, instead, to her son, and lest there be any confusion about the fact that Jeff has become the site of her repressed desire for Kirby, she kisses Jeff with the intimacy of a lover.

Song lyrics will become the medium of erotic exchange between Kirby and Kathleen. Lyrics not only affect their relationship, they carry it forward. In fact, the songs could be read as the emotional undercurrent coursing through Kirby, the expression of his repressed desire, which he denies on a number of levels, but which refuses to be silenced. "I'll Take You Home Again, Kathleen" provides the most obvious example, being a direct expression of the desire that Kirby outwardly denies. "I'll Take You Home Again, Kathleen" tells a story of a man's promise to his wife, Kathleen, who left her family home long ago as a young bride. The song looks both back into the past and forward into the future. The speaker, her husband, says that despite her homesickness, Kathleen has a heart "ever fond and true." Although he describes her as

Figure 15. Publicity still, Sons of the Pioneers in cavalry garb for *Rio Grande*: clockwise, from top, Lloyd Perryman, Tommy Doss, Ken Curtis, Karl Farr (with guitar), Hugh Farr, and Shug Fisher. In the center is the songwriter Stan Jones. Courtesy Lilly Library, Indiana University, Bloomington, IN.

aging ("The roses all have left your cheek"), he is devoted to her still and promises to take her back to her home himself. Although it is generally presumed to be Irish, it is not, having been written in Illinois by a music teacher, Thomas Westendorf, in 1875. By 1876, it was one of the most popular songs in America. Its lyrics, sung here by Sons of the Pioneers, with a few stuntmen in cavalry uniforms thrown in beside them,[80] address the narrative situation of Kirby and Kathleen and the singer's resolve—"Oh, I will take you back, Kathleen"—foreshadows Kirby's decision to reconcile, or attempt to, with Kathleen.

Earlier, Kirby and Kathleen are at loggerheads over their son Jeff, and their relations are cooling quickly. They sit, not speaking, while the Stan Jones song "Yellow Stripes" can be heard in the background, sung, presumably, by the regimental singers. The spirited song gives voice to the ambivalence of the cavalry soldier leaving his gal behind to ride out on patrol: "Kiss your gal and leave her there and hope she's gonna stay." Again, it's hard not to read that lyric as directly expressive of Kirby's desire for Kathleen. The song describes the anticipation and anxiety of delayed anticipation, evocative of Kirby's own feelings.

"Down by the Glenside" also evokes Kirby's emotional life, although more obliquely. After dinner with the officers, Kirby and Kathleen listen to yet another serenade by the regimental singers. "Down by the Glenside," as has been noted, is an Irish song commemorating the Fenian movement of the 1860s. The third verse, not sung in the film, and for obvious reasons, makes the song's political intent perfectly clear: "Some died on the glenside, / Some died near a stranger / And wise men have told us that their cause was a failure / They fought for old Ireland and they never feared danger / Glory O, Glory O, to the bold Fenian men." One of the most famous acts of the Fenian men was the bombing of Clerkenwell prison. There is no doubt in my mind that Ford knew the history of "Down by the Glenside," as well as the lyrics to all the verses. The moody, melancholy song speaks to the balancing act of Kirby's life as a soldier and to his psychic working through of the consequences of the demands of duty.

"My Gal Is Purple," another Stan Jones song, is performed around the campfire by soldiers on patrol (Sons of the Pioneers again) and is the clearest example of the way in which the songs give expression to Kirby's sexual longing. Kirby is off at a distance, walking along the bank of the Rio Grande, initially in long shot but concluding with a close-up of Yorke's face deep in thought; the song lyrics indicate the nature of those thoughts. "My Gal Is Purple" (which would turn out to be one of Sons of the Pioneers' hits of the 1950s) describes a soldier's thoughts of the gal he left behind him; he imagines her waiting patiently in the purple light of evening for him to return. But it is the soldier's melancholy and grief at having to leave her that provides the emotional ballast of the song: "My longing wrings my heart and tears get in my eyes." As the song concludes, the long shot has gradually become a close-up, with the song lyrics the direct expression of the thoughtful look on Kirby's face. In the very next shot, Kirby passionately kisses Kathleen when he finds her waiting in the darkness for him back at his tent in Fort Starke. The editing posits a direct cause-and-effect relationship between Kirby's sexual desire for Kathleen, expressed through the song lyrics, and his actions when he returns, despite the fact that the two shots thus connected would have to be separated by several days and many miles.

Music is an intrinsic part of the cavalry trilogy, the medium through which the films' meanings develop. Music speaks to many issues here: gender, the construction of masculinity, race, ethnicity, the legacy of Irish Americans in this country, and the founding of the nation itself. Ford would return to the cavalry as a subject in *Sergeant Rutledge, The Horse Soldiers,* and the Civil War segment of *How the West Was Won,* and the cavalry also figures in *The Searchers, Two Rode Together,* and *Cheyenne Autumn.* But none of these other endeavors can match the rich scores of the cavalry trilogy.

CHAPTER 7

"What Makes a Man to Wander"

The Searchers

Imagine hearing these lyrics, the original first verse to Stan Jones's title
song "The Searchers," as *The Searchers* begins:

> The horizon's like a woman
> With her arms flung open wide
> And a man that's tryin' to fill his heart
> Ain't got no place to hide.
> Ride away—Ride away—Ride away.[1]

It is the second verse of this song that found it way into the film and, with
its unanswered and unanswerable set of questions, dynamically alters the
film from a generic western to a metaphysical quest.

> What makes a man to wander
> What makes a man to roam
> What makes a man leave bed and board
> And turn his back on home.
> Ride away—Ride away—Ride away.

The argument of this book has been that song is a distinguishing feature
of Ford's westerns. Ford was well aware of the power of music; that was why
he concerned himself so closely with its use. Given that *The Searchers* is generally regarded as Ford's masterpiece, and the accompanying body of criticism is dazzling in its quantity and quality, the lack of in-depth attention to
the score is somewhat surprising. The music has much to reveal, enriching
an understanding of both the film and the culture in which it was produced.

All the verses to "The Searchers" were recorded by Sons of the Pioneers,[2] but someone chose verses two and seven, neither the expedient nor, without the benefit of hindsight, the obvious choices. Max Steiner, one of the architects of the classical film score and its most prolific practitioner, composed the original score, and Jones, a sometime member of Ford's stock company, wrote the song. But I'm putting my money on Ford.[3] For one thing, the paper trail leads there. Notorious for collaborating with other production personnel, whether they liked it or not, Ford expected compliance from those who worked for him. The lyrics for "The Searchers" can be found in Ford's files, not Steiner's, because that is where Jones sent them. Having worked for Ford before, Jones knew the drill; send the lyrics to Ford and let him decide what to use.[4] For another thing, Ford had a penchant for avoiding the obvious. The original first verse with its clear allusions to Martha and the original last verse with its conventional ending may have been too pointed. As he did with so many other aspects of this film, Ford chose not to "spell it out" for the audience.

Consider the way the lyrics for the second verse not only structure the narrative but set up an important connection between Ethan (John Wayne) and Scar (Henry Brandon) on which the film depends: "What makes a man to wander / What makes a man to roam / What makes a man leave bed and board / And turn his back on home." Ethan is established as a wanderer and the question of why he wanders is established as the central issue of the film. One immediately thinks of Ethan's own translation of Nawyecka Comanche: "Sorta like round about: man says he's going one place, means to go t'other." Alan LeMay, in the source novel, translates "Nawyecky" as "Them As Never Gets Where They're Going."[5] I favor James F. Brooks's translation of the Comanche term as "wanderer," because it highlights the similarities between Ethan and Scar.[6] Both are wanderers—Scar by tribal association, Ethan by nature and by circumstance. Even Chris the dog links them. He barks at only two people: Ethan and Scar. Wandering, a central connection between the two adversaries, sustained throughout the film in a variety of ways, is initially posited by song. Is this one of the reasons Ford chose the second verse of "The Searchers," with its focus on wandering?

The seventh verse of the song, the only other verse of the original eight used in the film, can be heard at the end. None of the questions the song initially posed are answered; in fact, the last verse offers only more questions: when will the searching end, and "Where, Oh lord, lord where?" The original last verse, although containing some ambiguity, provides much more closure:

> Me I go on searchin'
> For where there ain't no hate
> For a tender love I'm dreamin' of
> A'fore it gets too late.

The searcher charts his course for true love, "A'fore it gets too late," a creaky device to end the song and the quest that structures it. Jones's original first and last verses overtly shape the search around a woman and a man's desire for her, telegraphing a pedestrian message about true love conquering all. Succeeding verses map out this quest through a variety of different geographic locations. Without the frame of verses one and eight, the song is dramatically altered from a rather prosaic search for romantic love to a metaphysical search for what can never be found. This is Ford's hand at work.

Consider also the way in which verses two and seven frame the quest in terms of masculinity. Peter Lehman reminds us that, narratively, women are contained in *The Searchers,* limited in the expression of their desires and restricted in their actions: "Men search and women wait at home."[7] The choice of the second verse over the first provocatively shifts the focus from the feminine ("The horizon's like a woman / With her arms flung open wide") to the masculine: "What makes a man to wander / What makes a man to roam." Still, there is plenty left in the film to connect the frontier to the feminine: Martha (Dorothy Jordan), who "wouldn't let a man quit" a life on the frontier, Mrs. Jorgensen (Olive Carey), who gives the film's most impassioned speech about the wilderness and life "way out on a limb"; Laurie (Vera Miles), who voices the anger and frustrations of living on the edge. The music supports this connection in subtle ways: it is Martha whose presence is instilled into the leitmotif that represents the family on the frontier. I would like to suggest that traces of the original lyrics to Jones's first verse also find their way into the film: in the farewell scene between Ethan and Martha, Martha raises her arms ("flung open wide") as if to embrace Ethan but stops, her arms falling helplessly to her side.

The Searchers chronicles Ethan Edwards's search for his niece, Debbie (played at as a young girl by Lana Wood and as a young woman by Natalie Wood). Materializing out of the wilderness and under suspicious circumstances, Ethan clearly has a mysterious past, as well as an incestuous attachment to his brother's wife, Martha. The search, to which the title alludes, begins after the Comanches lure Ethan away from the ranch, abduct Debbie, and murder the rest of the family. Ethan and Martin Pawley (Jeffrey Hunter), adopted by the Edwards family, search for Debbie for seven years. As time passes and Debbie reaches sexual maturity, Ethan is committed to killing her. At the dramatic moment of his confrontation with her, however, Ethan embraces rather than murders her. He eventually returns her to a neighbor's ranch.

A number of period songs appear in the film, some that Ford had used before, "The Yellow Rose of Texas" (a personal favorite of Ford's), "Shall We Gather at the River?" and "The Girl I Left Behind Me," and some new ones: "Jubilo," "Bonnie Blue Flag," and the memorable "Lorena." Ford's participation in the scripting process was "very intense," as Arthur Eckstein has demonstrated,[8] and production records indicate a similar involvement with the music. When "Ethan" was still "Amos," the original name from Alan LeMay's novel, and casting had barely begun, Ford was already including musical selections in his story notes to the screenwriter, Frank Nugent, and the producer, Patrick Ford. Ford suggested "Blue Bonnet," "The Yellow Rose of Texas," and "The Bonnie Blue Flag" penciled in (an addition or a correction?) for the wedding sequence.[9] Neither "The Bonnie Blue Flag" nor "Blue Bonnet" was used in the wedding sequence (they were replaced by "Jubilo"), but "Bonnie Blue Flag" did find its way into the film, where it appears prominently in the famous opening sequence. "The Yellow Rose of Texas" can be heard exactly where Ford intended it—as the assembled wedding guests await Laurie's arrival. Studio publicity cited Ford's participation, crediting him with the choice of "The Yellow Rose of Texas" for a "nostalgic square dance scene," noting that Ford "picked the sentimental ditty from a dozen other favorites in his musical collection of Americana."[10] Of course, "The Yellow Rose of Texas" is hardly the "sentimental ditty" that Warner Bros. dubbed it. Perhaps they were thinking of the Mitch Miller version, widely circulating in 1955, which sanitized the lyrics.

The score of *The Searchers* begins with a mighty cymbal crash and a dramatic Max Steiner cue. But only moments into this classical film score, the quiet, melancholic, and folksy "The Searchers," sung by Sons of the Pioneers and accompanied by guitar strumming, displaces it. Guitars in Ford generally function as signifiers of Mexico. Sons of the Pioneers complicated this musical marker when they brought their own guitars. This is how guitars wind up in the hands of cavalry soldiers in *Rio Grande,* in which Sons of the Pioneers appear. It is, of course, Sons of the Pioneers who are singing "The Searchers" here too, but their contemporary use of the guitar converges in an interesting way with the guitar's more typical signification in Ford. Has Ethan returned from Mexico where he has been evading the law?

"The Searchers" will reappear where it crosses the diegesis from the conscious recognition of song to the less conscious perception of the background score, and there it enters the terrain of Max Steiner. Steiner scored three films for Ford in the mid 1930s: *The Lost Patrol, The Informer,* for which both men won their first Academy Awards, and *Mary of Scotland* (1936). Ford and Steiner had worked closely together on *The Informer.* Steiner composed the score's major leitmotif in preproduction so that Ford could film Victor McLaglen in perfect synchronization to it. Working in advance of a rough cut was an unusual practice for Steiner and not one he repeated with other directors: "I never read a script; I run a mile when I see one," he proclaimed.[11] Steiner and Ford parted professional company in 1937 when Steiner left RKO for Warner Bros., and it was not until 1955 that the two men's paths crossed again.

By the 1950s, Steiner was finding himself passed over in favor of younger composers with more contemporary scoring styles, and he left Warner Bros. in 1953 when his decades-old contract was not renewed. He moved into the more speculative world of music publishing, continuing to freelance as a composer. While Warner Bros. publicity described Steiner as "big league," he clearly was not playing in the majors anymore.[12] Exactly how Steiner came to score *The Searchers* is not documented, but the archivist James D'Arc suggests that it was "a kind gesture from old friend and *Searchers* producer Merian C. Cooper,"[13] the producer of *King Kong,* the film that had launched Steiner's Hollywood career over twenty years earlier. If this was the case, it was an easy enough favor to extend: Steiner had scored a number of prominent westerns, including *Dodge City* (Michael Curtiz, 1939), *The Oklahoma Kid* (Lloyd Bacon, 1939), *Virginia City* (Michael Curtiz, 1940), *Santa Fe Trail* (Michael Curtiz, 1941), *They Died with Their Boots On, The Treasure of the Sierra Madre* (John Huston, 1948), and *Pursued.*

This time, however, the collaboration did not go as smoothly. There is strong evidence that the final cut of the music was presided over by Ford. Steiner was apparently miffed to discover at a sneak preview that his music had been edited. A letter to Steiner from C. V. Whitney, credited as the film's producer, addresses those concerns: "I can assure you that the end result is typically American. This, I am sure, is what Mr. Ford wanted to achieve, and I feel he has done it. For my part, I understand your criticisms. I am satisfied, however, that the mood of reality in the picture is furthered by Mr. Ford's cuts."[14] It sounds as if Ford deleted some of Steiner's nondiegetic cues. The result privileged more of the "typically American" period music, giving the film a leaner sound than Steiner had originally created. Ford was in control here, and he exercised that control in matters large and small throughout the production.

Ford's longtime collaborators, such as screenwriter Frank Nugent, had learned to put up with this. But Steiner was clearly irritated.

Even after Ford's interventions, *The Searchers* remains among the most classical of Ford's film scores. Like Hageman's scores for *Fort Apache* and especially *3 Godfathers,* Steiner's score represents a distinctly different approach to musical accompaniment from earlier westerns such as *Stagecoach* and *My Darling Clementine,* which used a leaner approach and depended more upon diegetic music. The score for *The Searchers* also reflects another musical trend: the monothematic score, often based on the styles and idioms of popular music, which was beginning to infiltrate and even dominate the scoring scene. Theme songs had been a phenomenon in Hollywood since the 1920s, when movie studios bought music publishing houses to market sheet music generated as spin-off by their films. As studios saw the mechanical reproduction of music replacing actual performance in American homes, they began investing in the recording industry. Theme music could be simultaneously released as sheet music and on record. Some notable examples include Tara's Theme, recast as "My Own True Love," from *Gone with the Wind* (1939), "Laura" from *Laura* (1944), and "The Third Man Theme" from *The Third Man* (1949). But before the 1950s, theme songs remained largely the by-product of film scores. In the case of *Laura,* for instance, lyrics were hastily added to David Raksin's signature tune to accommodate public interest.

The phenomenal success of *High Noon*'s "Do Not Forsake Me, Oh, My Darlin'" alerted Hollywood to the vast potential revenue that could be harnessed through tie-in recording sales, and theme songs began to monopolize soundtracks.[15] The suddenly old-fashioned romanticism of the classical Hollywood film score gave way to more contemporary musical idioms. Sometimes tacked onto the beginning or ending of a film (a practice that continues to this day), sometimes endlessly recycled in every situation cued for musical accompaniment, theme songs became de rigeur in the Hollywood of the 1950s. One need only hear a film like *Comanche* (George Sherman, 1956), in content if not ambition related to *The Searchers,* to experience fully how wincingly inappropriate a theme score can be.[16] Steiner's score for *The Searchers,* featuring a song by a celebrated country-and-western composer, but steeped in classical scoring principles, provides an interesting flashpoint between the two institutional practices, reflected in the film's opening moments: Steiner's cymbal crash and symphonic cue juxtaposed with Jones's folksy theme song. For *The Searchers,* Steiner would develop, adapt, and weave Jones's song

into the nondiegetic score. To do so, Steiner recast Jones's song as a leitmotif and unleashed the full resources of the symphony orchestra in its
deployment.

The power of a leitmotif is demonstrated at the beginning of the film
through Steiner's treatment of Jones's song. Through its lyrics, its placement in the main title, and its association with Ethan in the film's opening, "The Searchers" becomes Ethan's leitmotif. When Ethan and his
brother Aaron first meet, the opening phrase of the song can be heard,
arranged for strings, with cellos deep in their register carrying the
melody. The silent, but attendant lyrics—"What makes a man to wander"—hang over this awkward meeting, suggesting that something has
transpired between the brothers that has sent Ethan "to wander." The
cellos further suggest a melancholic dimension to their meeting. Steiner
marked it *triste* (sad) in his original sketches.[17] The music continues as
Ethan approaches Martha to kiss her politely on the forehead, implicating her in his wanderings. Later, after Aaron remarks that Ethan's
money looks "fresh minted," thus implying that it is stolen, this same
musical phrase (with its unvoiced but present lyrics) can be heard. Is this
why Ethan has been made "to wander"?

Throughout the film, motivic material from "The Searchers" reappears and the attendant (unvoiced) lyrics provide commentary on
Ethan's motivations. For instance, moments before the posse happens
upon a Comanche grave, the orchestra plays the phrase accompanying
" . . . . where, oh Lord, Lord where . . ." in a slow reiteration, voicing
the men's frustrations in their futile search for the girls. (The score opens
up moments later when Ethan majestically guides his great horse down
a deep descent.) When Brad (Harry Carey Jr.) dies, the orchestra plays
the music accompanying the refrain, "Ride away, ride away, ride away,"
a commentary on Brad's fate and a reminder that the search will continue. And the music accompanying the opening questions, "What
makes a man to wander / What makes a man to roam" can be heard in
several key sequences, reminding us of Ethan's initial motivations for the
search: "heavier and more ominous,"[18] with a fuller orchestral deployment and excursions into the minor, as Ethan initially joins the search
and the posse rides off (and after Ethan has ignored Mrs. Jorgensen's
pleas to protect Martin and Brad); in a subdued string version when a
wounded Ethan is nursed by Martin; in an ominous arrangement when
Ethan and Martin view white scalps on Scar's lance; with strident instrumentation during the final attack on the Indian village (Steiner
marked the moment in the score when Ethan scalps Scar "as loud and

shrill as possible");[19] and strident again as Ethan tracks a terrified Debbie moments before he rescues her.

There is information to suggest that, at an early stage of production, "The Searchers" was intended to be reprised vocally. At one point, Ford must have considered having Ken Curtis sing it, because Curtis recorded it.[20] A studio press release announced that members of the cast, including John Wayne, Ward Bond, Jeffrey Hunter, and Harry Carey Jr., would sing it.[21] That Ford was thinking along these lines for *The Searchers* is an intriguing possibility. Was there going to be a reprise of "The Searchers" by the men, bonding them in their search for Debbie and Lucy? Stan Jones composed eight verses for the song; it makes sense that at least some of them were meant to be used throughout the film.

The Searchers' dependence upon leitmotifs extends beyond the use of its title song, however. The period song "Lorena" functions as a theme for Ethan's brother's family, including—and specifically—Martha. Choosing a song with this important a function in the film was typically Ford's prerogative. In fact, Steiner hadn't even been chosen as the composer when Ford directed his staff to find an appropriate period piece. He didn't want an original theme: "Let's not have it written overnight by Victor Young or Hageman" (an indication that at one point he was thinking of Young or Hageman for *The Searchers*), and he expected his researchers to look "exhaustively" for "a theme that is completely haunting . . . perhaps 'The Yellow Rose of Texas' is, after all, our theme song. . . . together with 'Bonnie Blue Flags' [sic]. . . . This is very important. ATTENTION ALL!"[22] Something changed Ford's mind, however, and while "The Yellow Rose of Texas" and "Bonnie Blue Flag" do appear in the film, neither provides the "haunting" melody Ford sought. "Lorena" did. It is quite likely that it was Steiner who suggested it. Of course, whoever made the suggestion, it was Ford who made the final choice.

Steiner frequently recycled musical cues from one film to another (some of the Indian music for The *Searchers*, for example, is recycled from *They Died with Their Boots On*), and he had used "Lorena" before in *Gone with the Wind* (Victor Flemming, 1939), where it can be heard as a waltz at a Confederate ball. "Lorena" is a Civil War–era song, first published in Chicago in 1857, that became a favorite with Confederate soldiers. I suspect that Steiner got it from the Margaret Mitchell source novel, where "Lorena" figures prominently at a Confederate ball and serves as a marker for lost love and tragedy.[23] Using period music as a major leitmotif is a scoring practice atypical of Steiner, who, especially

Example 5. "Lorena." Courtesy Archive of Popular American Music, UCLA.

in a film filled with period music, liked to compose his own leitmotifs. But it is entirely typical of Ford.

Lorena's lost love is a forbidden one, very probably adulterous: "We loved each other, then, Lorena, / More than we ever dared to tell." Later, the speaker confesses: "A duty, stern and pressing, broke / The tie which linked my soul with thee." While the lyrics of "Lorena" are not used in *The Searchers*, they would have been available to members of the audience who recognized the tune. The song was still popular in the South in the 1950s. Steiner and Ford both knew the song's Confederate attachments: Steiner used it in his score for *Gone with the Wind* to accompany a Confederate ball, and Ford used it in *The Horse Soldiers*, where it serves as a leitmotif for Miss Hannah Hunter (Constance Towers), a southern belle loyal to the Confederacy.

The use of "Lorena," especially in the opening moments of *The Searchers*, underscores the unspoken love between Ethan and Martha and telegraphs its forbidden nature and tragic outcome. Arthur Eckstein notes that the original version, written by J. P. Webster, was based on his own failed romance with a woman named Martha, who was forbidden by her brothers to continue the relationship. In the autobiographical story on which the song is based, the love is not adulterous per se, but in the song, there is a clear implication that this is the case.[24] Thus, "Lorena," while functioning generally as a leitmotif for the Edwards family hearth and home, specifically refers to Martha and forbidden love.

Narrative placement of "Lorena" points to Martha. We first hear it as the film begins and at the very moment when Martha opens the door revealing Ethan's arrival. The loss, encapsulated in the song's lyrics, is emphasized by the largely string instrumentation of this cue (entitled "Ethan's Return"), bridging nicely from the guitars of the main title. The initial performance of "Lorena" is followed by a lengthy quotation from another source, "The Bonnie Blue Flag," as Ethan materializes out of the wilderness. The bonnie blue flag in question is the flag of the Confederacy, and the song was a well-known Confederate anthem. Ford obviously knew its origins: it turns up in *The Horse Soldiers*, where it is sung by Confederate troops. "The Bonnie Blue Flag" was obviously meant to suggest Ethan's Confederate past and, like his relationship with Martha, another lost cause. The music establishes Ethan's status as defeated.

Gradually, "Lorena" begins to focus around Martha: it can be heard immediately after Ethan kisses her in greeting and later when he kisses her good-bye. We also hear "Lorena" when Ethan presents Debbie with his war medal. The connection between Martha and Debbie, posited in the music, will return at Debbie's rescue. A nostalgic parlor arrangement of "Lorena," with harpsichord and strings, accompanies Ethan's fraught glance at Aaron's entrance into the bedroom he shares with Martha, Martha's furtive fondling of Ethan's coat, and the good-bye kiss between Ethan and Martha. The good-bye scene is the only scene in the film where the melody is heard at length.

Steiner described the quality he wanted in the opening to the orchestrator Murray Cutter as "real old fashioned,"[25] and he specifically asked for a harpsichord with violins and violas for the good-byes. The parlor arrangement is revealing. Parlor arrangements were a common form of musical marketing in the nineteenth century, directed at women, who constituted a significant portion of amateur musicians. Parlor arrangements capitalized on the instruments typically found in an upper-middle-class parlor, such as the piano or harpsichord and stringed instruments, such as the violin. With its connotations of upward mobility, eastern refinement, and femininity, the parlor arrangement harkens back to a past that the film does not refer to, and points directly to Martha. When "Lorena" is heard in Ford's *Horse Soldiers,* it may also allude to lost love, specifically that of Colonel John Marlowe (John Wayne). There is even a pointed allusion to Martha in the film: when Miss Hunter scans the horizon to look for Marlowe, she shields her eyes from the sun with her arm exactly as Martha does in the opening scene of *The Searchers.* This gesture is accompanied by "Lorena."

"Lorena" returns, at various points in *The Searchers,* to flesh out the unspoken motivation and emotional content of several key sequences: Ethan's discovery of Martha's body, where it can be heard in the minor; the disbanding of the posse and the continued search by Ethan, Martin, and Brad; the first glimpse of a grown-up Debbie as she descends a cliff toward Martin, cut short by the intrusion of brass and percussion when Ethan spots her; Martin's embrace of Debbie when he rescues her in Scar's teepee; and Debbie's return to the Jorgenson ranch at the end of the film, displaced by a final reiteration of "The Searchers," now and only for the second time with lyrics.

Two instances merit more in-depth analysis. The first is when the posse realize that they have fallen for a Comanche trick to lure them away from their now unprotected homesteads: Ethan's glance offscreen over the back of his horse indicates his realization that his family is unprotected and as good as dead.[26] The use of "Lorena" as accompaniment here, performed low in the violin's register and cast into the minor, anchors Ethan's close-up specifically around his concern for Martha and

foreshadows her fate, soon confirmed when, upon his arrival at the site
of the massacre, he calls out her name and searches for her body.

"Lorena" also performs a similar function at one of the film's most
critical and ambiguous moments: when Ethan decides to rescue Debbie
instead of kill her. That it is Debbie's physical resemblance to her mother
that precipitates Ethan's sudden turnaround is clearly indicated in earlier versions of the script, where Ethan looks at Debbie and "says softly,
'You sure favor your mother.'"[27] In typical Fordian fashion, Ford deleted
the dialogue from the final shooting script and replaced it with "Let's go
home, Debbie," obfuscating Ethan's motives. Or perhaps Ford was simply being practical. Since Natalie Wood bears no physical resemblance
to Dorothy Jordan, he may have felt that the original dialogue strained
credibility. For whatever reason, a key moment, perhaps *the* key moment, in the film, is left unexplained. Peter Lehman reminds us "how
much that is central in the film is never spoken about or even hinted at
in the dialogue and how the visual information that cues our formula-
tion of an answer to those central questions is inherently ambiguous—
we simply do not see enough to know."[28] We are left to make inferences
from a variety of sources, including the music. It is "Lorena" that accompanies Ethan's lifting of a tense and terrified Debbie into the air.
"Lorena" functions as a specific aural marker for Martha. Thus, I would
argue that hearing "Lorena" at this moment brings us back to the figure
of Martha, who returns to the scene and supplies Ethan's motivation.
Still, does Ethan save Debbie because she looks like her mother or because a respect for the memory of Martha prevents him from harming
Debbie? Steiner was thinking otherwise. He entitled the cue "Reunion of
Ethan and Debbie,"[29] obviously referring to the earlier scene in which
Ethan lifts Debbie into the air, reenacted here.

The classical film score is identifiable, not only by its dependence on
leitmotifs, but, on a structural level, by its intricate interconnectedness
between music and narrative action, a characteristic epitomized by
Steiner's penchant for responding to the slightest narrative provocation
with music. Steiner's habit is noticeably toned down from earlier scores
(*The Informer* is a hyperexplicit case in point) but there are enough examples left in *The Searchers* to mark the score as vintage Steiner: Scar's
short leitmotif played sforzando and tremolo whenever his name is mentioned (in fact, a descending tremolo is a Steiner trademark for Indians);
the musical cue that simulates dripping water in the cave sequence where
Marty and the wounded Ethan seek cover; tremolo strings upon Aaron's
discovery that Ethan's money is "fresh minted"; falling cadences to ac-

company the tragic story of Martin Pawley's origins; a cymbal crash to represent Brad Jorgenson's death; a musical stinger to punctuate the comic business between Ethan and Reverend Clayton during the Indian attack on the posse; and even mickey mousing as Martin makes his first entrance, leaping off a horse, or later, when a harp glissando mimics the flight of birds moments before an Indian attack. There are no moments in *The Searchers* quite as intrusive as the one Ford describes in his condemnation of bombastic film scores. Nonetheless, Ford appears to have disliked the score intensely even after he had toned it down, much to Steiner's displeasure.[30]

Tag Gallagher describes *The Searchers* as "an atypical Ford movie in its concentration on a solitary hero rather than a social group."[31] But it seems to me that *The Searchers* is very insistently about social bonds or, rather, the lack of them. I read the film as recording the struggle and the failure of community facing the overwhelming odds of hostile Indians and inhospitable terrain. Defeat hovers over the film, from the personal (at the beginning, it is revealed that the Edwards' neighbors have given up and left, and the Edwards themselves are massacred and their ranch destroyed) to the public (the disintegrated nations that haunt the film: the Confederacy, the independent Republic of Texas, the Spanish New World, the Comanche nation). It is the vulnerability of the American nation on the edge of the western frontier that is chronicled in *The Searchers,* and the systemic use of interrupted song insistently marks the breakdown of the frontier community.

Surely there are few more inhospitable places on the American frontier to settle than Monument Valley, John Ford's stand-in for a particular corner of Texas in 1868. This was neither the first film nor the last that Ford shot there. But as Richard Hutson observes, in *The Searchers,* Monument Valley is presented as home, unlike in *Stagecoach,* where it is a place to be "passed through": "Monument Valley would never have tempted . . . white settlers into thinking that it could be developed for civilization. This land is outside of civilized assimilation, heavily marked by its inutility."[32] Mrs. Jorgensen says, "Texican is nothin' but a human man way out on a limb," but life among the buttes seems even more precarious than that. White settlers pay a heavy price for persisting there, and for their assault on the Indians who have made their peace with this land. Hostility emanates from both the landscape itself and the Comanches who inhabit it, and, as many critics have noted, the film often conflates the two. Lars Jorgensen (John Qualen) tells Ethan that it was "this country killed my boy," when, in fact, it was the Comanches, and in a stunning sequence, Comanches appear on a ridge above the posse as if springing from the rocks beneath their feet.

Community has been so whittled down that it seems to be made up of only two families—the Edwardses and the Jorgensens. The insularity is so complete that when marriageable offspring from one family seek a mate, they look no further than the other. Witness Lucy Edwards and Brad Jorgensen, or Laurie Jorgensen and Martin Pawley, or, more intriguingly, the case of Ethan and Martha, in which family members turn toward each other. In this world, with such a tenuous hold on civilization altogether, the rituals that have always been an important social mechanism on Ford's frontier take on increased importance. In *The Searchers,* ritual is a bulwark against the chaos and malevolence of the surroundings, not just ceremonial glue binding the community together.

Hence there is no surer sign of the community's fragility in *The Searchers* than the interruption of its rituals. Peter Lehman has argued persuasively for the structural significance of interruption in *The Searchers,*[33] but interruption is at its most dramatic when human voices raised in song are silenced. In one of the most profoundly antisocial gestures in all of Ford, Ethan interrupts the singing of "Shall We Gather at the River?" at the funeral of Martha, Aaron, and their son, Ben. His action is heightened by the choice of song, "Shall We Gather at the River?" at its most appropriate.

A Methodist hymn Ford had used before in *Stagecoach, My Darling Clementine, 3 Godfathers,* and *Wagon Master,* "Shall We Gather at the River?" embodies the Calvinist notion of predestination. The hymn's determinism, even fatalism—only those who will be judged worthy by God are allowed to cross the river Jordan and be judged by him—serve *The Searchers* well, especially at the Edwardses' funeral, with its discomforting sense that these deaths were fated once Ethan arrived. Vengeance transplants grief and reconciliation, both of which are interrupted, as is the ceremony itself. The mourners go their separate ways, and the search for the survivors commences. The film's own discomfort at this moment is reflected in the music. "Put an amen to it! . . . There's no more time for praying! AMEN," Ethan exclaims, and the score provides a final symphonic reiteration of the hymn that Ethan suspends, putting its own "Amen" to the ruptured ritual with church bells, no less, giving it that distinctive Steiner touch.

"Shall We Gather at the River?" returns at the aborted wedding of Laurie and Charlie McCorry (Ken Curtis). It is first heard, rather inappropriately and somewhat ominously (given that we last heard it at a fu-

neral), as the processional for Charlie and Captain Reverend Clayton.[34]
They await Laurie, who never enters, having been waylaid by the entrance of Ethan and Marty, and the music stops. After Marty and Charlie duke it out, a lone fiddler begins "Shall We Gather at the River?"
again. But this time the hymn is interrupted by Charlie who proclaims,
"There ain't going to be a wedding." And that's the end of that.

Interrupted music abounds in *The Searchers,* both diegetic and
nondiegetic. The castanet dance performed by a sultry Latina in the New
Mexican saloon is interrupted not once but twice by Martin Pawley,
whose sexual naïveté (or lack of interest?) blinds him to her intentions, and
thus not only her music but any possibility of a tryst between them is fore-
stalled. The "Skip to My Lou" number sung by Charlie McCorry is short-
ened; we hear only a single verse of a song with twelve.[35] Even a fiddle finds
itself in danger. During the fistfight between Charlie and Marty, the instrument has to be rescued by Reverend Clayton from sure destruction.

Then there are the nondiegetic interruptions: the theme song interrupted by a cymbal crash when the posse finds the seventh Comanche
grave and later, by "Lorena," when Ethan tracks Debbie to the mouth
of a cave. And, if one considers the lyrics of the title song and the questions with which it frames the text—"What makes a man to wander?
What makes a man to roam?"—the film itself becomes a kind of long,
unanswered question.

Like any product of culture, music bears a dynamic relationship to
ideology and is, in fact, part of the process through which ideology is
constructed. Music's relationship to social discourse is not always immediate or obvious, however, giving rise to the notion that music has
special status as an art form, free from the intervention of historical
forces. *The Searchers* offers a dramatic example of the way music carries
ideology's charge, and its songs open up avenues for reading the film in
terms of race.

Race is, in fact, the starting point of *The Searchers,* musically speaking. Although most listeners remember the title song as opening the film,
it is actually a Steiner cue, a romantic rendering of stereotypical "Indian"
music that begins *The Searchers:* a prominent tom-tom rhythm played on
the timpani under a descending melodic contour. This musical language,
lying outside the conventional rhythms, harmonies, and melodic design
of Western art music, is a powerful indicator of Otherness, with connotations of the primitive, the exotic, and the savage. Steiner described this
opening cue as an "an Indian *Tosca*" (an opera that famously opens with
the leitmotif of its villain, Scarpia).[36]

In *The Searchers,* tom-tom rhythms, modal melodies, striking instrumentation, and unusual harmonies are in abundant display whenever Indians are on the screen and sometimes when they are not. And yet I would argue that the representation of Indians in *The Searchers* is more complicated than it seems, and that at least one component in that complication is the music. Charles Ramirez Berg argues that Ford's insistence on multiculturalism in his westerns—in particular, his focus on the margins of American society, its immigrants and outcasts, instead of its WASP mainstream—counterbalances the undeniable stereotyping in Ford and provides a more "nuanced" approach to ethnicity than does much classical Hollywood cinema.[37] Music can be a part of this argument. Clearly, *The Searchers* falls into racist stereotypes through its deployment of conventional musical clichés. But the sheer amount of music devoted to Indians, including important leitmotifs, however stereotypical they may be, for two Indian characters, and the structural placement of that music opens up space for a more nuanced reading.

Musically speaking, it is the Indians who are allied with the frontier in *The Searchers,* an interesting development from earlier Ford westerns. In *Stagecoach,* for example, the music accompanying the awe-inspiring vista of Monument Valley is derived from the American folk idiom, with simple rhythms, lean texture, and familiar melody. This land is marked as white. Indians belong on the reservation; they are intruders into the landscape of Monument Valley, terrorizing the rightful heirs to the frontier, the white settlers. Indian music intrudes on the score as well. Written in a completely different idiom from the music that accompanies the stagecoach and its occupants, the music accompanying the Indians or their handiwork is menacing, depending on some of the most recognizable musical clichés for savagery: tom-tom rhythms, the exotic intervals of the fourth and fifth, and descending contours. The famous pan to Indians waiting to ambush the stagecoach could serve as an example here. When Indian music is heard in Monument Valley, we know there is trouble.

In *The Searchers,* the frontier belongs to the Indians, musically speaking—a reminder that the land is theirs and white settlers are the encroachers. Thus it is Indian music that opens the film and provides most of the aural accompaniment to scenes of the wilderness; even when Indians are not on screen, we can hear cues for their presence. Indian music, for instance, is heard during the scene following the departure of the posse, as the group descends into Monument Valley. Whereas in *Stagecoach,* Indian music seems out of place in Monument Valley, in *The Searchers,* it seems literally to emanate from it. I agree here with Hutson that whites are out of place in Monument Valley. Music dramatically underscores their intrusion on the frontier.

In Ford westerns, Anglo, Indian, and Mexican cultures often blend in interesting and sometimes provocative ways. In *The Searchers,* the conflation between Mexican and Anglo cultures is most evident when Ethan and Marty enter New Mexico Territory to meet a man, Emilio Fernandez y Figueroa (Antonio Moreno), who claims to know Scar. The cantina in which they meet, encoded as Mexican by its architecture and artifacts, as well as Ethan and Marty's dress, language, and even cuisine, signals the borders that have been crossed geographically and culturally. Music marks this transversal, too, with guitars forming the accompaniment. At Scar's encampment, the Spanish language becomes the point of mediation between the Indians and the Anglos, and the conversation with Scar takes place in a mix of Spanish, "American," and Comanche. The music now belongs to the Indians, beginning with the prominent tom-tom rhythm, once more indicating that this "medicine country" of sand dunes and stone monoliths is theirs. Indian music even accompanies the climactic scene in which Debbie appears in Scar's teepee and, following a reprise of "Lorena," the stand-off between Marty and Ethan, when Ethan attempts to kill Debbie.

Additionally, two Indian characters in *The Searchers* have leitmotifs: Scar and Look (Beulah Archuletta). Scar's leitmotif is little more than a musical cliché for savagery, a series of descending chromatic intervals heard whenever his name is mentioned. But Look's leitmotif is a more complicated and more interesting. The cue Steiner entitled "News of Debbie" is the second longest cue in the film (3:07). Although the title focuses on Debbie, and the cue itself accompanies the reading of Martin Pawley's letter to Laurie, it is Look who commands the soundtrack, not the white characters around whom, ostensibly, the narrative is organized. Look's leitmotif does incorporate many of the stereotypes of Indian music, but for Look, Steiner offers us an identifiable melody for an Indian character and opens up the orchestral palette to do so, using flutes and other woodwinds, and especially violins, instruments not typically associated with Indians. Look's portrayal in the film is as complicated as the music's representation of her and as ambivalent. One of the most deeply moving scenes in the film remains, as least for me, the discovery of Look's death at the hands of the cavalry. Even Ethan is touched. And yet this is the same character at whom we are expected to laugh when Marty kicks her.

A standard critical interpretation of *The Searchers* reads the film in terms of the civil rights movement of the 1950s. Given classic expression in Brian Henderson's, *"The Searchers:* An American Dilemma,"[38] this argument posits the film as displacing white-black relations onto the classic western standoff between cowboys and Indians. Hence the deeply troubling issue of miscegenation gets played out in *The Searchers* between Indians and whites.[39] *The Searchers* was made during a time of a tumultuous social drive for racial equality, and a number of indicators in the film do seem to facilitate this reading: Debbie's black-haired rag doll, Topsy (a clear reference to an African American character in *Uncle Tom's Cabin*); Mose Harper's (Hank Worden) racial ambiguity, and the minstrel music that forms the aural backdrop for the wedding: "The Yellow Rose of Texas" and "Jubilo." These songs function most obviously to authenticate the film's depiction of frontier life when they accompany the dance that precedes the wedding. But their origins on the minstrel stage mark these songs with another, older discourse, which needs to be uncovered. Recent biographical work on Ford makes the case that he intended *The Searchers* to be read as a film about racism. Joseph McBride, for instance, argues that "by dealing so directly with the miscegenatory fears of white Americans in *The Searchers,* Ford was tapping into more generalized contemporary racial anxieties."[40] If what *The Searchers* cannot express directly are the tensions of contemporaneous white-black race relations, then music may be one of the telltale markers of both Ford's intentions to address race and racism and the ultimate impossibility of doing so within the genre of the western in 1950s America. In *The Searchers,* minstrel song helps to push to the surface what is deeply buried in the film.

As I've argued in another context, minstrel music functions in western film scores as a mark of authenticity.[41] Blackface performance served to reinforce white superiority; its weapon was ridicule, and its function was nationalistic—to provide a definition of American identity at a historical moment when the young country was searching for one. Minstrelsy was a social construction, defining the image of an Other against which white Americans, many newly arrived from foreign shores, could measure themselves and feel superior. It was no coincidence that minstrelsy exploded onto the American scene during the Jacksonian era, when nationalism provided the justification for Manifest Destiny. Eric Lott, in his revisionary work on minstrelsy, describes whiteness in the nineteenth century as "precarious."[42] Minstrelsy helped to establish a connection in the popular imagination between whiteness and the American nation and allowed for the release of tension required in sustaining that definition. Given that the frontier was the forge where American character was supposedly hammered out, it should not be surprising that minstrel music found its way onto the frontier and into a number of texts about the frontier experience: dime novels, western fiction, Broadway plays, and films. Thus minstrelsy entered into a psychic and public discourse that helped to circumscribe the boundaries of American identity.

"The Yellow Rose of Texas"—a song originally about a mulatta—shows how minstrelsy reinforced white dominance. Given its origins in the nexus of race and sexuality, the song's appearance in a film obsessed with miscegenation is a complicated allusion to say the least. The song constructs an African American speaker (identified as a "darky" in the song's original lyrics) whose lack of education and inferior social status are signaled by the misspellings and ungrammatical constructions typical of minstrelsy peppering the verses. The song's narrative chronicles the loss the speaker experiences upon separation from his lover. That the speaker's grief is meant to be comic, or at the least not taken quite seriously, is marked by the buoyancy of the music. The spirited rhythm, derived from its use of eighth notes and the intermittent use of a sixteenth, undercuts, or is at least at odds with, the speaker's supposedly tragic emotions.

Yellow, of course, was a common nineteenth-century signifier for a person of mixed race, and indeed in the second verse of the song, the speaker identifies his "dearest" as "the sweetest rose of color this darky ever knew." Here we have yet another of the defining tropes of minstrelsy: the powerful and alluring sexuality of the African American female. References to this "rose's" sexual allure are oblique but unmistakable, including a provocative claim that she is superior to her white counterparts ("You may talk about your Clementine, and sing of Rosalee, / But the yellow rose of Texas is the only girl for me . . ."). Like many other minstrel songs, "The Yellow Rose of Texas" has become disconnected from its minstrel past and wrapped up in folklore and legend. Descriptions of "The Yellow Rose of Texas" as an authentic folksong, and sometimes even a "Negro folksong,"[43] abound during the twentieth century, and reports that it is a folk song that originally commemorated a notorious episode in Texas history persisted well into the 1990s.[44] "The Yellow Rose of Texas," was published in 1858 and performed in this country and Europe by, among others, the Christy Minstrels.[45] It was appropriated as an anthem by Confederate soldiers from Texas and later was sung by the Texas Rangers.

Of course, in order for "The Yellow Rose of Texas" to function as a Confederate patriotic song, references to its minstrel origin had to be elided. In the 1860s, "darky" thus became "soldier" and "sweetest rose of color" was changed to "sweetest little flower." It was probably this recontextualized version that Ford was thinking of when he requested it for the aborted wedding, resonating with the Confederate past of Texas and perhaps even foreshadowing Charlie McCorry's own lost cause—his quest for Laurie.

Alterations and embellishments that redefined "The Yellow Rose of Texas" from minstrel song to folk song continued throughout the twentieth century. During the 1930s, for instance, the art composer David Guion created a new melody and alternate lyrics as part of the centennial celebrations of Texas independence. This new version became a staple of the country-and-western music scene and was recorded by Sons of the Pioneers in 1943. In August 1955, Mitch Miller's even more sanitized version hit the charts and remained in the number one spot on the Lucky Strikes Hit Parade for six weeks (in fact during the film's shooting schedule), ending up the number five song in the country for that year. "The Yellow Rose of Texas" appears in *The Searchers* vocally, but without either the original minstrel lyrics, the Confederate lyrics, or the more thoroughly laundered Mitch Miller lyrics. I would characterize the lyrics of "The Yellow Rose of Texas" heard in *The Searchers* as somewhere "in between" the extremes of the nineteenth-century minstrel song and Mitch Miller's hit tune. While the minstrel origins of "The Yellow Rose of Texas" might not have been widely known, its attachment to the Confederacy was still pronounced. The cover of the sheet music for Mitch Miller's version features a photo of Miller in a Confederate uniform. Ford was well aware of the Confederate dimension of "The Yellow Rose of Texas," as shown by the fact that he coupled it with "The Bonnie Blue Flag" in production notes.[46]

The minstrel origin of "The Yellow Rose of Texas" is a slightly more complicated matter. The song was a favorite of Ford's, he clearly knew its Confederate ties, and it is possible that he knew or suspected its minstrel provenance. Song has a cultural life of its own, however, and comes attached to cultural meanings, of which Ford may or may not have been fully aware. "The Yellow Rose of Texas" may, in fact, be the most extreme example of buried ideological meaning in Ford's westerns, its associations of minstrelsy creeping into the film regardless of whether or not Ford or his audience had the slightest idea of what they were hearing.

Minstrel song was created to reinforce white superiority but its condensed representation of race did not function in a totalizing manner. Minstrelsy can be described as a multifaceted practice, one that contains

Figure 16. "The Yellow Rose of Texas." Cover of the 1955 sheet music featuring Mitch Miller as a Confederate officer. Author's collection.

virulent racism and sometimes ambiguity about that racism. Eric Lott
calls it an "unsettled phenomenon," a "mixed erotic economy of celebration and exploitation."[47] A standard minstrel song type focused on the
horrors of slavery, especially blighted love and the destruction of the family. Not surprisingly, this ambivalence is more pronounced in early minstrelsy. As the Civil War loomed and there was more at stake in voicing
abolitionist sentiments, references to the horrors of slavery decreased.
And yet one of the most successful songs in minstrelsy was just such a
song. "Jubilo" (aka "The Year of the Jubilo" and "Kingdom Comin'")
reached its greatest popularity during the Civil War. Its title, a permuta-
tion of "jubilee," carries a uniquely African American meaning, referring
to the liberation of slaves that would precede and inaugurate jubilation.
Composed by the noted abolitionist songwriter Henry Clay Work in
1862, complete with minstrel dialect, and transferred to the minstrel stage
shortly thereafter by the Christy Minstrels, for whom it was a monster hit,
"Jubilo" was deliberately created to further the cause of abolition. A year
in advance of the Emancipation Proclamation, its lyrics tell the story of a
plantation taken over by its slaves, awaiting Lincoln's soldiers.

The choice of "Jubilo," especially in juxtaposition to "Yellow Rose,"
complicates an already complicated discourse on race circulating through
the film. Ford clearly knew the abolitionist origins of "Jubilo." The song can
be heard in two other Ford westerns and in narrative situations that clearly
point to the song's abolitionist thrust: in *The Horse Soldiers,* a Civil War
film, it can be heard as Union troops pass an African American church, with
its congregation gathered outside; and in *Sergeant Rutledge,* it underscores
the dramatic escape of the African American soldier Rutledge. Steiner understood the abolitionist origins of "Jubilo" too. He had used it in *Virginia
City* as a dance-hall tune heard in a Union stronghold, and coupled it with
the popular Union anthem "The Battle-cry of Freedom." Douglas Pye argues that racism is "inherent" in the genre of the western, making "almost
any attempt to produce an antiracist western a paradoxical, even contradictory, enterprise. It is, in effect, impossible to escape the genre's inform-
ing white supremacist terms."[48] I think his argument is illuminated by the
music in *The Searchers* where an abolitionist song, "Jubilo," comes smack
up against an example of the racism more characteristic of the form in "The
Yellow Rose of Texas." *The Searchers* is struggling with the issue of race
and its representation, and that struggle is writ large in the musical score.

And there is something else. It is interesting to me that so much of the
source music in *The Searchers* is tied up with a minor plot point: Ethan's
past as a Confederate soldier. The Confederacy and its cause get stitched

into the film in a variety of ways, not the least of which is through the music, even music that is not, on the face of it, southern. "Lorena," a parlor ballad composed by a northern minister and published in Chicago, was, nonetheless, a favorite of Confederate soldiers (hence Margaret Mitchell's reference to it in *Gone with the Wind*). "The Bonnie Blue Flag," a Confederate patriotic song, composed by Harry Macarthy,[49] commemorates the unofficial flag of the Confederacy, a blue flag with a single white star, used earlier by the sovereign state of Texas from 1836 to 1839 and often carried by Texas Confederate cavalry. "The Yellow Rose of Texas," with changed lyrics, was adopted by Texas recruits and other Confederate soldiers. There's something disturbing about what these songs get attached to: the family and the unrequited love between Ethan and Martha ("Lorena"), Ethan's heroic appearance, materializing as he does from the wilderness itself ("The Bonnie Blue Flag"), and communal life on the frontier ("The Yellow Rose of Texas").

There is a kind of diffused melancholy for the antebellum South circulating in *The Searchers* that the music focuses into a nostalgia for a less complicated and more graceful time.[50] I would not want to argue that *The Searchers* represents the Confederacy unproblematically. Certainly, Ethan's destructive racism is connected to his status as a former Confederate soldier. And the use of "Jubilo," with its unmistakable abolitionist context, provides a marker for slavery and the condition and status of African Americans, in a film in which such issues seem absent. But, in attaching the Confederacy, through its historic roots in song, to moments in the film that encapsulate heroism, family values, noble sacrifice, and community, the antebellum South cannot help but be ennobled in the process.[51] I am reminded here of Douglas Pye's comment: "The film probably goes further than any other western in dramatizing and implicating us in the neurosis of racism. But in wrestling with the ideological and psycho-sexual complex that underlies attitudes to race, it is working within almost intractable traditions of representation."[52]

"A Man will search his heart and soul / Go searching way out there / His piece [sic] o' mind he knows he'll find / But where oh Lord, Lord where." The film ends with a question, and one expressed musically at that. The search is not over; its terrain has simply changed from the literal to the figurative, from the wilderness to the recesses of the human mind. That this shift into the metaphysical has been signaled by the music indicates the importance of the score in the film's design. The prominence of the song in the film's final moments reminds us of how central music is to the meaning of *The Searchers*.

CHAPTER 8

In the Shadow of
The Searchers

Two Rode Together and *Sergeant Rutledge*

The Quiet Man may be John Ford's most enduringly popular film with the moviegoing public and his most successful from a financial standpoint, but it is *The Searchers* that is considered his masterpiece. Two films lurk in its shadow: *Two Rode Together* and *Sergeant Rutledge*. *Two Rode Together* is generally regarded as among Ford's worst, a film Ford himself called "the worst piece of crap I've directed in twenty years."[1] Both *The Searchers* and *Two Rode Together* are captivity narratives that gave Ford the opportunity to reexamine America's frontier past in terms of the confrontation between whites and Indians. Both films come to the same conclusion: racism is deadly. The films reach this point, however, in very different ways. *The Searchers* is rich in imagery, subtle in its storytelling, and overpowering in its emotional reverberations. Its score contributes, significantly, to the film's power. *Two Rode Together* deploys recycled images, pedestrian storytelling, and tepid emotion. Largely abandoning the folk songs and period music of other Ford westerns, the film also lacks the rich nondiegetic score of *The Searchers*. In its unconventional use of the guitar, however, the score of *Two Rode Together* anticipates later developments in the western film score. *The Searchers* received good reviews and did more than respectable business. It was generally thought of as a solid Ford western, hardly a message film. With *Sergeant Rutledge*, Ford put race on the front burner, and no one who saw the film could doubt his intentions. Musically, however, *Sergeant Rutledge* has more in common with *Two*

Rode Together than with *The Searchers,* with little in the way of the characteristic folk and period music so intrinsic to earlier Ford westerns. But the score does have its one big moment.

Two Rode Together revisits some of the same plot elements as *The Searchers.* At the center of the film is a cynical, mercenary sheriff, Guthrie McCabe (James Stewart) recruited by the U.S. cavalry but hired by the families of whites held by the Comanches to get back their loved ones. McCabe gruesomely recounts the probable fate of the captives, but he is willing to negotiate with the Comanches if paid to do so. Among the hopeful is Marty Purcell (Shirley Jones), who has traveled to the fort for the return of her brother, captured ten years earlier. McCabe, accompanied by Lieutenant Jim Gary (Richard Widmark), who is more enlightened but ultimately an ineffectual check on McCabe's baser instincts, rides to the Comanche camp and finds three captives still alive: two women who refuse to return (one who describes herself as "dead" and another who is insane) and a young man, Running Wolf, whom they rescue against his will. A fourth captive joins McCabe and Gary voluntarily—Stone Calf's woman, a Mexican captive named Elena (Linda Cristal), who returns with them but seems to have little will of her own. None of the families can identify Running Wolf, who so aggressively lashes out against his captors that he has to be restrained. It is clear that he will never to able to reintegrate into white American culture. When he murders a woman who attempts to help him, he is lynched. On his way to his death, he recognizes Marty's music box; he is Marty's brother after all, but the mob is unstoppable. Elena, also rejected by the Anglo society, decides to leave for California, and McCabe, witness to her humiliation and confronted by the ugliness of racism, decides to leave with her.

It's a toss-up who is worse in this dark and cynical tale—the Indians, who abuse their captives and willingly sell one who begs to stay, or the white settlers, who lynch one young captive and cannot disguise their fascination and disgust with another. Reintegration of the former captives into white society is impossible. "Good God, this is a lousy script," Ford himself complained,[2] and Harry Carey Jr., was neither the first nor the last to comment upon the images, narrative devices, and dialogue recycled from previous Ford westerns. "*Two Rode Together* seems to me to be a hodgepodge of incidents and pieces of business from every western Jack ever made," Carey writes.[3] Working for hire at Columbia Pictures, Ford did not shoot the film in Monument Valley, but in Brackettville, Texas, using the same location and even some of the same sets as John Wayne's epic film *The Alamo* (John Wayne, 1960) which had recently finished production there.[4] Despite its location shooting, *Two Rode Together* has the look of a film made on the back lot. The one interesting moment from a cinematographic standpoint is a lengthy two-shot of McCabe and Gary talking out their principles. Ford set up the camera in the middle of a river to get it.

The musical score is by George Duning, a veteran Columbia Pictures composer in 1961, with orchestration by Arthur Morton. The classically trained Duning had made his name in popular music in the 1930s working with Kay Kayser's band as an arranger and orchestrator. After a stint in the Navy during World War II, Duning arrived in Hollywood, where he went to work for Columbia, remaining there for fifteen years and earning three Academy Award nominations.[5] Duning scored a few westerns at Columbia—a Randolph Scott vehicle, *The Doolins of Oklahoma* (Gordon Douglas, 1949), and two Delmer Daves westerns: *3:10 to Yuma* (1957) and *Cowboy* (1958). Daves would say of Duning's work that it was "quintessential for the genre,"[6] but it was probably Duning's Navy experience that forged the connection to Ford. Duning would work on all of Ford's Columbia ventures, scoring *Two Rode Together* and *The Last Hurrah*; he is credited with "Musical Adaptation" for *The Long Gray Line.*

With the exception of "Buffalo Gals," there are no Anglo American folk tunes in the score of *Two Rode Together*. Neither is there any American period music. At an early stage of the film's development, Sid Cutner, an orchestrator at Columbia, had arranged a medley of folk tunes and period music, including "Red River Valley," "Dear Evalina," and "Drink to Me Only with Thine Eyes," but it was not used. As he usually did, Ford shot the dance sequences, using period music of his own choice, before the score was composed. Duning had to write to Ford to ask him what "tunes" he had chosen.[7] It was Ford's usual practice to use American period music for the traditional dances but for the Bachelors' Hop at Fort Grant, several waltzes by Johann Strauss Jr. were used instead: "Tales from the Vienna Woods," "The Blue Danube," and "Roses from the South." Perhaps Ford was thinking of the dance sequence in *The Long Gray Line,* which also uses Strauss's "Roses from the South." At any rate, the Strauss waltzes in *Two Rode Together* function much like Stephen Foster's "Beautiful Dreamer" in *Fort Apache,* encoding aristocratic privilege and class status, and thus setting up the (racist) inhabitants of Fort Grant for disapproval. Even Marty's music box lacks an American soundtrack: it plays the famous minuet from Boccherini's *String Quintet in E Major.*[8] Duning even queried Ford on the choice of the tune for the music box, and it appears that Ford provided the answer.[9]

Other divergences from past musical practices include a stagecoach entering the frame without "Oh, Bury Me Not on the Lone Prairie," and Dan Borzage playing a role in the film instead of the accordion, at least on camera. Of all things, he plays a drunk (Francis Ford having passed on by then), standing with what appears to be a barrel organ, a street instrument popular in nineteenth-century America. Given the instruments assembled in this sequence, it is surprising that no one plays or sings. In fact, there are no diegetic performances of song in the film. There is some conventional Indian music, nicely orchestrated in the sequence when Stone Calf is killed, but there is only one Fordian musical moment: at the dance held outside Fort Grant, "Buffalo Gals," an authentic piece of American period music, can be heard.[10] "Buffalo Gals" contrasts nicely with the Strauss waltzes, underscoring the class issues that divide the military from the settlers. Of course, the settlers prove to be as racist as the military.

The instrument that is exploited in *Two Rode Together* is the guitar, distinctively used to play the score's theme, presented initially in the main title and reiterated throughout the film. Although Mark Twain owned one and Thomas Eakins painted one, the guitar played a rather insignificant role in nineteenth-century music-making on the American frontier.[11] The most popular and widely used instruments were the banjo, the fiddle, and the mandolin, played by cowboys, soldiers, miners, farmers, and ranchers alike and featured in entertainments from minstrel shows to frontier saloons and from country dances to military balls. Guitars were not generally used by cowboys (who favored more portable instruments, such as the Jew's harp or the harmonica),[12] or much by westerners in general, until the twentieth century when they were adopted by country-and-western singers. Guitars became the ubiquitous western instrument only after they accompanied singing cowboys on the radio, in recordings, and in films. Nevertheless, in a kind of projection backwards, guitars became synonymous with the nineteenth-century American West, strummed by cowboys in countless Hollywood westerns, including some of Ford's.[13] It is worth noting that in silent Ford westerns predating the country-and-western phenomenon, cowboys don't play guitars: in *Straight Shooting,* they listen to phonograph records, and in *Bucking Broadway,* in 1917, they strum the mandolin or play the piano.

In Hollywood film scoring, the guitar was central to a set of stereotypical musical markers for Mexico, which also included the instrumen-

Figure 17. James Stewart, on the right, playing the accordion on the set of *Two Rode Together*. That's Danny Borzage looking on. Courtesy Lilly Library, Indiana University, Bloomington, IN.

tation and harmonies of mariachi bands: trumpets, guitars, and castanets in the characteristic harmonies of parallel thirds. Although the guitar was not prevalent in the nineteenth-century American West, it was well known in the Spanish New World where conquistadors imported it as early as the sixteenth century. The guitar has had a rich history in the Middle East, North Africa, and Europe, especially Spain, where it developed into an instrument of art music. But when transplanted to the Spanish New World, the guitar would eventually develop as a folk instrument in Latin America and especially Mexico. Both the guitar and the mariachi band with which it is often configured are deeply rooted in Mexican popular culture. I would not want to argue that the guitar is an authentic signifier for Mexico, although there is more historical basis to make the claim for Mexico than there is for the western United States, or that the use of the guitar does not come trailing along with it a set of potentially negative ethnic stereotypes. Ford was well read in nineteenth-century American history, and he knew the music of the period. The vast majority of his westerns do not use the guitar as a western instrument, but rather as a marker for Mexico.

Ford often alluded in his westerns to the multicultural mix of Mexico and the United States that characterized the borderlands. He included the Spanish language, Mexican characters, Mexican songs, and Mexican actors, and when he did so, the score generally responded with some or all of the musical signifiers of Mexico.[14] The classical Hollywood film score depended upon this kind of musical stereotyping to establish and authenticate historical era, geographic place, and national identities quickly and reliably. K. J. Donnelly describes these stereotypes as "the musical counterpart to an establishing shot. A limited musical vocabulary furnishes a sense of place and people for films whilst also supplying significant boundary markers, which set zones of difference and national or other border lines."[15]

Some of the time, the guitar in *Two Rode Together* functions in this conventional way, connoting Mexico in the leitmotif for Elena, for instance.[16] But most of the time, I think, the guitar functions differently. In *Two Rode Together,* the guitar is a prominent feature of the nondiegetic score in several scenes involving the white protagonists, blunting the stereotypical function of the guitar as a general signifier of Otherness and a specific signifier of Mexico. While the film opens with a shot of a man in his serape and sombrero, accompanied by two nondiegetic guitars, the introduction of Guthrie McCabe is also accompanied by those guitars, including a nice guitar stinger for the first utterance of his name. Guitars accompany the arrival of the cavalry in *Two Rode Together;* the first meeting between old friends Jim Gary and McCabe; the settlers' descriptions of their captive family members; the appearance of the town madam; and McCabe's final appearance in the film. A mariarchi arrangement accompanies the cavalry fording the river, and mariarchi horns accompany McCabe and Gary's entry into the pioneer camp, as well as

Gary's dramatic exit to join McCabe. The Mexican *corrido* "El Corrido de Cananea" accompanies McCabe's replacement, Deputy Ward Carby (Chet Douglas). A *corrido* is a kind of Mexican ballad, popular in the nineteenth century, usually dealing with contemporary events. This one is about a man, arrested in the middle of the night, "American-style" and unjustly thrown into prison.[17] The parallel to the plot of *Two Rode Together* is a bit tenuous (Ward has unjustly seized McCabe's job and paramour), but the song was clearly chosen with the film in mind.

In uncoupling the connection between the guitar and Otherness, *Two Rode Together* anticipates later revisionist westerns that "allowed new ethnicities to be brought into the fore and old ones to be rethought."[18] Music is a critical part of this process. In Sam Peckinpah's *The Wild Bunch* (1969), for instance, Mexican music is not ghettoized as a signifier of Otherness but becomes part of the structural mix of the score, even used to accompany white characters.

Two Rode Together shares with other late Ford westerns, such as *The Searchers, Sergeant Rutledge, The Man Who Shot Liberty Valance,* and *Cheyenne Autumn,* a revisionary impulse to take account of what is usually repressed when the dominant culture controls the historical narrative of the American West. In *Two Rode Together,* music helps to bring into focus the history of Mexico and the role of its culture in the development of the American nation. James Brooks points out that Hispanic captives far outnumbered Anglo American captives of Indians in the southwestern borderlands and argues that although *Two Rode Together* "is a far lesser work of art than *The Searchers,* less psychologically profound (though still an exploration of racism), [it is] . . . more in line with historical reality."[19] Elena's ethnicity is a construction of the film. In the source novel, she is Janice Tremain, a white woman, the niece, in fact, of a U.S. senator. The change allows the film to reference Hispanic history in the West and to probe racism. The music in *Two Rode Together* does more than simply resist stereotypes that encode ethnicity; the music also points to this other, often marginalized, historical reality.

Two Rode Together is a confused polemic against racism, ostensibly decrying racist responses to white captives returned to Anglo culture, while simultaneously representing Indians as stereotypical savages. Some critics have read the film, à la *The Searchers,* as an allegory of black-white relations during the era of the civil rights movement.[20] Figured in the casting of the African American Woody Strode as the Indian Stone Calf, this reading of the film, however, is as fraught with contradictions as its surface message.[21] Two years earlier, Strode had played Sergeant

Rutledge, an African American cavalryman falsely accused of rape and murder. Yet in *Two Rode Together*, he appears to commit these very crimes, portraying a murderous savage who has repeatedly raped his Mexican captive, Elena. Stone Calf is mourned by Elena, but his death is seen as her salvation.

Just two years earlier, Ford had been able to deliver his message about race and racism with more clarity and impact in *Sergeant Rutledge*. Few critics have treated the film in depth.[22] The eponymous protagonist, Sergeant Braxton Rutledge (Woody Strode),[23] a so-called buffalo soldier in the U.S. cavalry, is accused of the murder of the white post commander, Major Dabney, and the rape and murder of his daughter, Lucy (Toby Richards). The narrative takes the form of Rutledge's court-martial, with witnesses narrating their testimonies as flashbacks to the actual events. Among those providing evidence are Mary Beecher (Constance Towers), a white woman whose life Rutledge has saved, Lieutenant Tom Cantrell (Jeffrey Hunter), Rutledge's white commanding officer and lawyer advocate, who praises Rutledge's ethical conduct, high principles, and fine soldiering, and Rutledge, who defends himself as best he can, justifying the murder of the commander as self-defense, but who is at a loss to explain or account for the crimes against Lucy. Justice is served when the actual criminal, a white shopkeeper, Chandler Hubble (Fred Libby), comes forward and is tricked into confessing by Cantrell. The film was not a success either with critics or with audiences of any color. Armond White offers this explanation: "Filmgoers in 1960 weren't prepared to accept Ford turning the Western into a psychological thriller, using the form's historical reference to probe our customs and ethics."[24] I suspect that audiences were not quite ready either for Ford first to unleash and then to defuse the cultural myth of black male sexuality.

Essentially a courtroom drama, *Sergeant Rutledge* nonetheless engages critically with generic expectations of the western, inserting the history of African American soldiers on the frontier into dominant cultural myths about the West and its settling. The Indian wars in the latter half of the nineteenth century were fought by ten cavalry units stationed on the Great Plains, two of which, the Ninth and the Tenth, were made up of segregated African American units commanded by white officers.[25] Thus, roughly 20 percent of post–Civil War U.S. cavalry troops were black.[26] This is a not a small proportion. Historically, the military, and in the nineteenth century, the cavalry, functioned as something of a safe haven for African American males, providing them with a steady job and pay and benefits such as medical care and education.[27] Buffalo soldiers, so named by the Indians because of the perceived resemblance between African American hair and buffalo hides,[28] however, often faced the very racism they joined the cavalry to escape, from within the military and outside it.[29] The crusading journalist, editor, and publisher Oswald Garrison Villard, who in 1903 wrote one of the first chronicles of the buffalo soldiers, described African Americans in the military as "on trial," producing a soldier "who must worry incessantly about his relations to his white comrades."[30] Yet desertion rates for buffalo soldiers in the Ninth and Tenth Cavalry were among the lowest on the frontier.

Ford has a tendency to idealize the military, and he does so here in the enlightened relationships between Rutledge and his commanding officer, Cantrell, and between Rutledge and Mary Beecher.[31] But Ford shies away neither from championing the buffalo soldiers for their valor and loyalty in fighting for American interests on the frontier nor from indicting racism as a real and terrifying condition that African American soldiers had to endure. The disillusion and cynicism that might result from these conditions are voiced by a dying buffalo soldier—"We fools to fight the white . . . man's war"—and answered with the idealism of Rutledge: "It ain't white man's war. We're fighting to make us proud." At his court-martial, Rutledge defends the military as worthy of African American loyalty and sacrifice ("the Ninth Cavalry was my home, my real freedom, and my self-respect") opening up the film to charges that it was a recruitment vehicle for the war in Vietnam.[32] Of course, the assimilation of the African American into the military is at the expense of the Indians, who continue to function as the savage embodiment of everything that needs to be conquered for civilization to exist. As Rutledge explains to Mary Beecher in the face of an Indian attack, "They'll have no mercy on you, lady. They'll have no mercy."

The original screenplay for *Sergeant Rutledge* by James Warner Bellah and Willis Goldbeck was based on an original idea inspired by Frederic Remington's sketches of buffalo soldiers. Remington accompanied the Tenth Cavalry on patrol in 1886 and the sketches of his experience first appeared in *Century* magazine. Goldbeck did the legwork here, putting the Warner Bros. research department on the trail of the original *Century* publication, as well as Remington's *Crooked Trails* (1898) and Harold McCracken's *Frederic Remington, Artist of the Old West* (1947), a standard reference.[33] Warner Bros. publicity got on the bandwagon, noting that Remington's sketches "were used for reference in preparing the uniforms worn by the actors."[34] There was a lot to interest Ford in the material: a facet of western history that had been ignored by Hollywood; a western artist whom Ford had long admired and who clearly influenced Ford's visual composition; and Ford's growing social conscience, reawakened by the civil rights movement. According to Bellah, Ford was initially enthusiastic about the film and "delighted to take on the project."[35] Dan Ford, however, reports that his grandfather's "enthusiasm was less than complete," and even Bellah noticed a waning of Ford's interest and energy during the course of their writing sessions. The film became, according to Dan Ford, "just another job of work."[36] Eighty percent of the film was shot in the studio, and even location shooting in his beloved Monument Valley didn't seem to perk Ford up. Still, Ford thought of the film as Academy Award material ("a hell of a picture") and tried to get Warner Bros. to move up the release date in order for the picture to be considered for an Oscar in 1959.[37]

Sergeant Rutledge captures some of the spirit and sometimes the look and feel of the earlier cavalry trilogy. The critics Armond White and Frank Manchell speak of the film's "unexpected, authentic complexity about race, history, and American social temperament," praising it as a conscientious attempt to "revise the Western's racial iconography" and calling it "revolutionary."[38] Warner Bros. appears to have had some trepidation about promoting the film, realizing that it would be a tough sell. The front office decreed that the initial trailers for *Sergeant Rutledge* were to show "*no scenes* from the picture."[39]

The score was composed by Howard Jackson, with orchestration by Jackson, Leo Shuken, and Jack Hayes. Jackson conducted, although David Buttolph was on hand for one of the recording sessions. Howard Jackson (aka Howard Manuey Jackson and Howard M. Jackson), a career film and television composer and sometime songwriter, staff arranger, orchestrator, and composer for various studios, spent a good part of his creative life at Paramount. He worked on over 300 film scores, the vast majority uncredited. Jackson's first credit, in 1929, is for *Broadway* and his work extends through the early 1960s. *Sergeant Rutledge* was one of his last films. Although he was also a songwriter (he composed, among other popular songs, "Hearts in Dixie"), Jackson did not provide the song "Captain Buffalo." That was supplied by the songwriting team of Jerry Livingston and Mack David, who both individually and together provided a wealth of music during the theme song craze of the 1950s and 1960s and penned memorable themes for the television shows *77 Sunset Strip* and *Hawaiian Eye,* and a number of television westerns such as *Sugarfoot, Cheyenne, Bronco,* and *Lawman.*

Although Ford may have treated the film as "just another job of work," he was still in control of the music. Demo recordings were made of the song "Captain Buffalo" in July 1959 for Ford's approval. The Warner Bros. music department was thinking along the lines of either "The Ballad of Davy Crockett," an upbeat theme song for a popular television series, or a jaunty arrangement in "the style of . . . Mitch Miller."[40] In fact, there had been conversations and correspondence with Miller about recording the song for the soundtrack and simultaneously releasing it on record. The music department was happy to provide "additional verses written to suit the pop market" if Miller was interested.[41] Ford was thinking otherwise. He requested that "Captain Buffalo" be recorded a cappella; "he wanted to see how it would sound sung slowly," not in the upbeat tempi characteristic of Miller's arrangements.[42] Victor Blau, head of Warner's music department, cautioned Miller that "Mr. Ford leans to not too professional singing, and would like to utilize colored voices in keeping with his film."[43] At one point, the music department was nervous about whether Ford would even use "Captain Buffalo" in the main and end titles, a virtual requirement for marketing the song. "Dealing with John Ford is rough," Blau confessed to an associate.[44] Ultimately, Mitch Miller was not used, and Ford got a recording with harmonica only. Margaret Hairston and Florence Brantley were contracted by the studio to provide and coach the choir for the recording of "Captain Buffalo." Twelve male singers came in on November 4, 1959, to record the main and end titles and the bivouac scene. Margaret Hairston was the wife of the noted African American choral director Jester Hairston, who directed the first integrated choir in Hollywood and who prepared the choruses for *3 Godfathers* and *She Wore a Yellow Ribbon*. Margaret frequently collaborated with her husband, and I suspect that Jester left the conducting duties to his wife because he was engaged elsewhere.[45]

The score for *Sergeant Rutledge*, at moments, engages with the film's intentions in a powerful way. There is no nondiegetic score during any of the trial itself, not even during Rutledge's impassioned defense of his humanity: " . . . . I am a man." Some of the suspenseful moments (the film, in some ways, has more in common with Hitchcock than with Ford) are scored with typical thriller devices: tremolo strings, stingers, crescendo and decrescendo. There is conventional Indian music as well, used sometimes in a fairly sophisticated way to invoke the Indian presence when they are absent from the screen. Most of the music, however, is reserved for the location sequences in Monument Valley featuring the buffalo soldiers.

The score's most powerful moment comes during Rutledge's escape, where it depends upon use of American period music to make its point. As Rutledge, under arrest, breaks for freedom, the song "Jubilo" can be heard instrumentally in a lush orchestration accompanying his getaway. (Listen for a brief instrumental foreshadowing of "Jubilo" and a quotation from "Battle Hymn of the Republic" when Rutledge rides after Moffatt, a wounded buffalo soldier.) The use of the abolitionist minstrel song "Jubilo" in *Sergeant Rutledge* to mark a black man's escape shows Ford's clear understanding of its contents and intent.

With the exception of "Jubilo," period song, so richly utilized in the earlier cavalry trilogy and typical of military life in the nineteenth-century cavalry, is missing. Like the Seventh Cavalry, depicted in *Fort Apache*, the Ninth and Tenth Cavalry had regimental songs of their own. The Ninth Cavalry sang "The Monkey Married the Baboon's Sister" to a recycled folk tune and "The Indian Ghost Dance and War," a ballad composed by a soldier in the Ninth. The Tenth Cavalry adopted "The Buffaloes," sung to the tune of Stephen Foster's "Camptown Races."[46] None of these regimental songs are used in *Sergeant Rutledge,* although research for the film turned up "The Indian Ghost Dance and War" as well as the song "The Colored Troops at Petersburg" composed to commemorate the valor of an African American division at the Battle of the Crater in the Civil War. The pop tune "Captain Buffalo" seems to have taken the place of a period song: when the buffalo soldiers out on patrol sing, it's "Captain Buffalo."

Music was a part of African American soldiers' experience in the military as much as, or perhaps more than, their white counterparts'. There was seemingly no end of music in the ranks of the buffalo soldiers. Benjamin Grierson, who commanded the Tenth Cavalry, had been a music teacher in civilian life and recruited a regimental band that played evening concerts "keenly anticipated and much enjoyed by the officers and the men."[47] When the Tenth departed Fort Riley, Kansas, for their posting on the frontier, they were accompanied by the regimental band. According to Villard: "There was always 'a steady hum of laughter and talk, dance, song, shout, and the twang of musical instruments.'"[48] Music, however, is largely absent from *Sergeant Rutledge.*

As I have argued throughout this book, songs in Ford westerns serve an important function beyond simply authenticating time and place. Sometimes song expresses what the dialogue cannot. In *Rio Grande,* for instance, song constitutes an interior monologue literally voicing what Kirby Yorke cannot: his repressed sexual desire. "Captain Buffalo" functions in a similar way: it brings to the surface a controversial representation that it would be difficult for the film to represent more directly.

"Captain Buffalo" is sung nondiegetically as a main title song during the opening credits. It is sung once diegetically by the buffalo soldiers, and it is reprised at the end of the film, first instrumentally and then vocally, against an image of the buffalo soldiers on patrol in Monument Valley. The song expresses what the film cannot depict: a powerful black male. Race is so fraught in this film, so controversial a subject, that the professional and even awe-inspiring "top soldier" that Rutledge must have been before the events of the film transpire is almost entirely repressed. (And imagine Warner Bros. trying to create a trailer with no scenes from the film!) What we know of Rutledge's past position can only be glimpsed secondhand through the testimonies of the white characters who are in a position to frame Rutledge, some literally.

The song "Captain Buffalo" speaks to another reality, the powerful buffalo soldier, a Paul Bunyanesque figure, who is larger than life, an inspirational figure who is the master of every task: "He'll march all night, and he'll march all day, and he'll wear out a twenty mule team along the way. . . ." Here is the displaced representation of the powerful, commanding, authoritative, "top soldier" Sergeant Rutledge, safely contained in the theme song. White argues that the representation of race in *Sergeant Rutledge* is "so controversial, so psychically disruptive, it is hardly spoken in plain terms."[49] I think he's right. It is sung instead.

Historically, music has been resistant to critical analysis. Listeners and producers alike have tended to perceive music as free of the intervention of social forces. But as the scores for *Two Rode Together* and *Sergeant Rutledge* remind us, music is never innocent; it carries with it the seeds of its culture. As I've argued for *The Searchers,* the use of minstrel songs functions as a displacement for what the film and the genre of the western as a whole, did not and perhaps could not address directly: contemporary black-white race relations. In *Sergeant Rutledge,* the song "Captain Buffalo" serves a similar displacement, depicting the powerful, competent African American male that racist cultural myths prevent the film from representing directly. In *Two Rode Together,* the score's allusions to and exploitation of Mexican musical culture underscore the film's multicultural focus on Hispanic as well as Anglo captives. All three films remind us of how central—and how fraught with tension—the issue of race was in America in the 1950s and 1960s.

CHAPTER 9

Cheyenne Autumn

A Conclusion

This book's central argument has been that John Ford's choices of folk song, hymnody, and period music significantly affect the meaning of his westerns, and that readings of his films ignore the scores at their peril. Even in his last films, Ford continued to exert control over the music, delegating responsibility when his diminishing energies and enthusiasms demanded it but asserting his authority when it became necessary.

Ford's last western was *Cheyenne Autumn*. The musical aesthetics of Ford's western canon constitute a continuum, from the lean, sparse sound of *My Darling Clementine,* with its virtual dependence upon the diegetic use of folk song, hymnody, and period music, to the lush Hollywood sound of *The Searchers,* in which the folk songs, hymns, and period music are embedded in a wall-to-wall nondiegetic score. Ford, cantankerous to the end, lumped *Cheyenne Autumn* with *The Searchers:* "I thought it was a bad score and too much of it."[1] But *Cheyenne Autumn* also depends upon period music, and, in fact, uses little else in the central Dodge City section. I see the score for *Cheyenne Autumn* more as a combination of both ends of the Ford musical continuum. As a conclusion to Ford's career, the score holds a few surprises. For the first time, Ford initiated research on Native American music, and in his attempt to incorporate it into the film, he anticipates Hollywood's discovery of world and ethnic music.

Ford's last western is based on the history of the Cheyenne's doomed flight in 1878 from a barren reservation in Indian Territory in Oklahoma across 2,000 miles to their native lands in the Dakotas. The subject matter gave Ford the opportunity to return to America's frontier past and, as he did in *Sergeant Rutledge,* to tell a story wrested from the margins of the dominant historical narrative. The treatment of the Cheyenne at the hands of the U.S. government was nothing less than tragic. When 286 Cheyenne left the reservation, they fled an uninhabitable place, where they had been racked by disease and hunger and reduced to almost complete dependence on the government. Hounded by the cavalry, beset by internal rivalries, after one of their bands was tricked into surrendering at Camp Robinson, Nebraska, hundreds of miles from their destination, the Cheyenne generated national attention. Even previously hostile western newspapers were now sympathetic. An editorial in the *Omaha Herald* intoned: "It means starvation for them. I implore you for justice and humanity to those wronged red men. Let them stay in their own country."[2] While army officials such as Lieutenant General Philip Sheridan remained obdurate ("unless they are sent back to where they came from, the whole reservation system will receive a shock which will endanger its stability"),[3] the public outcry was loud and strong, and the Indian Bureau finally yielded to the pressure: the Cheyenne could return to their homelands. Fifty-eight of them were left.

Like so many of Ford's westerns, however, *Cheyenne Autumn* is based only very loosely on this history, fictionalizing participants in the drama, and even changing the course of events where necessary. In fact, the film was based on fiction: the historical novels *Cheyenne Autumn* by Mari Sandoz (credited) and *The Last Frontier* by Howard Fast (uncredited).[4] In Ford's film, the Cheyenne begin their trek accompanied by a beautiful young Quaker schoolteacher, Deborah Wright (Carroll Baker), and they are pursued, half-heartedly, by the cavalry and an officer in love with her, Captain Thomas Archer (Richard Widmark). An awkward interlude in Dodge City features a card game between Wyatt Earp (James Stewart), Doc Holliday (Arthur Kennedy), and a Major Jeff Blair (John Carradine), as well as a comic rout of the townspeople occasioned by the appearance of a single Cheyenne. Escaping a winter encampment, the dying and wounded Cheyenne make it as far as Victory Cave. There, in a deus ex machina ending, Secretary of the Interior Carl Schurz (Edward G. Robinson) personally saves them from massacre and promises a better future from the government. With their fates seemingly settled, jealous rivalries explode, and Dull Knife (Gilbert Roland) kills Red Shirt (Sal Mineo). The film ends with a young Cheyenne girl being returned to the tribe.

Although some of its imagery is still striking, *Cheyenne Autumn* never quite came together. At the end of his career, Ford was finding himself out of step with new ways of doing business in the wake of the studio system's breakup, fighting to get films produced, and unconnected to a new generation of stars audiences flocked to see. Even the old dependable stalwarts of the John Ford stock company were disappearing, many of his longtime cast and crew dead, retired, or siphoned off by television, or worse, becoming such huge stars, like John Wayne, that Ford could no longer count on their unquestioned participation. A Ford film, even a Ford western, was no longer a sure bet. Studios were hesitant to commit to Ford's projects, and some even turned a deaf ear to them. Warner Bros., which had initially passed on the project, eventually gave Ford an unenthusiastic go-ahead. The tremendous effort to get *Cheyenne Autumn* into production took its toll in a number of ways. There were script problems, and filming began before the screenplay was complete. Legal problems loomed over the production as a result of the surreptitious use of Fast's novel. Only a few Ford regulars were engaged for the film, and the cast was largely not of Ford's choosing. Spencer Tracy was supposed to star as Secretary of the Interior Carl Schurz, and even shot some footage; Ford had to do some fancy camera work to finesse Edward G. Robinson into his place.[5] Ford had wanted to use Navajo actors for the main parts, as well as Woody Strode, who was part Native American, but the studio balked and Ford ended up with the Mexicans Gilbert Roland, Ricardo Montalban, and Dolores Del Rio, the Italian American method actor Sal Mineo, and the Canadian Victor Jory. Carroll Baker was cast in a role Ford had envisioned as a middle-aged Quaker. Ford was absent from the set for portions of the filming, too ill or depressed to carry on even in Monument Valley and Moab. During the snow sequences filmed at Gunnison, Colorado, Ford broke his ankle. Warner Bros. edited Ford's cut without his knowledge or approval. Most American critics disliked the film intensely, and it was not a success.

It has become commonplace to interpret *Cheyenne Autumn* as Ford's apology for his treatment of Indians on screen, a culminating statement on his western oeuvre. His comments at the time of the film's release reinforced this interpretation: "I've killed more Indians than Custer, Beecher, and Chivington put together. . . . There are two sides to every story, but I wanted to show their point of view for a change."[6] But, as usual, Ford knew how to tell a good story, especially one that would promote his film. Given the representation of Indians in *Fort Apache, Wagon Master,* and even *The Searchers,* Ford's claim is a bit disingenuous, and *Cheyenne Autumn* is not technically told from the Cheyenne's point of view. It is the white cavalry officer who is the focal point of the narrative. But in the music, Ford made a genuine attempt at showing the Cheyenne "point of view for a change." This quest for authentic Cheyenne music, however, was at the expense of folk song, hymnody, and period music. With the exception of a brief nondiegetic quotation from "Battle Hymn of the Republic," only in the Dodge City set piece, a self-contained narrative sequence focusing on a comic incident and showcasing James Stewart, is there any American folk or period music.

As early as August 1963, Ford initiated research into authentic Cheyenne song and chant. It would neither be the first time nor the last that Ford incorporated ethnic music into a film. *Mogambo* (1953) is scored almost entirely with native African music. (This being Ford, there is a song too: "Coming through the Rye," sung by Ava Gardner, no less.) And *7 Women,* his last film, would incorporate Chinese musical elements, albeit with a strong whiff of orientalism. For *Cheyenne Autumn,* Danny Borzage was put in charge of source music; in October, he requested a book on nineteenth-century bugle calls and copies of popular songs of the period. "Drill, Ye Terriers, Drill" and "Oh, We've Lost the Trail, O" were among the period songs considered for the soldiers to sing. "Drill, Ye Terriers, Drill" was not used; "Oh, We've Lost the Trail, O" came close to being included. Borzage got as far as distributing lyrics to the actors. But nothing ultimately came of it.

Alex North must have seemed an inspired choice to compose the score. He had come to Hollywood in the 1950s and helped to revolutionize classical scoring practices, writing in musical idioms that were still relatively new to Hollywood: jazz in *A Streetcar Named Desire* (Elia Kazan, 1951) and modernist and traditional Mexican music in *Viva Zapata* (Elia Kazan, 1952). North was classically trained—he had studied with Ernest Bloch, Aaron Copland, and the Mexican composer Silvestre Revueltas—but he cut his teeth in the New York dance and theater worlds, where he worked with the modern dancer Anna Sokolow and the director Elia Kazan. For a time, he was the go-to composer for psychological dramas, and he scored a string of them, including *Death of a Salesman* (Lázló Benedek, 1951), *The Bad Seed* (Mervyn LeRoy, 1956), *The Long, Hot Summer* (Martin Ritt, 1958), *The Misfits* (John Huston, 1961), *The Children's Hour* (William Wyler, 1961), and *Who's Afraid of Virginia Woolf* (Mike Nichols, 1966). Since he wasn't known for westerns, perhaps it was the Zapata score, with its distinctive use of Mexican folk melodies, that brought him to Ford's attention. Although Ford's power was waning in the Hollywood of the 1960s, he still controlled enough of the production to approve the composer. Warner Bros. waited for Ford to authorize North's hiring personally before they signed him on December 9, 1963. North conducted the score, but he did not orchestrate it; Henry Brant and Gil Grau did, although neither is credited.[7]

The research on Cheyenne and other Indian music was turned over to North on January 29, 1964. There was a fairly substantial amount of research for North to digest.[8] Ken Darby, a musical arranger at Warner Bros., adapted a number of authentic Cheyenne and Cree Indian chants. But for all of that effort, North's music is more Indianesque than Indian. In a score containing over an hour and a half of music, less than six minutes are comprised of actual Cheyenne chant, all of it diegetic: 86 seconds during the opening sequence, 37 seconds after the death of Tall Tree (Victor Jory), about 3 minutes prior to the Cheyenne escape from the fort, and 30 seconds during the final sequence. These performances of authentic Cheyenne music found their way into the film via Ford. As was his habit, Ford chose music he wanted in the film and sometimes recorded it during filming. In his music notes, North observes that all the occurrences of actual Cheyenne music were "recorded on set" or "recorded on location";[9] North inherited these cues when he prepared his film score. Certainly, North utilized the research on Indian music and incorporated some of these elements into his nondiegetic film score: his use of drum rhythms, for instance, were clearly created with an ear to actual Cheyenne rhythms. But some of the old stereotypes creep in too, such as a reliance upon fourths and fifths in the harmonic texture when Indians are on screen.

North's score for *Cheyenne Autumn* is marked by a modernist musical vocabulary: dissonance, unusual rhythms, a pared-down medium,[10] the incorporation of jazz elements, and an avoidance of conventional melody. North did pull out all the stops, however, for a beautiful leitmotif for Deborah. Warner Bros. actually marketed the song, retitled "Autumn's Ballad," via its publishing arm, M. Witmark. Recently released on CD, the score for *Cheyenne Autumn* has not fared well with critics. Mark Hockley's comments, in *Film Music CD Reviews,* are typical: "Alex North is not everyone's cup of hemlock. There is a startlingly bleak and remote quality to his work at times and this score bears that out. . . . [F]or all its artistic integrity [this score] is rather hard to sit through."[11]

There appears to have been a good amount of push-and-pull between North and Ford, with Ford generally retaining the upper hand. For instance, North queried Ford at one point as to whether he could make the diegetic drums that Ford had already recorded live on the set "continuous" with the drums in his nondiegetic score. Ford responded: "not continuous."[12] In another instance, North wanted to know whether he could add instruments to the funeral chant of the "voices already recorded." The answer must have come back, "no," since the chanting remains unaccompanied in the release print. The score was recorded in late April and early May of 1964, although Warner Bros. production records indicate that "considerable" changes were still being made to it as late as the following September.[13] Despite Ford's clear antipathy for North's work, Bernard Smith, Ford's partner and producer, contacted North about scoring "Chinese Finale," the working title of Ford's last film, *7 Women*. Ford's relationship to Smith's offer is unclear, but North did not score the film.

North did not select or arrange either the folk and period songs used in *Cheyenne Autumn* during the Dodge City sequence or the Ukrainian folk song briefly crooned by the Ukrainian American Mike Mazurki, playing Stanislaw Wichowsky, described in a memo as an "American sergeant of Russian descent" (although clearly identified as Polish in the film).[14] Mazurki suggested "Oi Vidsi Gora," and Warner Bros. music department scrambled to track down the song and confirm that it was in the public domain. Ford, of course, chose the American songs, and Ken Darby and Sid Cutner arranged them. All of the American folk and period songs were in the public domain: "Oh! Dem Golden Slippers," by James K. Bland, "Early in de Mornin'," by William Shakespeare Hays, "Angelina Baker" and "Camptown Races" by Stephen Foster, and the traditional songs "Dandy Jim of Caroline," "Buffalo Gals," "Quadrille," "The Yellow Rose of Texas," "Little Brown Jug," "The Big Rock Candy Mountain," "Dixie," and "Poor Lonesome Cowboy." The astonishing cost for music clearances in a film with a substantial amount of source music was zero.

There was concern on the part of Warner's music department about increased costs for what was turning out to be a lengthy nondiegetic score. The producer, Bernard Smith, had initially hoped to minimize large orchestral cues and depend more upon "small orchestra" combinations, such as woodwinds and percussion.[15] North appears to have heeded Smith's advice (or was it a directive?), but he liked to paint with a big brush, and some cues were recorded by as many as fifty-seven players. The score was so lengthy that it took four days to record. Ensuring that the period music was in the public domain was at least one way to economize on music costs.

The Dodge City sequence, which features virtually all of the film's folk and period music, was among the first sequences to be shot, with the small ensemble that appears in the film, three banjo players and a piano player, recorded on the set over a period of two to three days in late September 1963. Wingate Smith, Ford's longtime associate and assistant director, specifically requested a "negro group."[16] Ford's recognition of the African American contribution to the settling of the West in *Sergeant Rutledge,* as well as his profound friendship with the actor who portrayed Rutledge, Woody Strode, had changed Ford, and the two westerns he made after Rutledge both feature African Americans. I cannot imagine that the request for a "negro group" to perform American folk and period music in *Cheyenne Autumn* came from anyone other than Ford.

Ultimately, the score of *Cheyenne Autumn* is a hybrid: some authentic Cheyenne chant, classical Hollywood wall-to-wall scoring, but employing a modernist idiom, and the distinctive folk and period songs omnipresent in Ford to the end. The last song to appear in a Ford film is "Shall We Gather at the River?" led by an American missionary and sung by Chinese schoolchildren in *7 Women,* Ford's final film. Could there have been a more appropriate coda, musical or otherwise, to his career?

Ken Curtis, one-time singing star of Sons of the Pioneers and member of the John Ford stock company, put it simply: "Ford liked having songs in his films."[17] In a studio system designed to limit his directorial signature, John Ford was able to exert control over the musical score, most profoundly through his selection of the songs that formed so central a part of his films. Ford's musical choices were strikingly original and deeply constitutive of filmic meaning in the westerns. The core of his principles—the privileging of song, the use of song and dance to bind the community on the frontier, and a dependence upon American folk song, hymnody, and period music—produced the distinctive scoring that I have described as Fordian. Song is deeply imbricated with the ideological content of Ford's films. Historically and culturally informed, Ford's musical choices function as a force field through which issues of race, ethnicity, gender, and national identity swirl. I do not believe that it is an overstatement to claim that Ford's musical choices are responsible, in large part, for the success and continued popularity of his films.

Unfortunately, much of the cultural context necessary to understand the ideological operation of the music has been elided. Who knew that "The Yellow Rose of Texas" is a minstrel song, or that the music accompanying the "Grand March" in *Fort Apache* is a Catholic hymn? A defining part of this book has been an argument, if only implicitly made, that Ford criticism and scholarship needs to refocus its lens to include the music. But that project only becomes possible through a commitment to putting the cultural context of Ford's films on the front burner, reconstructing the production and reception of these films within social, political, artistic, institutional, and economic frameworks.

Much of the cultural context attached to the music in Ford's films has been lost, but there is a powerful residue of recognition that remains, even today, in many of the songs Ford chose. *How the West Was Sung* is, I hope, a catchy title, but it was chosen at least partly because the geographic space of the American West is an important part of the power of song in Ford. Filmic westerns adopted a number of codes to signify the real. Costumes, settings, props, and historical references functioned as shorthand to the audience that the representations on the screen were historically accurate. Music, and especially song, may be the most powerful of those markers. When audiences recognized a song as western, or thought they did, the film seemed more genuine. But the use of period music in the filmic western is anything but simple. Many frontier songs are not western in the way that we have assumed them to be and are authentic only in a deeply complex way. Western songs trail in their wake a multifaceted discourse that helped to produce and continues to sustain powerful cultural fictions about the West, about America's defining relationship to it, and about American character, identity, and destiny. Much more work needs to be done into the sources of music's power as a historical marker and especially into song as a site of complicated definitions of authenticity. There is much left to be told in the story of how the West was sung.

Notes

INTRODUCTION

1. Tag Gallagher, *John Ford: The Man and His Films* (Berkeley: University of California Press, 1986), 55.

2. A list of monographs in English devoted to John Ford that refer to music would include Peter Bogdanovich, *John Ford* (Berkeley: University of California Press, 1968, rev. ed. 1978); John Baxter, *The Cinema of John Ford* (London: A. Zwemmer; New York: Barnes, 1971); Peter Stowell, *John Ford* (Boston: Twayne, 1986); Joseph McBride and Michael Wilmington, *John Ford* (London: Secker & Warburg, 1974; New York: Da Capo Press, 1975); Andrew Sarris, *The John Ford Movie Mystery* (Bloomington: University of Indiana Press, 1975); Lindsay Anderson, *About John Ford . . .* (New York: McGraw-Hill, 1983); Andrew Sinclair, *John Ford* (New York: Dial Press, 1979); Janey Place, *The Western Films of John Ford* (Secaucus, N.J.: Citadel Press, 1974); William Darby, *John Ford's Westerns: A Thematic Analysis with a Filmography* (Jefferson, N.C.: MacFarland, 1996); Brian Spittles, *John Ford* (New York: Longman, 2002); Scott Eyman, *John Ford: The Searcher, 1894–1973*, ed. Paul Duncan (Cologne: Taschen, 2004); and Peter Cowie, *John Ford and the American West* (New York: Abrams, 2004).

3. Claudia Gorbman, "Scoring the Indian: Music in the Liberal Western," in *Western Music and Its Others: Difference, Representation, and Appropriation in Music,* ed. Georgina Born and David Hesmondhalgh (Berkeley: University of California Press, 2000), 234–53, and in a revised version, "Drums along the L.A. River," in *Westerns: Films through History*, ed. Janet Walker (New York: Routledge, 2001), 177–96; K. J. Donnelly, "The Accented Voice: Ethnic Signposts of English, Irish, and American Film Music," in *The Spectre of Sound: Music in Film and Television* (London: British Film Institute; Berkeley: University of California Press, 2005), 55–87; William Darby, "Musical Links in *Young Mr. Lin-*

coln, *My Darling Clementine,* and *The Man Who Shot Liberty Valance,*" *Cinema Journal* 31, 1 (Fall 1991): 22–36; Lane Roth, "Folk Song Lyrics as Communication in John Ford's Films," *Southern Speech Communication Journal* 46 (Summer 1981): 390–96; and Edward Buscombe, *Stagecoach* (London: British Film Institute, 1992) and *The Searchers* (London: British Film Institute, 2000).

4. Kathryn Kalinak, "The Sound of Many Voices: Music in John Ford's Westerns," in *John Ford Made Westerns: Filming the Legend in the Sound Era,* ed. Gaylyn Studlar and Matthew Bernstein (Bloomington: Indiana University Press, 2001), 169–92, and "'Typically American': Music for *The Searchers,*" in *The Searchers: Essays and Reflections on John Ford's Classic Western,* ed. Arthur M. Eckstein and Peter Lehman (Detroit: Wayne State University Press, 2004), 109–44.

5. Dan Ford, *Pappy: The Life of John Ford* (Englewood Cliffs, N.J.: Prentice Hall, 1979; repr. New York: Da Capo Press, 1998); Joseph McBride, *Searching for John Ford* (New York: St. Martin's Press, 2001); Scott Eyman, *Print the Legend: The Life and Times of John Ford* (Baltimore: Johns Hopkins University Press, 1999); Ronald L. Davis, *John Ford: Hollywood's Old Master* (Norman: University of Oklahoma Press, 1995); and Gallagher, *John Ford.*

6. John Ford quoted in Walter Wagner, "One More Hurrah," in *John Ford Interviews,* ed. Gerald Peary (Jackson: University of Mississippi Press, 2001), 157.

1. HOW THE WEST WAS SUNG

1. Dan Ford told me (conversation in Portland, Maine, October 7, 2005) that Ford's brother, Frank, was supposed to have played the piano and may have played one of the pianos in the Ford household.

2. Dan Ford, interview with the author, Los Angeles, July 28, 2005.

3. Andrew Sarris, *The American Cinema: Directors and Directions 1929–1968* (New York: Dutton, 1968), 19, 43–49.

4. See, e.g., William Darby's *John Ford's Westerns: A Thematic Analysis with a Filmography* (Jefferson, N.C.: MacFarland, 1996).

5. Peter Wollen, "The Auteur Theory," in *Signs and Meaning in the Cinema* (Bloomington: Indiana University Press, 1969, 1972), 74–115.

6. A few additions of note: "Oh! Dem Golden Slippers," in *My Darling Clementine, The Man Who Shot Liberty Valance,* and *Cheyenne Autumn;* "The Monkeys Have No Tails in Zamboanga" in *Seas Beneath* and *They Were Expendable;* "Buffalo Gals," in *My Darling Clementine, Two Rode Together,* and *Cheyenne Autumn;* "Hail, Hail, the Gang's All Here" in *Steamboat Round the Bend, The Sun Shines Bright, The Last Hurrah, The Long Gray Line,* and *The Man Who Shot Liberty Valance;* "Camptown Races" in *My Darling Clementine, The Man Who Shot Liberty Valance,* and *Cheyenne Autumn;* "Four Little White Doves," "Carmela," "Little Brown Jug," and "Ring, Ring de Banjo" in *My Darling Clementine* and *The Man Who Shot Liberty Valance.*

7. John Ford quoted in George J. Mitchell, "Ford on Ford," in *John Ford Interviews,* ed. Gerard Peary (Jackson: University of Mississippi Press, 2001), 66.

8. John Ford quoted in Burt Kennedy, "A Talk with John Ford," *Action! The Magazine of the Director's Guild of America* 3, 5 (September–October 1968): 6.

9. There is virtually no mention of music in any of the James Warner Bellah stories that provided the source material for the cavalry trilogy (in the source story for *Rio Grande,* the Kirby Yorke prototype plays the violin, a detail not used in the Ford adaptation), or in Will Cook's *Comanche Captives,* the source for *Two Rode Together.* In the Cook novel, there are no specific references to music, although there is an informal dance with "the sound of music," some "off-key singing" from one of the characters, and a formal dance, obviously with music. See Will Cook, *Comanche Captives* (New York: Bantam Books, 1960), 25, 80. There are no references to music in Herman Whitaker's *Over the Border,* the source for *3 Bad Men,* Ernest Haycox's story "Stage to Lordsburg," the source for *Stagecoach,* Alan LeMay's *The Searchers,* or Dorothy Johnson's "The Man Who Shot Liberty Valance." Stuart Lake's biography, *Wyatt Earp, Frontier Marshall,* the source for *My Darling Clementine,* includes numerous references to saloons, dance halls, variety shows, gambling houses, touring theater companies, and the unidentified music that emanates from them, but refers specifically to only one piece of music: the opera *Stolen Kisses* performed in Abilene by the Lingard Opera Company. See Stuart N. Lake, *Wyatt Earp, Frontier Marshall* (Boston: Houghton Mifflin, 1931), 319. Howard Fast's *The Last Frontier* and Mari Sandoz's *Cheyenne Autumn,* the sources for *Cheyenne Autumn,* both contain references to Indian music-making, Sandoz to fictional Indian songs, all sung in English, and Fast to generic death chants. Typical of an "Indian" song from Sandoz is the following: "Eyia-ah-ah, Powers help us! / Powers that live in the winds of the storming! / In all the Great Directions, and in the earth and the sky, / Help us!" Mari Sandoz, *Cheyenne Autumn* (New York: Avon, 1953), 183. Peter B. Kyne's *The Three Godfathers* does describe one of the cowboys singing a lullabye to a newborn, but it is not "The Streets of Laredo," as in Ford's film *3 Godfathers.* "The Holy City" figures in the novel as it does in the Ford film when Hightower arrives in New Jerusalem. See Kyne, *The Three Godfathers* (New York: Cosmopolitan Press, 1922), 94–95.

10. Rick Altman, *Silent Film Sound* (New York: Columbia University Press, 2004), 372.

11. John Ford quoted in Axel Madsen, "Ford on Ford," in *John Ford Interviews,* ed. Peary, 84.

12. *Mother Machree,* which has not survived in its entirely, apparently contained both silent and sound sequences.

13. John Ford quoted in Peter Bogdanovich, *John Ford* (Berkeley: University of California Press, 1978), 99.

14. Robert Parrish quoted in Bogdanovich, *John Ford,* 9.

15. Harry Carey Jr. quoted in Dan Ford, *Pappy: The Life of John Ford* (New York: Da Capo Press, 1998), 222–23.

16. This is according to Harold Schuster, production assistant and film editor. See Kevin Brownlow, *The War, the West, and the Wilderness* (New York: Knopf, 1978), 388.

17. *Fox Folks Junior* 1, 3 (January 5, 1924), unpaginated, John Ford Archive, Lilly Library, Indiana University.

18. *Fox Folks Junior* 1, 15 (January 15, 1924), unpaginated, John Ford Archive.

19. Maureen O'Hara quoted in review of *'Tis Herself, Newsweek,* June 28, 1999, 49.

20. Rudy Behlmer, *America's Favorite Movies: Behind the Scenes* (New York: Frederick Ungar, 1982), 116.

21. Pippa Scott in the 2006 PBS *American Masters* television documentary *John Ford / John Wayne: The Filmmaker and the Legend.*

22. John Wayne in the documentary *Directed by John Ford,* written and directed by Peter Bogdanovich (1971, revised 2006).

23. Borzage also appears on screen briefly in *My Darling Clementine,* in a scene cut from the final release print but remaining in the preview version.

24. John Ford Phonograph Disk Collection, Brigham Young University.

25. Patrick Ford quoted in James D'Arc, "What's in a Name: The John Ford Music Collection at Brigham Young University," *Cue Sheet* 5 (1988), 115.

26. A variant of "Oh, Bury Me Not on the Lone Prairie."

27. Dan Ford, interview with the author, Los Angeles, July 28, 2005.

2. HEARING THE MUSIC IN FORD'S SILENTS

1. Edwin L. Sabin, *Building the Pacific Railway* (Philadelphia: Lippincott, 1919), 13.

2. Robert Louis Stevenson, *Across the Plains* (New York: Scribner, 1900), 49–50.

3. I use the term "Native American" when referring to America's indigenous population but "Indian" when referring to the representation Hollywood created for them. As Richard Maltby so succinctly puts it: "In the Hollywood western, there are no 'real' Indians . . . only Hollywood Indians." See Maltby, "A Better Sense of History: John Ford and the Indians," in *The Book of Westerns,* ed. Ian Cameron and Douglas Pye (New York: Continuum, 1996), 35.

4. The Fox Pictures souvenir program "William Fox Presents *The Iron Horse*" states that railroads employed 5 percent of American workers in the 1920s; Norm Cohen, *Long Steel Rail: The Railroad in American Folksong* (Urbana: University of Illinois Press, 1981), 6, says it was one out of every twenty-eight workers.

5. See Lynne Kirby, "National Identity in the Train Film," in *Parallel Tracks: The Railroad and Silent Cinema* (Durham, N.C.: Duke University Press, 1996), 189–219.

6. Train use crested in 1920, when Americans rode the rails an average of 445 miles per year. By 1970, that number had declined to 77 miles per year, about one-sixth of the 1920 total. See Cohen, *Long Steel Rail,* 5, 14.

7. Ford's film *The Iron Horse* pulled in profits of over two million dollars.

8. George J. Mitchell, "Ford on Ford," *Films in Review* 15, 6 (July–August 1964), 329. Even late in life, Ford continued to confirm the story about having torn ten pages out of the script for *The Iron Horse,* saying: "It's all true."

9. Ibid., 329.

10. The *Los Angeles Times,* March 9, 1925, called *The Iron Horse* Ford's "crowning triumph"; quoted in souvenir program "William Fox Presents *The Iron Horse.*"

11. Dan Ford, *Pappy: The Life of John Ford* (New York: Da Capo Press, 1998), 34.

12. For a survey of railroad fiction, see Frank Donovan Jr., *The Railroad in Literature* (Boston: Railway and Locomotive Historical Society, Baker Library, Harvard Business School, 1940).

13. Among many parallel incidents in the novel and film is the one in which the young surveyor is almost killed when he is lowered by rope down a ravine. In the novel, the rope breaks; in the film, it is cut; in both, the protagonist's fall is broken by a tree. See Zane Grey, *The U.P. Trail* (New York: Harper and Brothers, 1918).

14. John Ford quoted in Mitchell, "Ford on Ford," 328.

15. Ibid., 327–28.

16. Ibid., 327.

17. Dan Ford told me that he didn't believe the Uncle Mike story either.

18. Also contestable is the meaning of the key word: "tarriers," in Casey's version, "terriers" in Ford's. Does "tarriers" refer to laggards slowing down the work pace and hence exhorted to work more quickly or does it refer to terriers, dogs known for their digging abilities. Both seem to work in the context of the song.

19. Maxwell F. Marcuse, *Tin Pan Alley in Gaslight: A Saga of the Songs That Made the Gray Nineties "Gay"* (Watkins Glen, N.Y.: Century House, 1959), 84.

20. Cohen, *Long Steel Rail,* 555.

21. See Zane Grey, *U.P. Trail,* 192, 247, 381, 389.

22. Griffith co-wrote the love theme for *Birth of a Nation* with the composer Joseph Carl Breuil.

23. That new score was composed by none other than Erno Rapee. See Richard Fehr and Frederick G. Vogel, *Lullabies of Hollywood: Movie Music and the Movie Musical, 1915–1922* (Jefferson, N.C.: MacFarland, 1993), 10.

24. According to an undated, untitled contemporaneous review, Chamberlin scrapbooks, Margaret Herrick Library, Academy of Motion Picture Arts and Sciences.

25. B. Heggie and R. L. Taylor, "Idea Flourisher," *New Yorker* 19 (February 5, 1944), 32.

26. "Erno Rapee, 55, Dies; Conductor at Music Hall," *New York Herald Tribune,* June 27, 1945, 16.

27. Heggie and Taylor, "Idea Flourisher," 34.

28. Ibid., 32.

29. Ibid., 32.

30. Rapee's work during this period also includes other Ford scores: the 1925 reissue of *Straight Shooting, Mother Machree,* and a song for *Four Sons.* He is also credited as musical director for *Riley the Cop,* although S. L. "Roxy" Ropthafel is credited with the musical arrangements.

31. James D'Arc, archivist at BYU, reported that a copy of the score existed as a "12-record set of the original score for Ford's 1924 epic, *The Iron Horse,* played by the Grauman's Theatre Orchestra in Los Angeles." That report proved incorrect. See D'Arc, "What's In a Name: The John Ford Music Collection at Brigham Young University," *Cue Sheet* 5 (1988): 116. What BYU holds is a two-

disk set entitled "Echoes of *The Iron Horse*," totaling 6:23 minutes of music which is very likely a recording of the music for the stage show that preceded the film's Los Angeles premiere.

32. The titles included on the disks are: "Turkey in the Straw," "When Johnny Comes Marching Home," "Pop! Goes the Weasel," "Old Black Joe," "Listen to the Mockingbird," "Columbia, the Gem of the Ocean," "Dixie," "Old Folks at Home," and "Yankee Doodle Dandy."

33. Paul Murray, "Erno Rapee: Musical Educator," *Musical Courier*, January 3, 1929, 39.

34. Reviews of *The Iron Horse*, *New York Times*, August 29, 1924; *Variety*, September 3, 1924.

35. Undated review of *The Iron Horse*, Chamberlin scrapbooks, Academy of Motion Picture Arts and Sciences.

36. Review of *The Iron Horse*, *Film Daily*, September 7, 1924.

37. "The Iron Horse, #2" (undated and unpaginated scenario).

38. *The Covered Wagon* does the same with "Oh! Susannah."

39. "The Iron Horse, #2."

40. In the British release print, Private Schultz is renamed Private MacKay.

41. Thomas Flanagan, "The Irish in John Ford's Films," in *The Irish in America*, ed. Michael Coffey (New York: Hyperion, 1997), n.p.

42. Sabin, *Building the Pacific Railway*, 111.

43. Kevin Brownlow, *The War, the West, and the Wilderness* (New York: Knopf, 1978), 245, 273n.

44. "The Iron Horse, #2."

45. Ibid.

46. Sabin, *Building the Pacific Railway*, 297.

47. According to Harold Schuster, "Indian teepees encamped on the left of the town towards the mountains. They were the real thing, and the various nations brought their own. The Chinese were housed in tents back of the town. But most of the cast were housed in the circus train." Quoted in Brownlow, *War, the West, and the Wilderness*, 388.

48. In the British release print, Deroux is renamed Bauman.

49. Zane Grey, *U.P. Trail*, 409.

50. Virginia Wright Wexman, *Creating the Couple: Love, Marriage, and Hollywood Performance* (Princeton: Princeton University Press, 1993), 88.

51. Quinn Martin, undated review of *3 Bad Men*, Chamberlin scrapbooks, Academy of Motion Picture Arts and Sciences.

52. Review of *3 Bad Men*, *New York Times*, August 29, 1924.

53. Undated unidentified review of *3 Bad Men*, Lilly Archive, *3 Bad Men* file.

54. The property master Lefty Hough, standing just out of the camera's range on the running board of a car poised to take off, was supposed to grab the baby. He quickly devised a backup plan: if he couldn't grab the baby in time, or if he couldn't grab the baby at all, he would fall near the tot and use his body to shield it from the onslaught!

55. Quoted in Brownlow, *War, the West, and the Wilderness*, 392.

56. See Joseph McBride, *Searching for John Ford* (New York: St. Martin's Press, 2001), 157.

57. Erno Rapee was back in the United States by 1928 and working again in musical accompaniment. He would eventually become the resident conductor at Radio City Music Hall.

58. Jean Mitry, "The Birth of Style," trans. William T. Conroy Jr., *Wide Angle* 2, 4 (1978): 7.

59. Theodore Roosevelt, *Ranch Life and the Hunting Trail* (1888; reprint, Lincoln: University of Nebraska Press, 1983), 100.

60. Ibid., 6.

61. Gaylyn Studlar, *This Mad Masquerade: Stardom and Masculinity in the Jazz Age* (New York: Columbia University Press, 1996), 8.

62. Miriam Hansen, *Babel and Babylon: Spectatorship in American Silent Film* (Cambridge, Mass.: Harvard University Press, 1991), 254.

63. *New York Daily Mirror,* November 7, 1934.

64. *Women Have Been Kind: The Memoirs of Lou Tellegen* (New York: Vanguard Press, 1931) is unfortunately out of print. The *New York Daily Mirror,* however, serialized it after Tellegen died by his own hand in 1934. Dorothy Parker is supposed to have suggested that *of Dumb* be added to the title.

65. Quoted in *New York Daily Mirror,* November 19, 1934.

66. "I shall never marry, I never intended to marry," Geraldine Farrar is quoted as saying. "I am old-fashioned enough to think that a woman should be subordinate to her husband, and I must have freedom or I can't work." Sumiko Higashi, *Cecil B. DeMille and American Culture: The Silent Era* (Berkeley: University of California Press, 1994), 136.

67. *New York Daily Mirror,* November 2, 1934.

68. Burt A. Folkart, "Athlete and Film Actor George O'Brien, 86, Dies," *Los Angeles Times,* September 8, 1985.

69. *Daily Telephone,* August 1, 1927.

70. The studio claimed that George O'Brien did all his own stunts; he didn't, although he did perform all of them in *The Iron Horse.*

71. Fox Pictures souvenir program "William Fox Presents *The Iron Horse.*"

72. Herman Whitaker, *Over the Border* (New York: Harper & Brothers, 1917).

3. "BASED ON AMERICAN FOLK SONGS"

1. That George Antheil's score for *The Plainsman* foreshadows *Stagecoach*'s in some key respects (its selective use of folk tunes, reliance upon the banjo, an archetypal western instrument, and incorporation of some folk harmonies) suggests the powerful pull of Americana in scoring westerns. Antheil, a modernist and the self-proclaimed "bad boy of music," whose *Ballet mécanique* (1924) called inter alia for sixteen player pianos, four bass drums, three xylophones, a tam-tam, seven electric bells, a siren, and three airplane propellers, was one of a number of serious art composers lured to Hollywood in the 1930s. The sequence in *The Plainsman* where the supply train is attacked by Indians displays Antheil's modernist idiom. Antheil's score for *The Plainsman* seems not to have generated a great deal of attention (it wasn't, for instance, nominated for an Academy Award), and Antheil did not continue to score westerns. Although he was ini-

tially assigned to *Union Pacific,* another DeMille western, Antheil did not complete the score, although he composed some music for it. (DeMille apparently was displeased.) By 1939, the year of *Stagecoach,* Antheil had left Hollywood to return to the concert hall. He would resume his Hollywood career after the war but not in westerns.

2. Scott Simmon estimates that there were 50 A westerns produced during the 1930s compared to over 1,000 B westerns; Edward Buscombe puts the numbers slightly differently: between 1930 and 1941, he finds 66 A westerns out of a total of 1,336 produced during the period. By anyone's count, A westerns represented a minuscule proportion of the production of westerns in the era. See Scott Simmon, *The Invention of the Western Film: A Cultural History of the Genre's First Half-Century* (Cambridge: Cambridge University Press, 2003), 100, 315n2, and Edward Buscombe, "The Western: A Short History," in *The BFI Companion to the Western,* ed. id. (New York: Atheneum, 1988), 39.

3. Paul Rosenfeld, "'Americanism' in American Music," *Modern Music* 17, 4 (1940): 226.

4. See Krin Gabbard, *Jammin' at the Margins: Jazz and the American Cinema* (Chicago: University of Chicago Press, 1996), 8–19.

5. Louis Gruenberg quoted in Robert F. Nisbett, "Louis Gruenberg's American Idiom," *American Music* 3, 1 (Spring 1985): 25.

6. Even in the silent era, jazz did not seem to be particularly well suited to westerns. Erno Rapee, conductor in residence at the Fox flagship theater in Philadelphia, who composed a score for *The Iron Horse,* experimented with jazz as an accompaniment to Fox's westerns, but feedback from both audiences and William Fox was apparently negative. See B. Heggie and R. L. Taylor, "Idea Flourisher," *New Yorker* 19 (February 5, 1944): 34.

7. See Timothy E. Scheurer, *Born in the U.S.A.: The Myth of America in Popular Music from Colonial Times to the Present* (Jackson: University Press of Mississippi, 1991), 147.

8. Beth E. Levy, "'The White Hope of American Music': or, How Roy Harris Became Western," *American Music* 19, 2 (Summer 2001): 149.

9. Virgil Thomson, *American Music since 1910* (New York: Holt, Rinehart & Winston, 1970), 16.

10. Roy Harris studied with the famed Nadia Boulanger in Paris during the 1920s.

11. Levy, "White Hope of American Music," 151.

12. Missing from this list is Charles Ives, whose important work using American hymnody and folksong predates the work of American composers in the 1930s by decades. Ives was not recognized until much later in life, however, more or less after he had given up composing, and his music was not a major influence during the 1930s.

13. Peter Stanfield, *Horse Opera: The Strange History of the Singing Cowboy* (Urbana: University of Illinois Press, 2002), 154.

14. Ibid., 57.

15. Aaron Copland, *Our New Music* (New York: McGraw-Hill, 1941), 260.

16. Inasmuch as anyone produced for Ford; generally, Ford produced his own films and Wanger was fairly "hands off" on *Stagecoach.*

17. *New York Post,* January 24, 1939.

18. Rudy Behlmer comes to the same conclusion in *America's Favorite Movies: Behind the Scenes* (New York: Frederick Ungar, 1982), 117.

19. Gruenberg quoted in Robert F. Nisbett, "Louis Gruenberg: His Life and Work" (Ph.D. diss., Ohio State University 1979), 65.

20. Roy Prendergast, *Film Music: A Neglected Art* (New York: Norton, 1977), 29.

21. A rough approximation of the contributions of each composer, as indicated by the Paramount cue sheet, is as follows: Leipold, 17 minutes; Shuken, 11; Carbonara, 10; Harling, 7; Hageman, 4 1/2; Pasternacki, 6 1/2.

22. The rules regulating nominations for Academy Awards during this period were byzantine. The studios themselves made the nominations in the music categories and were supposed to poll the musicians in their employ in order to arrive at a nominee. Each studio was limited to one nomination in each of two categories: Best Original Score (scores with "primary emphasis on original composition") and Best Scoring (scores chosen "without regard to the source of the music"). *Stagecoach* was nominated in the latter category by Walter Wanger himself. Nominations came from the studio, not individual producers, but Wanger argued that this was a special case, since neither Walter Wanger Productions nor United Artists had a music department. Wanger nominated Hageman, Harling, Leipold, and Shuken. Gruenberg's name is not included in the nominating letter, most likely an oversight.

23. See Kathryn Kalinak, "How the West Was Sung," in *Westerns: Films Through History,* ed. Janet Walker (New York: Routledge, 2001), 151–76. Peter Stanfield reaches the same conclusion in "Country Music and the 1939 Western," in *The Book of Westerns,* ed. Ian Cameron and Douglas Pye (New York: Continuum, 1996), 33, although he deals with *Drums Along the Mohawk* not *Stagecoach.*

24. There are many variants of this song title: "Bury Me Not on the Lone Prairie," "O Bury Me Not on the Lone Prairie," and the one John Ford owned in his record collection, "Bury Me Out on the Lone Prairie." It is also sometimes referred to as "The Dying Cowboy." Richard Hageman referred to it as "O Bury Me Not on the Lone Prairie."

25. Foster almost went broke trying to break out of blackface according to Ken Emerson, *Doo-Dah! Stephen Foster and the Rise of American Popular Culture* (New York: Da Capo Press, 1998), 174.

26. See John Quincy Wolf, "Who Wrote Joe Bowers?" *Western Folklore* 29, 2 (1970): 77–89. Typical of so many minstrel songs, "Joe Bowers" has acquired a historical patina and is frequently cited as a Texas folk song or a traditional Gold Rush tune. "Joe Bowers" might indeed have been sung by miners in California (and it was a favorite of Confederate soldiers), but its folk heritage seems highly suspect for a number of reasons. While the actual origins of the song are lost, musicologists now point to a much more likely source: minstrel troupes touring the West in the 1850s, possibly Johnson's Pennsylvanian minstrels, in whose published songbook "Joe Bowers" first appears.

27. There is no record that "I Love You" was used by any of *Stagecoach's* composers. In fact, one of them, Leo Shuken, signed an affidavit claiming its au-

thorship (itself a bit fishy). Still, I feel confident in stating that the chorus of "I Love You" was the inspiration and very possibly the direct source for Dallas and Ringo's love theme. It wouldn't be the first time or the last that studio music departments infringed on copyright.

28. See Edward Buscombe, *Stagecoach* (London: British Film Institute, 1991), 48; Behlmer, *America's Favorite Movies*, 117.

29. Rudy Behlmer generously shared information with me about the score for *Stagecoach* and brought the Carson Robison song to my attention.

30. Richard Hageman, *She Wore A Yellow a Yellow Ribbon,* RKO Music Archive, UCLA.

31. Gary Wills, *John Wayne's America* (New York: Simon & Schuster, 1997), 78.

32. Joseph Kerman quoted in *Ethnicity, Identity, and Music: The Musical Construction of Place,* ed. Martin Stokes (Providence, R.I.: Berg, 1994), 1.

33. Caryl Flinn, *Strains of Utopia: Gender, Nostalgia, and Hollywood Film Music* (Princeton: Princeton University Press, 1992), 9.

34. Bruno David Ussher, review of *Stagecoach* in the *Hollywood Spectator,* February 18, 1939, 17.

35. *New York Post,* January 24, 1939.

36. Gaylyn Studlar, "Class, Gender, and Frontier Democracy in *Stagecoach,*" in *John Ford's Stagecoach,* ed. Barry Keith Grant (New York: Cambridge University Press, 2003), 134.

37. Tag Gallagher, *John Ford: The Man and His Films* (Berkeley: University of California Press, 1986), 150.

38. Ibid.

39. Peter Stowell, *John Ford* (Boston: Twayne, 1986), 106, and Joseph W. Reed, *Three American Originals: John Ford, William Faulkner, Charles Ives* (Middletown, Conn.: Wesleyan University Press, 1984), 120.

40. John A. Lomax and Alan Lomax, *Cowboy Songs and Other Frontier Ballads,* rev. ed. (New York: Macmillan, 1938), 114. "Ten Thousand Cattle" does not appear in John Lomax's original 1910 edition, and when it did appear in 1938, Lomax credited the song to Margaret Larkin's *Singing Cowboy* (New York: Knopf, 1931), 151.

41. Several sources argue that Wister may have based the song upon folk ballads circulating in the northern Plains states in the years following the notorious winter of 1886–87, which killed thousands of cattle. But if Wister borrowed "Ten Thousand Cattle," he also copyrighted it, and it is Wister's version of the song that made its way into several folk collections, including Lomax's. For the thorny history of Wister's song, see Jim Bob Tinsley, *He Was Singin' This Song* (Orlando: University Presses of Florida, 1981), 88–91; Glenn Ohrlin, *The Hell-Bound Train: A Cowboy Songbook* (Urbana: University of Illinois Press, 1973), 15–17; and John I. White, *Git Along, Little Dogies: Songs and Songmakers of the American West* (Urbana: University of Illinois Press, 1975), 27–37.

42. Dudley Nichols, final revised screenplay for *Stagecoach,* November 11, 1938. Walter Wanger Collection, Wisconsin Center for Film and Theater Research, Madison.

43. Matthew Bernstein, *Walter Wanger, Hollywood Independent* (Berkeley: University of California Press, 1994), 149.

44. That fee for permission to use "Ten Thousand Cattle" was initially $2,500.

45. K. J. Donnelly, *The Spectre of Sound: Music in Film and Television* (London: British Film Institute, 2005), 57. See also Georgina Born and David Hesmondhalgh, eds., *Western Music and Its Others: Difference, Representation, and Appropriation in Music* (Berkeley: University of California Press, 2000), esp. the Introduction, 1–58.

46. Michael Pisani, "'I'm an Indian, too': Creating Native American Identities in Nineteenth- and Early Twentieth-Century Music," in *The Exotic in Western Music,* ed. Jonathan Bellman (Boston: Northeastern University Press, 1998), 218–57.

47. Claudia Gorbman, "Scoring the Indian: Music in the Liberal Western," in *Western Music and Its Others,* ed. Born and Hesmondhalgh, 234–53; Pisani, 220–33.

48. See Pisani, "I'm an Indian, too," 231.

49. Gorbman, "Scoring the Indian," 236.

50. Ibid.

51. Ibid.

52. Charles Ramirez Berg, "The Margin as Center: The Multicultural Dynamics of John Ford's Westerns," in *John Ford Made Westerns: Filming the Legend in the Sound Era,* ed. Matthew Bernstein and Gaylyn Studlar (Bloomington: Indiana University Press, 2001), 75.

53. J. P. Tellote, "'A Little Bit Savage': *Stagecoach* and Racial Representation," in *John Ford's Stagecoach,* ed. Grant, 125.

54. Buscombe, *Stagecoach,* 54.

55. Ibid. Buscombe's translation.

56. *Stagecoach,* final continuity screenplay, n.d., n.p.

57. Berg, "Margin as Center," 76.

4. TWO FORDIAN FILM SCORES

1. I am not the first to pair *My Darling Clementine* and *The Man Who Shot Liberty Valance.* Several Ford critics have done so, largely reading the latter as a cynical revision of the former's frontier mythos. See, e.g., Joseph McBride and Michael Wilmington, *John Ford* (1974; New York: Da Capo Press, 1975), 180; Joseph McBride, *Searching for John Ford* (New York: St. Martin's Press, 2001), 631–32; Peter Stowell, *John Ford* (Boston: Twayne, 1986), 95–120; Jon Tuska, *The Filming of the West* (Garden City, N.Y.: Doubleday, 1976), 515; Mike Yawn and Bob Beatty, "John Ford's Vision of the Closing West: From Optimism to Cynicism," *Film & History* 26, 1–4 (1996): 6–7, 10; Scott Simmon, *The Invention of the Western: A Cultural History of the Genre's First Half-Century* (Cambridge: Cambridge University Press, 2003), 136–37.

2. The country fiddle and the guitar were associated with the West, and the accordion (played by Danny Borzage, of course) was close to hand.

3. "Buffalo Gals" was performed by Cool White, who published the song under his own name in 1844.

4. Alfred Newman, letter to John Ford, November 16, 1945, John Ford Archive, Lily Library, Indiana University. Contacting Newman directly seems to have been Ford's usual practice. According to correspondence at Lilly Library, Ford did the same for *When Willie Comes Marching Home* (1950). Daryl F. Zanuck, letter to John Ford, November 17, 1949.

5. Press book for *My Darling Clementine*, n.p.

6. Dan Ford, in conversation with the author, July 28, 2005.

7. See esp. Stowell, *John Ford*, 106, and Joseph W. Reed, *Three American Originals: John Ford, William Faulkner, Charles Ives* (Middletown, Conn.: Wesleyan University Press, 1984), 119.

8. Lindsay Anderson, *About John Ford* . . . (New York: McGraw-Hill, 1981), 114.

9. See, e.g., Paul Giles, "John Ford and Robert Altman: The Cinema of Catholicism," in *Unspeakable Images: Ethnicity and the American Cinema,* ed. Lester D. Friedman (Urbana: University of Illinois Press), 140–66.

10. See Reed, *Three American Originals,* 20–21, for more on the religious symbolism of "Shall We Gather at the River?"

11. *The Play-party in Indiana: A Collection of Folk-songs and Games,* ed. Leah Jackson Wolford (Indianapolis: Indiana Historical Commission, 1916), 2.

12. Ford used at least some of the traditional play-party pattern for "The Cuckoo Waltz" in *Young Mr. Lincoln* when dancers cross hands and circle the dance floor changing partners with each cross.

13. This version was arranged by Arthur Kingsley and J. E. Jonasson.

14. "Nelly Bly" was composed by Stephen Foster for the minstrel stage, but like many sentimental minstrel ballads, it is quite different from the standard minstrel song. With the exception of the dialect, "Nelly Bly" could pass as a parlor song of the period.

15. Simmon, *Invention of the Western,* 265.

16. Darryl F. Zanuck quoted in *Memo from Darryl F. Zanuck: The Golden Years at Twentieth Century-Fox,* ed. Rudy Behlmer (New York: Grove Press 1993), 104.

17. The DVD release of *My Darling Clementine* from Twentieth Century–Fox "Studio Classics" contains both versions of the film, the preview and the final release version as well as a comparison of the two by Robert Gitt of the UCLA Film and Television Archive, who supervised the restoration.

18. See, e.g., Joseph McBride who argues that the film's revisionist impulse "ruthlessly exposes the mythmaking apparatus that underlies much of the history and much of the director's own work in the Western genre"; or Scott Eyman, who writes: "in *Liberty Valance,* he begins with myth and methodically dismantles it on the way to a mournful irony." Or Yawn and Beatty who describe the film as a "bitter statement about the price of progress." See McBride, *Searching for John Ford,* 633; Scott Eyman, *Print the Legend: The Life and Times of John Ford* (Baltimore: Johns Hopkins University Press, 1999), 491; Yawn and Beatty, "John Ford's Vision," 14.

19. Stowell, *John Ford,* 108, McBride, *Searching for John Ford,* 626.

20. Dan Ford, *Pappy: The Life of John Ford* (New York: Da Capo Press, 1998), 292

21. Eyman, *Print the Legend,* 69.

22. William Darby has written an interesting analysis of the connections between these films in "Musical Links in *Young Mr. Lincoln, My Darling Clementine,* and *The Man Who Shot Liberty Valance*," *Cinema Journal* 31, 1 (Fall 1991): 22–36.

23. Cyril Mockridge is also credited with the scores of Ford's *Judge Priest, The Prisoner of Shark Island, Wee Willie Winkie* (1937), and *Donovan's Reef* (1963).

24. The second, revisionary shootout sequence, this time narrated by Tom, does contain music, and here Mockridge pulls out all the stops: stingers, tremolo strings, vibraphone, and an accordion solo by Danny Borzage.

25. Given that Arizona was formally declared a territory in 1863 (and a state in 1912), the songs Ford chose are not historically accurate, not the first or the last time Ford would ignore history in choosing songs. "The Gang's All Here" became popular during World War I, "(There'll Be) A Hot Time in the Old Town Tonight" was composed in 1886, and "Home on the Range" wasn't generally known until the 1920s. Ford didn't care. The songs worked to bring specific meaning to the convention sequence, and dramatic necessity was always more important to Ford than historical verisimilitude.

26. "The Gang's All Here" is a reworking of a song from Gilbert and Sullivan's *Pirates of Penzance* (1879), itself a parody of the Anvil Chorus from Verdi's *Il Trovatore* (1853). The version we know today was first published in 1917 with new lyrics by D. A. Estron and music credited to Theodore Morse and Arthur Sullivan.

27. In 1934, an injunction against the performance of "Home on the Range" was issued as part of a federal lawsuit brought by William and Mary Goodwin, who alleged that they had written and published the song in 1904. Other would-be progenitors popped up and numerous variants surfaced. The lawyer representing the Music Publishers Protection Association, Samuel Moanfeldt, was able to trace all published versions to Lomax's 1910 anthology, with the exception of the Goodwins', whose publication preceded Lomax. For a while it looked good for the Goodwins. But they were eventually to drop the suit when Moanfeldt produced a "Home on the Range" written by Brewster Higley, an Ohio-born minister, and set to music by Dan Kelley, a Rhode Islander, in 1873, which preceded the Goodwins' 1904 publication date.

28. On the history of "Home on the Range," see Jim Bob Tinsley, *He Was Singin' This Song* (Orlando: University Presses of Florida, 1981), 212–15; John I. White, *Git Along, Little Dogies: Songs and Songmakers of the American West* (Urbana: University of Illinois Press, 1975), 153–66; and Kirke Mechem, "Home on the Range," *Kansas Historical Quarterly* 17, 4 (November 1949): 313–39.

29. John Wayne netted $750,000 from *The Man Who Shot Liberty Valance,* plus a percentage of gross profits.

30. Dan Ford, *Pappy,* 292.

31. Peter Bogdanovich, *John Ford* (Berkeley: University of California Press, 1968, rev. ed. 1978), 99.

32. Ford added the character of the African-American Pompey. In the original source story by Dorothy M. Johnson, there are no African Americans, and the Doniphon character, Bert Barricune, has no servant. Ford's awakening interest in the place of both African Americans and Indians in histories of the West is more centrally featured in films such as *The Searchers, Sergeant Rutledge,* and *Cheyenne Autumn,* but Pompey in *The Man Who Shot Liberty Valance,* played by Woody Strode, who had starred so memorably in *Sergeant Rutledge* two years earlier, indicates Ford's intention to redress the historical elision of African Americans.

33. Bogdanovich, *John Ford,* 34.

5. "WESTERN AS HELL"

1. Quoted in Harry Carey Jr., *Company of Heroes: My Life as an Actor in the John Ford Stock Company* (Lanham, Md.: Madison Books, 1996), 90.

2. *The Quiet Man* and *The Sun Shines Bright* would be Ford's final Argosy productions.

3. Richard Hagemen, letter to John Ford, October 2, 1946, John Ford Archive, Lilly Library, Indiana University.

4. Ibid. Hageman to Ford. Between *The Long Voyage Home* and *Angel and the Badman,* Hageman has only two score credits: *Paris Calling* (Edwin L. Marin, 1941) and *The Shanghai Gesture* (Josef von Sternberg, 1941), and one song credit: *This Woman Is Mine* (1941). However, he contributed to dozens of other films uncredited.

5. After working on *Stagecoach,* Gruenberg scored a documentary for Pare Lorentz, *The Fight for Life,* and completed a couple of freelance scores, among them *So Ends Our Night* (John Cromwell, 1941), *Commandos Strike at Dawn* (John Jarrow, 1942), *An American Romance* (King Vidor, 1944), *Counter-Attack* (Zoltan Korda, 1945), and *Arch of Triumph* (Lewis Milestone, 1948). His work on many other films was uncredited.

6. Hageman, letter to Ford, October 2, 1946, John Ford Archive

7. Donald Dewar, letter to Floyd Henrickson, May 6, 1948, Argosy Pictures Archive, Brigham Young University.

8. Jester Hairston was told that a studio executive said: "Who the hell ever heard of n—— singing Russian music." According to Hairston, it was Dimitri Tiomkin who "forced the producers to relent." See Henry Wiencek, *The Hairstons: An American Story in Black and White* (New York: St. Martin's Press, 1999), 222.

9. It was Hairston who arranged and sang "Amen" for Sidney Poitier in *Lilies of the Field.* In later life, he enjoyed a successful career as an actor. On television, he is best known for his recurring role in the 1980s sitcom *Amen.*

10. In 1960, Hairston appeared with John Wayne in *The Alamo,* playing Jethro. Perhaps this is why he was tied up and not available to direct the choir for *Sergeant Rutledge.*

11. These terms refer to techniques for starting and stopping musical cues without drawing the audience's conscious attention to them, such as beginning or ending cues at low volume, under lines of dialogue, or with distracting on-screen movements or loud sound effects.

12. Richard Hageman, musical sketches for *3 Godfathers,* Cinema-Television Library, USC.

13. Peter B. Kyne, *The Three Godfathers* (1913; New York: Cosmopolitan Books, 1922), 65.

14. Ford even sent staffers scurrying to find recordings of "The Yellow Rose of Texas." Meta Sterne, telegram to Mrs. George Stafford, February 11, 1948, John Ford Archive.

15. His name is spelled Kearny in the source novel.

16. Kyne, *Three Godfathers,* 54.

17. Bob Hightower is Bob Sangster in the source novel; Ford renamed him after one of his favorite stunt men.

18. Francis Henry Maynard quoted in Jim Hoy, "F. H. Maynard, Author of 'The Cowboy's Lament,'" *Mid-America Folklore* 21, 2 (Fall 1993): 61.

19. Thanks to Jim Hoy for this information in correspondence with the author.

20. Carey, *Company of Heroes,* 33.

21. Ibid.

22. Richard Hageman, sketches for *3 Godfathers,* Richard Hageman scores, USC.

23. "Silent Night" was written by a young Catholic priest, with the melody supplied by his music teacher, Franz Guber.

24. "Hark! The Herald Angels Sing" was actually created by William Cummings, who linked the previously composed melody by Mendelssohn to previously written lyrics by Charles Wesley, brother of John Wesley, founder of the Methodist Church.

25. Kyne, *Three Godfathers,* 94–95.

26. Michael Maybrick, a concert singer, who wrote under the pen name Stephen Adams, is credited with the lyrics of "The Holy City," and Frederick E. Weatherly, a London barrister, with the music.

27. According to Krin Gabbard, it was Bubber Miley who appropriated "The Holy City" for "Black and Tan Fantasy," which he co-wrote with Ellington in 1926. The song had become a part of American church music in this country, and it seems likely that Miley heard it first in this context. "Black and Tan Fantasy" was a hit for the Ellington band in 1927, and Ellington played it frequently thereafter at dance concerts and in radio broadcasts. It is interesting to speculate on whether Ford or Hageman heard it played by Ellington. Thanks to Krin Gabbard for this information.

28. Stephen Adams (Michael Maybrick), lyrics, "The Holy City" (1892).

29. Another Mormon migration, to the San Juan Valley in southeastern Utah in 1880, forms the basis of *Wagon Master.*

30. "Rock of Ages" does appear in Ford's World War II documentary, *December 7th.*

31. Quoted in Peter Bogdanovich, *John Ford* (Berkeley: University of California Press, 1978), 108.

32. Carey, *Company of Heroes,* 2, 4.

33. Scott Eyman, *Print the Legend: The Life and Times of John Ford* (Baltimore: Johns Hopkins University Press, 1999), 370.

34. Quoted in Bogdanovich, *John Ford,* 88.

35. Carey, *Company of Heroes,* 90.

36. George O'Brien had starred in many Ford silent and early sound era films, including *The Iron Horse* and *3 Bad Men.* After a reconciliation with Ford, prompted by his wife, he went on to appear in *Fort Apache, She Wore Yellow Ribbon,* and *Cheyenne Autumn.*

37. Carey, *Company of Heroes,* 92.

38. Ford quoted in ibid., 93.

39. In *3 Godfathers,* Sons of the Pioneers were augmented with the Bob Mitchell Choirboys. Donald Dewar, letters to Bicknell Lockhart, April 6 and August 1, 1950, Argosy Archive.

40. For a reliable history of Sons of the Pioneers, see Ken Griffis, *Hear My Song: The Story of the Celebrated Sons of the Pioneers* (Los Angeles: UCLA Folklore and Mythology Center, 1974).

41. Instead, Sons of the Pioneers joined Roy Rogers on the soundtrack of the "Pecos Bill" section of Disney's *Melody Time* (1948).

42. Correspondence from Stan Jones to John Ford included the song lyrics for the three songs Jones wrote for *3 Godfathers.* Stan Jones, letter to John Ford, November 10, 1949, John Ford Archive.

43. Tag Gallagher, *John Ford: The Man and His Films* (Berkeley: University of California Press, 1986), 263–64.

44. Meta Sterne, interoffice memo to Wingate Smith, October 31, 1949, and Fulton Brylawski, letter to Katherine Cliffton, November 2, 1949, John Ford Archive.

45. Joseph I. Breen, letter to John Ford, December 5, 1949, Argosy Archive.

46. Paul E. Dahl, "'All is Well'". . . . The Story of 'The Hymn That Went Around the World,'" *Brigham Young University Studies* 21, 4 (1981): 515–27.

47. Quoted in Bogdanovich, *John Ford,* 99.

6. "THE GIRL I LEFT BEHIND ME"

1. Quincannon, played by Dick Foran, appears to have been killed on the suicide mission with the rest of the Seventh Cavalry in *Fort Apache,* but he was resurrected, now played by Victor McLaglen, for *She Wore a Yellow Ribbon* and *Rio Grande.* And if Quincannon has been with Nathan Brittles since their days together in the Civil War in *She Wore a Yellow Ribbon,* how can he also have been in the Civil War with Kirby York, who appears in two films (as Captain Kirby York in *Fort Apache* and—apparently the result of a screenwriter's typo— as Lieutenant Colonel Kirby Yorke in *Rio Grande*)? Tyree is a recruit in *Rio Grande* but a sergeant in *She Wore a Yellow Ribbon,* which chronologically takes place earlier. The list could go on.

2. Tag Gallagher, *John Ford: The Man and His Films* (Berkeley: University of California Press, 1986), 55.

3. Scott Eyman, *Print the Legend: The Life and Times of John Ford* (Baltimore: Johns Hopkins University Press, 1999), 332.

4. Richard Slotkin, *Gunfighter Nation: The Myth of the Frontier in*

Twentieth-Century America (Norman: University of Oklahoma Press, 1998), 722n54, further compares Colonel Thursday to General Douglas MacArthur.

5. Charles Ramiriz Berg, "The Margin as Center: The Multicultural Dynamics in John Ford's Westerns," in *John Ford Made Westerns: Filming the Legend in the Sound Era,* ed. Gaylyn Studlar and Matthew Bernstein (Bloomington: Indiana University Press, 2001), 88.

6. The source stories for the cavalry trilogy by James Warner Bellah contain no singing or dancing. The only Bellah source story to contain any reference to music is "Mission with No Record," the source of *Rio Grande,* which mentions the violin playing of Colonel Massarene, the Yorke character.

7. Literally dozens of books related to the history of Arizona and the cavalry were consulted, including the first-person memoirs of George Armstrong Custer's widow, Elizabeth Custer, *Boots and Saddles, or, Life in Dakota with General Custer* (1885) and *Following the Guidon* (1890); H. H. McConnell's *Five Years a Cavalryman, or, Sketches of Regular Army Life on the Texas Frontier, Twenty Odd Years Ago* (1889); and John D. Billings's *Hardtack and Coffee, or, The Unwritten Story of Army Life* (1887). Books on Frederic Remington and Charles Schreyvogel were circulated. Spaatz also interviewed women, including her own grandmother, who had experienced army life in the Seventh Cavalry.

8. Frank Nugent quoted in Joseph McBride, *Searching for John Ford: A Life* (New York: St. Martin's Press, 2001), 447.

9. John Ford quoted in Peter Bogdanovich, *John Ford* (Berkeley: University of California Press, 1978), 86.

10. Songs under consideration at one point included "Captain Jinks [of the Horse Marines]," "The Cuckoo Waltz," "Fiddlers' Green," "For Her Lover Who Was Far Far Away [aka (Round Her Neck) She Wore A Yellow Ribbon]," "For Seven Long Years" [aka "The Wide Missouri" and "Shenandoah"], "Garry Owen," "The Girl I left Behind Me," "The Regular Army O!" "Sweet Genevieve," "Army Blue," "We're the Boys of the Thirty-First," "The Old Ninth Infantry," "A Son of a Musketeer," and "Old Arizona Again."

11. Joseph Breen, letter to Argosy Pictures (Katherine Cliffton), July 29, 1947. Argosy Pictures Archive, Brigham Young University.

12. Given Ford's involvement with the music in his westerns, it seems implausible that he would have left the task of rewriting the lyrics to anyone else. A copy of the lyrics can be found in Ford's papers at Lilly Library, but the smoking gun here is the correspondence from Argosy's lawyer, Donald Dewar, in response to a pending lawsuit over the song "(Round Her Neck) She Wore a Yellow Ribbon," in which he named Ford as the lyricist. Donald Dewar, letter to Gordon Young, February 9, 1950, Argosy Pictures Archive.

13. Regimental bands served a dual purpose in the frontier cavalry—piping the soldiers into battle and waiting to attend the wounded and bury the dead afterwards.

14. John D. Billings, *Hardtack and Coffee, or, The Unwritten Story of Army Life* (Boston: Hard Tack Publishing, 1889), 69.

15. H. H. McConnell, *Five Years a Cavalryman, or, Sketches of Regular Army Life on the Texas Frontier, Twenty Odd Years Ago* (Jacksboro, Texas: J. N. Rogers, printers, 1889), 19, 99, 133.

16. See Elizabeth B. Custer, *Boots and Saddles, or, Life in Dakota with General Custer* (1885; reprint, Norman: University of Oklahoma Press, 1961), 182.

17. Elizabeth B. Custer, *Following the Guidon* (1890; reprint, Norman: University of Oklahoma Press, 1966), xxx.

18. Thanks to Krin Gabbard for bringing Felix Vinatieri to my attention. Vinatieri's music for Custer has now been recorded and issued with extensive liner notes: *Custer's Last Band: The Original Music of Felix Vinatieri, Custer's Legendary Band Leader* (National Music Museum, University of South Dakota, 2001).

19. Edward A. Dolph, *"Sound Off!": Soldier Songs from the Revolution to World War II* (New York: Farrar & Rinehart, 1942), an anthology of military music published in association with the U.S. Military Academy at West Point, is the most reliable source on "Fiddlers' Green." Dolph cites written records and oral testimony, including testimony that "Fiddlers' Green" was sung by the Sixth and Seventh Cavalry during the Indian Wars. See ibid., 25–26.

20. The cavalry version of "Fiddlers' Green" is quite different from the sea chantey in melody, lyrics, and tone.

21. Dolph, *"Sound Off!"* 25.

22. Katherine K. Preston's excellent introduction to Edward Harrington and David Braham in *Irish American Theater,* ed. Preston (New York: Garland, 1994), argues that many of their songs failed to achieve lasting popularity "in part because they date from a time just prior to the advent of sound recordings and the mass marketing techniques of Tin Pan Alley" (xv).

23. See William H. A. Williams, "The Theater and Songs of Edward Harrigan," in *'Twas Only an Irishman's Dream: The Image of Ireland and the Irish in American Popular Song Lyrics, 1800–1921* (Urbana: University of Illinois Press, 1996), 158–74.

24. The other jobs to which the Irish gravitated were the federal public works projects—roads, canals (and the Erie Canal, in particular), and railroads.

25. For work on Ford's Irishness and its relationship to his films, see especially Jack Morgan, "The Irish in John Ford's Cavalry Trilogy—Victor McLaglen's Stooge-Irish Caricature," *Melus* 22, 2 (Summer 1997): 33–43; Thomas Flanagan, "The Irish in John Ford's Films," in *The Irish in America,* ed. Michael Coffey (New York: Hyperion, 1997), 191–95; and Lee Lourdeaux, *Italian and Irish Filmmakers in America: Ford, Capra, Coppola, and Scorcese* (Philadelphia: Temple University Press, 1990). Oddly, Lordeaux does not explicitly address the cavalry trilogy.

26. Morgan, "The Irish in John Ford's Cavalry Trilogy," 34–35.

27. Berg, "Margin as Center," 81–82.

28. Paul Giles, "The Cinema of Catholicism: John Ford and Robert Altman," in *Unspeakable Images: Ethnicity and the American Cinema,* ed. Lester D. Friedman (Urbana: University of Illinois Press, 1991), 150.

29. John Ford, "Story Notes," Argosy Pictures Archive.

30. Martin Stokes, ed., *Ethnicity, Identity, and Music: The Musical Construction of Place* (Providence, R.I.: Berg, 1994), 5.

31. See McBride, *Searching for John Ford,* 763.

32. Flanagan, "Irish in John Ford's Films," 191–95, argues that what is generally considered his most Irish film, *The Quiet Man,* could be thought of as a western that transplants Ford's archetypal western hero, in the form of the cavalry trilogy star John Wayne, to Ireland.

33. I believe this is the same Miles Keogh to whom Nathan Brittles refers in *She Wore A Yellow Ribbon.*

34. George Armstrong Custer, *My Life on the Plains, or, Personal Experiences with Indians* (1874; reprint, Norman: University of Oklahoma Press, 1962), 240.

35. Joseph Breen to John Ford, July 22, 1947, Argosy Pictures Archive, Brigham Young University.

36. "Londonderry Air" is more commonly known today as "Danny Boy," a version of "Londonderry Air" with new lyrics written by the Briton Fred Weatherly and published in 1913, effectively depoliticizing its content. Most Irish and Irish American immigrants would not have known the melody as "Danny Boy," although it was immensely popular under that title. For a history of "Londonderry Air" and its relationship to "Danny Boy," see "The Provenance of the Londonderry Air," *Journal of the Royal Musical Association* 125, 2 (Fall 2000): 205–47.

37. In *The Quiet Man,* Michaleen O'Flynn remembers Sean Thornton's grandfather as having been "hung in Australia," where many Fenians were transported in 1867, making it possible and even likely that Thornton's grandfather was a Fenian himself.

38. Thanks here go to K. J. Donnelly for bringing my attention to the republican nature of "Down by the Glenside."

39. See McBride, *Searching for John Ford,* 16, 137; Gallagher, *John Ford,* 29; Dan Ford, *Pappy: The Life of John Ford* (1979; reprint, New York: Da Capo Press, 1998), 23–24. Andrew Sinclair, *John Ford* (New York: Dial Press, 1979), 32, claims that Ford was both a "contributor and collector of funds for the IRA."

40. Ford had originally wanted "The Wearing of the Green," another patriotic Irish song, to be played on a banjo and sung by the Irish troopers in *She Wore a Yellow Ribbon.*

41. "Goodnight, Ladies," the traditional last dance in the nineteenth century, ends the ball.

42. In an early version of the screenplay, "The Cuckoo Waltz" was to have been played along with "Beautiful Dreamer." At some point, "The Cuckoo Waltz" was dropped because an original composition by Hageman occupies that place. I suspect that copyright problems surfaced in connection with the song. When RKO Legal researched the provenance of "The Cuckoo Waltz," they determined that it was in the public domain. It was not. "The Cuckoo Waltz" was under copyright to the Indiana Historical Society, which Twentieth Century–Fox paid not once but twice for the privilege of using it, in *Young Mr. Lincoln* and *My Darling Clementine.*

43. The parlor ballad was a musical form designed for the upper- and upper-middle-class homes, which generally had a piano in the parlor.

44. This according to Katherine Cliffton.

45. Elizabeth Custer, *Boots and Saddles,* 218.

46. Gaylyn Studlar, "Sacred Duties, Poetic Passions," in *John Ford Made Westerns,* ed. id. and Bernstein, 43. Wendy Chapman Peek has argued along similar lines for the western which "often demands that the Western hero negotiate between the poles of masculine and feminine performance to find the mean of behavior that will ultimately achieve . . . success." See Peek, "The Romance of Competence: Rethinking Masculinity in the Western," *Journal of Popular Film and Television* 30, 4 (Winter 2003): 208.

47. Studlar, "Sacred Duties, Poetic Passions," in *John Ford Made Westerns,* ed. id. and Bernstein, 46.

48. See Steven Cohan, "'Feminizing' the Song-and-Dance Man: Fred Astaire and the Spectacle of Masculinity in the Hollywood Musical," in *Screening the Male: Exploring Masculinities in Hollywood Cinema,* ed. Steven Cohan and Ina Rae Hark (New York: Routledge, 1993), 46–69; id., "Dancing with Balls: Sissies, Sailors, and the Camp Masculinity of Gene Kelly," in *Incongruous Entertainment: Camp, Cultural Value, and the MGM Musical* (Durham, N.C.: Duke University Press, 2005), 149–99; Carol J. Clover, "Dancin' in the Rain," in *Hollywood Musicals: The Film Reader,* ed. Steven Cohan (New York: Routledge, 2002), 157–73; and Peter Wollen, *Singin' in the Rain* (London: British Film Institute, 1992).

49. Susan McClary, *Feminine Endings: Music, Gender, and Sexuality* (Minneapolis: University of Minnesota Press, 1991), 17.

50. "Sweet Genevieve" was composed by George Cooper, a friend and sometime collaborator of Stephen Foster's. It was published in 1869 and remains a favorite of barbershop quartets.

51. *Fort Apache,* screenplay, revised July 10, 1947, 144. RKO Screenplay Collection, UCLA. The sequence appears to have been shot but at some later point relegated to a foreign version.

52. See, e.g., Joan Dagle, "Linear Patterns and Ethnic Encounters in the Ford Western," in *John Ford Made Westerns,* ed. Bernstein and Studlar, 102–31; Barry Keith Grant, "John Ford and James Fenimore Cooper: Two Rode Together," ibid., 193–219; McBride, *Searching for John Ford,* 457; Eyman, *Print the Legend,* 341, Douglas Pye, "Genre and History: *Fort Apache* and *The Man Who Shot Liberty Valance*," in *The Book of Westerns,* ed. Ian Cameron and Pye (New York: Continuum, 1996), 111–22; Leland Poague, "All I Can See Is the Flags: *Fort Apache* and the Visibility of History," *Cinema Journal* 27, 2 (Winter 1988): 8–26; Joseph McBride and Michael Wilmington, *John Ford* (New York: Da Capo Press, 1975); Gallagher, *John Ford,* 249–54; Kenneth J. Nolley, "Printing the Legend in the Age of MX: Reconsidering Ford's Military Trilogy," *Literature/Film Quarterly* 14, 2 (1988): 82–88; Slotkin, *Gunfighter Nation,* 341–43. Of these, only McBride and Wilmington mention "Battle Hymn of the Republic."

53. Many sources claim the tradition of the yellow ribbon continues in the modern practice of tying a yellow ribbon around a tree trunk as a signifier of solidarity with the nation. But the practice seems more likely a direct descendent of the hit song "Tie a Yellow Ribbon Round the Old Oak Tree," recorded by Tony Orlando and Dawn in 1973. The song, which inspired Americans to support the American hostages held in Iran by tying yellow ribbons around tree trunks, made

a comeback in 1981 when the hostages were released. "Tie a Yellow Ribbon Round the Old Oak Tree" has a cloudy generation myth of its own; its songwriters have made numerous (confusing) statements about the genesis of the song, some alluding to the cavalry connection and some not.

54. See Tad Tuleja, "Closing the Circle," in *Usable Pasts: Traditions and Group Expressions in North America* (Logan: Utah State University Press, 1997), ed. id., 311–28; Gerald E. Parsons, "Yellow Ribbons: Ties with Tradition," *Folklife Center News* 4, 2 (Summer 1981): 1, 9–11, and "How the Yellow Ribbon Became a National Folk Symbol," *Folklife Center News* 13, 3 (Summer 1991): 9–11; Linda Pershing and Margaret Yocum, "The Yellow Ribboning of the USA: Contested Meanings in the Construction of a Political Symbol," *Western Folklore* 55, 1 (1996): 41–85; Jack Santino, "Yellow Ribbons and Seasonal Flags: The Folk Assemblage of War," *Journal of American Folklore* 105, 1 (1992): 19–33. The musicologist Sigmund Spaeth writes about "All Round My Hat" in *A History of Popular Music in America* (New York: Random House, 1948), 83–84.

55. Parsons, "Yellow Ribbons," 10.

56. Ibid.

57. Tuleja, "Circle," in *Usable Pasts,* 317.

58. See Dolph, *"Sound Off!"* 19.

59. Hageman assured Argosy's lawyer, Donald Dewar, that "She Wore a Yellow Ribbon" was in the public domain, having taken the song from "an old book of soldier's songs which I got from the Music Department of RKO." The "old book of soldier's songs" was almost certainly Edward Dolph's *"Sound Off!"* Hageman probably got it from Clifford, who explicitly refers to the book in her research notes for the film. Richard Hageman, letter to Donald Dewar, n.d. (but sometime after September 30, 1949), Argosy Pictures Archive.

60. Argosy's lawyer, Donald Dewar, writes: "The lyrics used in the picture are the original work and/or arrangement of John Ford." Dewar, letter to "Tubby" Youngman, February 9, 1950, Argosy Pictures Archive. Of course, it was typical of Ford to take the responsibility of writing the lyrics himself.

61. "She Wore a Yellow Ribbon" had appeared in exactly the same form in *Fort Apache* one year earlier to no complaint. Dewar believed that it was the print and recorded versions of the song that "caused the trouble." Dewar, letter to K. B. Umbreit, November, 11 1949, Argosy Pictures Archive.

62. Dolph writes of his version of the song: "I don't know how old this is or where it came from but I do know that it originated before the World War." See Dolph, *"Sound Off!"* 19.

63. Richard Hageman, score for *She Wore A Yellow Ribbon,* RKO Music Archive, UCLA.

64. Dolph, *"Sound Off!"* 25–26.

65. Nonetheless, I have found several articles extremely useful. Debra Thomas has an insightful section on *Rio Grande* in her article, "John Wayne's Body," in *The Book of Westerns,* ed. Ian Cameron and Douglas Pye (New York: Continuum, 1996), 80–83; K. J. Donnelly treats the score in a chapter entitled "The Accented Voice: Ethnic Signposts of English, Irish and American Film Music," in *The Spectre of Sound: Music in Film and Television* (London: British

Film Institute; Berkeley: University of California Press, 2005), 55–87; Barton Palmer reads the film through masculinity studies in "A Masculinist Reading of Two Western Films: *High Noon* and *Rio Grande*," *Journal of Popular Film and Television* 12, 4 (1984): 161, as does Robert D. Leighninger Jr. in "The Western as Male Soap Opera: John Ford's *Rio Grande*," *Journal of Men's Studies* 6, 2 (Winter 1998): 135–48.

66. *The Quiet Man* turned out to be Ford's most successful film at the box office.

67. Palmer, "A Masculinist Reading of Two Western Films," 161.

68. Leighninger, "The Western as Male Soap Opera," 146.

69. James Warner Bellah, "Mission with No Record," *Saturday Evening Post*, September 27, 1947, 29.

70. Debra Thomas, "John Wayne's Body," 83, argues that the Indian arrow is meant to be seen as "Cupid's arrow," and I'm inclined to agree with her.

71. Leighninger, "The Western as Male Soap Opera," 143.

72. The opening of the main theme that Victor Young composed for *Rio Grande* sounds tantalizing close, to me, to the Irish song by Richard Farrelly that appears prominently in *The Quiet Man*, "The Isle of Innisfree" (aka "The Lake Isle of Innisfree"). It is tempting to see a connection here. Was Young inspired by "Innisfree" when he wrote the theme for *Rio Grande?* The film after all features a feisty Irish heroine, and Young used several other Irish songs in the film. But, of course, there is no way to know.

73. Victor Young Collection, Robert D. Farber University Archives and Special Collections, Brandeis University, Waltham, Massachusetts.

74. Joseph McBride reports that there were some Apaches used in *Stagecoach* for the close-ups. See McBride, *Searching for John Ford*, 294.

75. Bodie Thoene and Rona Stuck, "Navajo Nation Meets Hollywood: An Inside Look at John Ford's Classic Westerns," *American West* 20, 5 (1983): 38–44, describes a screening of *The Searchers* on the Navajo reservation that was greeted by gales of laughter from the Navajo. The Native American writer Tony Grayson Colonnese describes a similar response in "Native American Reactions to *The Searchers*," in *The Searchers: Essays and Reflections on John Ford's Classic Western*, ed. Arthur Eckstein and Peter Lehman (Detroit: Wayne State University Press, 2004), 335–42.

76. McBride, *Searching for John Ford*, 505, also points out that film departs significantly from the historical events on which it is based. In the actual confrontation with the Apache, it is Indian women and children who were kidnapped by the cavalry and returned to the reservation.

77. Dale Evans recorded "Aha! San Antone" with Majestic Records in 1946.

78. Quoted in Eyman, *Print the Legend*, 392.

79. Thomas, "John Wayne's Body," 82.

80. "Bad Chuck" Roberson was one of those stuntmen pressed into service with Sons of the Pioneers. He was given no directives regarding whether or not he was supposed to sing, and he decided to sing along when the song was recorded live. Apparently, his voice blended in with Sons of the Pioneers; Ford never said a word to him about it. See his autobiography, *The Fall Guy* (North Vancouver, B.C.: Hancock House, 1980), 66–67.

7. "WHAT MAKES A MAN TO WANDER"

1. Stan Jones, lyrics to "The Searchers," John Ford Archive, Lilly Library, Indiana University.

2. The song was recorded for RCA Victor on March 28, 1956. Sons of the Pioneers at that time was comprised of Bob Nolan, who was called out of retirement by RCA to record the song, Lloyd Perryman, Ken Curtis, Hugh Farr, Karl Farr, and Pat Brady. They were backed by a fourteen-piece orchestra.

3. So does Tag Gallagher, who claims that Ford chose the verse that ends the film; he does not, however, cite any evidence for his claim. See Gallagher, *John Ford: The Man and His Films* (Berkeley: University of California Press, 1986), 331.

4. Jones routinely routed his lyrics to Ford. On *Wagon Master,* for instance, Jones wrote to Ford enclosing the lyrics to the three songs for the film. Stan Jones, letter to John Ford, John Ford Archive.

5. Alan LeMay, *The Searchers* (New York: Harper Brothers, 1954), 104.

6. James F. Brooks, "'That Don't Make You Kin!': Borderlands History and Culture in *The Searchers,*" in *The Searchers: Essays and Reflections on John Ford's Classic Western,* ed. Arthur M. Eckstein and Peter Lehman (Detroit: Wayne State University Press, 2004), 281.

7. Peter Lehman, "You Couldn't Hit It on the Nose," in *John Ford Made Westerns: Filming the Legend in the Sound Era,* ed. Gaylyn Studlar and Matthew Bernstein (Bloomington: Indiana University Press, 2001), 246.

8. See Arthur Eckstein, "Darkening Ethan: John Ford's *The Searchers* (1956) from Novel to Screenplay to Screen," *Cinema Journal* 38, 1 (1998): 3–24.

9. John Ford, "Story Notes," to Pat Ford and Frank Nugent, January 27, 1955, John Ford Archive.

10. Publicity Release, Warner Bros. Archive, USC. A typical example of studio ballyhoo, in this case, turns out to be surprisingly accurate.

11. Max Steiner, "The Music Director," in *The Real Tinsel,* ed. Bernard Rosenberg and Harry Silverstein (New York: Macmillan, 1970), 392.

12. Walter MacEwen, memo to J. L. Warner, December 5, 1955, Warner Bros. Archive.

13. James D'Arc, "Max Steiner and the Searchers," introductory essay to the liner notes for the sound recording *The Searchers: Composed and Conducted by Max Steiner.*

14. C. V. Whitney, letter to Max Steiner, December 9, 1955, Max Steiner Archive, Brigham Young University.

15. Struck by Ethan's signature line "That'll be the day," Buddy Holly, unknown to Warner Bros. or C. V. Whitney Pictures, composed his own theme song with that title, which became a hit.

16. Thanks to Arthur Eckstein for calling this film to my attention.

17. Max Steiner, pencil sketches, *The Searchers,* Warner Bros. Archive.

18. Ibid.

19. Ibid.

20. John Ford Phonograph Disk Collection, Brigham Young University.

21. Studio Publicity Release, June 24, 1955, Warner Bros. Archive.

22. John Ford to Pat Ford, Frank Nugent, Wingate Smith, and Frank Beetson, "Notes on *The Searchers*," January 28, 1955, John Ford Archive.

23. Scarlett, buried at the back of the hall behind a concession stand, hears
the orchestra break into "the sweet melancholy of 'Lorena': What a beautiful
waltz. She extended her hands slightly closed her eyes and swayed with the sad
haunting rhythm. There was something about the tragic melody and Lorena's
lost love that mingled with her own excitement and brought a lump into her
throat." Margaret Mitchell, *Gone with the Wind* (New York: Macmillan, 1936),
168.

24. See Eckstein, "Darkening Ethan," 23–24n70.

25. Steiner, pencil sketches, *The Searchers*, Warner Bros. Archive.

26. Janet Walker describes this moment as one of "'prospective pastness.' . . .
At the moment of Wayne's/Ethan's close-up, the family may still be alive, but by
the time Ethan gets there, the family *will have been* killed (or abducted). It's already too late, even though it hasn't happened yet." Walker, "Captive Images in
the Traumatic Western: *The Searchers, Pursued, Once Upon a Time in the West,*
and *Lone Star*," in *Westerns: Films through History*, ed. id. (New York: Routledge, 2001), 223.

27. Frank Nugent, Revised Screenplay, *The Searchers*, March 1956, 140,
Warner Bros. Archive. See also Synopsis, *The Searchers*, Production Code
Archive, Academy Of Motion Picture Arts and Sciences. In this later version, the
words "he says," are changed to "he thinks." See Eckstein, "Darkening Ethan,"
14 for a more detailed analysis.

28. Lehman, "You Couldn't Hit It on the Nose," 250.

29. Steiner, pencil sketches, *The Searchers*, Warner Bros. Archive.

30. See John Baxter, *The Cinema of John Ford* (London and New York: A. S.
Barnes, 1971), 26.

31. Gallagher, *John Ford*, 328.

32. Richard Hutson, "Sermons in Stone: Monument Valley in *The
Searchers*," in *The Searchers*, ed. Eckstein and Lehman, 100.

33. Peter Lehman, "Texas 1868 / America 1956," in *Close Viewings: An Anthology of New Film Criticism*, ed. Peter Lehman (Tallahassee: Florida State University Press, 1990), 387–415.

34. Danny Borzage recorded "All Is Well," the Mormon hymn of celebration
heard in *Wagon Master* on a studio playback recording for *The Searchers*. It was
not used in the film. My guess is that it was originally intended for the wedding
(I can't imagine where else it would be appropriate) but I don't know for sure.

35. Ford's production notes include a copy of all twelve verses of "Skip to
My Lou." John Ford Archive.

36. Steiner, pencil sketches, *The Searchers*, Warner Bros. Archive.

37. Charles Ramirez Berg, "The Margin as Center: The Multicultural Dynamics of John Ford's Westerns," in *John Ford Made Westerns*, ed. Studlar and
Bernstein, 75–101.

38. See, e.g., Brian Henderson, "*The Searchers*: An American Dilemma,"
Film Quarterly 34, 2 (Winter 1980–81): 9–23.

39. I would hasten to add here, however, that this allegorical reading of *The
Searchers* does not negate a non-allegorical reading of the film. Clearly there are

also ways to read the film in terms of its response to and treatment of native Americans. In particular see Janet Walker, "Captive Images in the Traumatic Western: *The Searchers, Pursued, Once Upon a Time in the West,* and *Lone Star,*" in *Westerns: Films Through History,* ed. Walker, 219–51, and Steve Neale, "Vanishing Americans: Racial and Ethnic Issues in the Interpretation and Context of Post-war 'Pro-Indian' Westerns," in *Back in the Saddle Again: New Essays on the Western,* ed. Edward Buscombe and Roberta Pearson (London: British Film Institute, 1998), 8–28.

40. Joseph McBride, *Searching for John Ford: A Life* (New York: St. Martin's Press, 2001), 560.

41. See Kathryn Kalinak, "How the West Was Sung" in *Westerns: Films through History,* ed. Walker, 155–76. Much of my argument here is derived from this earlier article.

42. Eric Lott, *Love and Theft: Blackface Minstrelsy and the American Working Class* (New York: Oxford University Press, 1993), 6.

43. See Martha Anne Turner, "Emily Morgan: Yellow Rose of Texas," in *Legendary Ladies of Texas,* ed. Francis Edward Abernethy (Denton: University of North Texas Press, 1994), 28.

44. The legend attached to and elliding the minstrel origins of "The Yellow Rose of Texas" centers around a mulatta whose sexual prowess supposedly won the battle of San Jacinto for Texas under the command of Sam Houston. For her part in seducing Mexican General Santa Anna and thereby delaying his preparations for battle, this woman, possibly named Emily, who may or may not have been a slave, supposedly inspired a folk song in her honor. This was largely hearsay until the late 1950s, when a nineteenth-century manuscript by the English traveler William Bollaert was published reporting the story as true. Whether or not it is, there is no definitive link between this woman and the genesis of the song.

As Margaret Swett Henson persuasively argues, the legend surrounding "Emily" masks a threatening historical reality: the pervasive and largely condoned rape of African American women by white men. According to Henson, if any sexual congress did occur between General Santa Anna and "Emily," it was almost certainly not consensual, at least not on the part of "Emily" and she offers historical circumstances to substantiate her claim. For more on the genesis of "The Yellow Rose of Texas," see esp. Margaret Swett Henson, "West, Emily D.," entry in *The Handbook of Texas* (Austin: Texas State Historical Society, 1997), and Francis E. Abernethy, *Singin' Texas* (Dallas: E. Heart Press, 1983).

45. I have read numerous sources reporting that a handwritten copy of the lyrics held in the archives of the University of Texas at Austin dates the song to 1836 and thus predates the publication of the minstrel song by two decades. I have my doubts. While, of course, it is possible that the published minstrel song drew upon folk origins, I remain unconvinced by the arguments put forward to support this interpretation. In any event, the actual manuscript in question bears no date and to my knowledge has not been definitively dated. For a summary of these arguments, see Martha Anne Turner, *The Yellow Rose of Texas: Her Saga and Her Song* (Austin, Texas: Shoal Creek, 1976), 41–47.

46. See John Ford, "Story Notes," to Pat Ford and Frank Nugent, January

27, 1955, where Ford pairs the songs in discussion of a musical theme for the film, and Patrick Ford, interoffice memo to John Ford, M. C. Cooper, Frank Nugent, and Frank Beetson, February 1, 1955, which pairs the songs in notes on musical selections for the aborted wedding, both in the John Ford Archive.

47. Lott, *Love and Theft*, 6.

48. Douglas Pye, "Double Vision: Miscegenation and Point of View in *The Searchers*," in *The Searchers*, ed. Eckstein and Lehman, 223.

49. Harry Macarthy was famous for his "personation concerts" and is often described as a "variety entertainer." I suspect he entertained on the minstrel stage. Macarthy borrowed the melody from the song "The Irish Jaunting Car."

50. Ford's interest in "martyrology" helps explain his Confederate sympathies, according to Paul Giles, "John Ford and Robert Altman: The Cinema of Catholicism," in *Unspeakable Images: Ethnicity and the American Cinema*, ed. Lester D. Friedman (Urbana: University of Illinois Press, 1991), 146. Giles focuses on *The Horse Soldiers*, but I would not discount his argument for *The Searchers*.

51. I am reminded of two other Ford westerns in which another song identified with the Confederacy, "Dixie," works in similar ways: in *She Wore a Yellow Ribbon*, it provides a moving tribute for a dead Confederate veteran, and in *Rio Grande* it invokes the happiness of Kirby and Kathleen's marriage in the distant past and foreshadows their ability to recapture that happiness in the future.

52. Pye, "Double Vision," in *The Searchers*, ed. Eckstein and Lehman, 223.

8. IN THE SHADOW OF *THE SEARCHERS*

1. John Ford quoted in Dan Ford, *Pappy: The Life of John Ford* (New York: Da Capo Press, 1998), 290.

2. John Ford quoted in Peter Bogdanovich, *John Ford* (Berkeley: University of California Press, 1978), 98.

3. Harry Carey Jr., *Company of Heroes: My Life as an Actor in the John Ford Stock Company* (Lanham, Md.: Madison Books, 1996), 179.

4. Ford had visited the *Alamo* set a few months earlier and shot some footage for the film with a second unit.

5. George Duning's Academy Award nominations were for *No Sad Songs for Me* (Rudolph Maté, 1950), *From Here to Eternity* (Fred Zinnemann, 1953), and *Picnic* (Joshua Logan, 1955).

6. Delmer Daves quoted in John Stanley, "Celebrating the Rich Legacy of Film Composer George Duning,"www.thecolumnists.com/stanley10.html (accessed October 18, 2006).

7. George Duning, music notes, penciled annotation, *Two Rode Together*, George Duning Papers, Cinema-Television Library, University of Southern California, Los Angeles.

8. Luigi Boccherini's *String Quintet in E Major*, from which the minuet is extracted, is variously labeled Opus 11 No. 5 and Opus 13 No. 5. Apparently discrepancies involving edition numbers account for the difference. See James J. Fuld, "Minuet—Boccherini" in *The Book of World-Famous Music: Classical, Popular, and Folk*, 5th ed. (New York: Dover, 2000), 370.

9. In Duning's music notes, the question "what tune?" appears next to the cue for the music box; "Bocherrini" *[sic]* is penciled in over the question. George Duning, music notes, pencil annotation, *Two Rode Together*, George Duning Papers, Cinema-Television Library, University of Southern California, Los Angeles.

10. "Sally Brown," a nineteenth-century sea chantey sung by American lumberjacks was, at one point, considered, but it was not used in the film.

11. For a history of the guitar in the Americas, see Tim Brookes, *Guitar: An American Life* (New York: Grove Press, 2005).

12. See Charlie Seeman, "The American Cowboy: Image and Reality," liner notes to *Back in the Saddle Again: American Cowboy Songs,* New World Records, NW 314–NW 315.

13. In *Wagon Master, The Searchers,* and *Rio Grande,* the guitar is motivated by the presence on the soundtrack of the contemporary singing group Sons of the Pioneers. In *Rio Grande* Sons of the Pioneers, dressed as cavalry extras, wield guitars onscreen. In *My Darling Clementine,* a guitar is used in the accompaniment of the title song; Dick Foran sings "Sweet Genevieve" in *Fort Apache* accompanied by a guitar.

14. Ford used the Mexico City Symphony to record the score for *The Fugitive.*

15. K. J. Donnelly, *The Spectre of Sound: Music in Film and Television* (London: British Film Institute, 2005), 81.

16. The guitar does the same for Yakima in *Stagecoach* and Chihuahua in *My Darling Clementine,* both of whose songs are accompanied by guitars.

17. Linda Ronstadt recorded "Corrido de Cananea" on her album of Mexican songs *Canciones de mi padre* (1987), Asylum 60765–2.

18. Donnelly, *Spectre of Sound,* 78.

19. Brooks, "Borderlands History and Culture," in *The Searchers: Essays and Reflections on John Ford's Classic Western,* ed. Arthur Eckstein and Peter Lehman (Detroit: Wayne State University Press, 2004), 272.

20. See Richard Maltby, "A Better Sense of History: John Ford and the Indians," in *The Book of Westerns,* ed. Ian Cameron and Douglas Pye (New York: Continuum, 1996), 34–37, 42–44, and Philip French, *Westerns* (London: Secker & Warburg, 1973), 82.

21. Strode claimed to be a "Negro-Indian" with Creek, Blackfoot, and Cherokee ancestry on both his mother's and father's sides. He refers to himself as a "mixed breed" in Woody Strode and Sam Young, *Goal Dust: An Autobiography* (Lanham, Md.: Madison Books, 1990), 1–7. Yet his mixed racial background was largely ignored in the press and by the public at the time of his work with Ford. According to Strode, Ford once pointedly asked him, "Woody, why don't you ever talk about your Indian blood?" Strode's response was that no matter how he described himself, he would be identified as black by the public. "In America, if you have one drop of black blood you're colored." Ibid., 206.

22. Other than Ford's major biographers, Eyman, McBride, Gallagher and Dan Ford, few critics have addressed the film at length and in depth. Four who do are Armond White, "Stepping Forward, Looking Back," *Film Comment* 36, 2 (2000): 32–36; Joseph McBride and Joseph Wilmington, *"Sergeant Rutledge,"*

Velvet Light Trap 2 (August 1971): 16–18; and Frank Manchell, "Losing and Finding John Ford's *Sergeant Rutledge*," *Historical Journal of Film, Radio and Television* 17, 2 (1997): 245–60. Surprisingly, Thomas Cripps devotes less than a paragraph to the film in *Making Movies Black: The Hollywood Message Movie from World War II to the Civil Rights Era* (Oxford: Oxford University Press, 1993), 270.

23. Ford nixed both Poitier and Belefonte in favor of Strode, who had a small part in *The Horse Soldiers.* Walter MacEwen, letter to Steve Trilling, April 10, 1959, Warner Bros. Archive. University of Southern California, Los Angeles.

24. White, "Stepping Forward, Looking Back," 34.

25. For historical background on the buffalo soldiers, see William H. Leckie, *The Buffalo Soldiers: A Narrative of the Negro Cavalry in the West* (Norman: University of Oklahoma Press, 1967); William Loren Katz, *The Black West* (New York: Touchstone Books, Simon & Schuster, 1987), 199–245; and Fairfax Downey, *Buffalo Soldiers in the Indian Wars* (New York: McGraw-Hill, 1969).

26. African American officers are another story. The first African American man to graduate from West Point and serve in the cavalry, Henry Flipper, was court-martialed for conduct unbecoming an officer, ending his military career. Flipper believed fraternization with a white woman was the unspoken cause.

27. Bob Marley and King Sporty's "Buffalo Soldier" (1983), on the Bob Marley & The Wailers album *Confrontation* (Island Records 90085) was one of Marley's most popular songs. Its appeal in Marley's native Jamaica may well have stemmed from the fact that the buffalo soldiers succeeded in a world dominated by whites.

28. In the film *Sergeant Rutledge,* Lieutenant Cantrell explains the derivation of the name differently, explaining that the buffalo soldiers were so named because to the Indians their overcoats made them resemble buffalo. This is also the explanation offered by one of the earliest books on the buffalo soldiers, Cyrus Townsend Brady's *Indian Fights and Fighters: The Soldier and the Sioux* (New York: McClure, Phillips, 1904), 351, as well as Leckie, *Buffalo Soldiers,* 26. Later historians have revised this explanation. See Katz, *Black West,* 202 and Downey, *Buffalo Soldiers,* 10. White soldiers called African Americans "Brunettes."

29. White officers, for instance, such as George Armstrong Custer, refused to serve with the buffalo soldiers, and settlers often refused their help or, worse, attacked them.

30. Oswald Garrison Villard, "The Negro in the Regular Army," *Atlantic Monthly* 91 (1903): 727.

31. Does the name "Mary Beecher" perhaps reference the noted abolitionist writer Harriet Beecher Stowe?

32. See Manchell, "Losing and Finding John Ford's *Sergeant Rutledge*," 249.

33. Frederic Remington, *Crooked Trails* (New York: Harper, 1898); Harold McCracken, *Frederic Remington, Artist of the Old West; with a Bibliographical Check List of Remington Pictures and Books* (Philadelphia: Lippincott, 1947).

"Requisition for materials" (n.d.), Warner Bros. Archive, University of Southern California, Los Angeles.

34. Warner Bros. publicity (n.d.), Warner Bros. Archive, University of Southern California, Los Angeles.

35. This according to Dan Ford, *Pappy*, 284.

36. Ibid., 284–85.

37. Willis Goldbeck appears to have been given the job of approaching Warner Bros. with Ford's request to advance the release of *Sergeant Rutledge*. "Ford seems to feel he has a hell of a picture," the producer Walter MacEwen noted in an interoffice communication to Steve Trilling dated September 18, 1959 (Warner Bros. Archive, University of Southern California, Los Angeles).

38. "[U]nexpected, authentic complexity about race, history, and American social temperament," seeking to "revise the Western's racial iconography": White, "Stepping Forward, Looking Back," 32, 38; "revolutionary": Manchell, "Losing and Finding John Ford's *Sergeant Rutledge*," 246.

39. Tom Buchanan, letter to Victor Blau, March 22, 1960, Warner Bros. Archive, University of Southern California, Los Angeles.

40. Victor Blau, letter to Herman Starr, July 10, 1959, Warner Bros. Archive, University of Southern California, Los Angeles.

41. Victor Blau, letter to Herman Starr, July 10, 1959, Warner Bros. Archive, University of Southern California, Los Angeles.

42. Victor Blau, letter to Herman Starr, July 10, 1959, Warner Bros. Archive, University of Southern California, Los Angeles.

43. Victor Blau, letter to Mitch Miller, October 19, 1959, Warner Bros. Archive, University of Southern California, Los Angeles.

44. Victor Blau, letter to Herman Starr, July 10, 1959, Warner Bros. Archive, University of Southern California, Los Angeles.

45. Jester Hairston may have been unavailable due his involvement in John Wayne's *The Alamo*, in which he plays the part of Jethro.

46. Those lyrics are: "Goin' to drill all day / Goin' to drill all night, / We got our money on the Buffaloes / Somebody bet on the fight."

47. Quoted in Leckie, *Buffalo Soldiers*, 50.

48. Villard, "Negro in the Regular Army," 725. With the ending of the Indian wars, the buffalo soldiers were sent to various trouble spots such as Cuba, where they fought in the Spanish-American War and rode with the Rough Riders. Villard describes their experiences in Santiago, where music is inextricable from their experiences: "As soon as the army settled down in the trenches before Santiago, smuggled musical instruments—guitars, banjos, mouth organs, and what not—appeared among the negro troops as if by magic, and they were ever in use. It was at once a scene of cheerfulness and gayety, and the officers had their usual trouble in making the men go to sleep instead of spending the night in talking, singing, and gaming." Ibid.

49. White, "Stepping Forward, Looking Back," 39.

9. *CHEYENNE AUTUMN*

1. John Ford quoted in Peter Bogdanovich, *John Ford* (Berkeley: University of California Press, 1978), 104–6.

2. The *Omaha Herald* quoted in Ralph K. Andrist, *The Long Death: The Last Days of the Plains Indian* (New York: Macmillan, 1964), 324.

3. General Philip Sheridan quoted in Andrist, *Long Death,* 323.

4. Howard Fast had been a member of the Communist party and served prison time for his refusal to cooperate with the House Un-American Activities Committee (HUAC) in 1950. Fast was blacklisted and hounded by the FBI for years. Columbia Pictures owned the screen rights to his novel *The Last Frontier,* but dropped the idea of producing it when Fast got into hot water with HUAC. Ford was determined to use Fast even if he was blacklisted and his novel optioned by another studio. Columbia threatened a lawsuit and Warner Bros. settled out of court, but not before several elements from Fast had found their way into *Cheyenne Autumn.* For more details on Fast's relationship to *Cheyenne Autumn,* see Joseph McBride, *Searching for John Ford: A Life* (New York: St. Martin's Press, 2001), 644–45.

5. Scott Eyman, *Print the Legend: The Life and Times of John Ford* (Baltimore: Johns Hopkins University Press, 1999), 502, reports that the real problem was that Tracy didn't like the script.

6. John Ford quoted in Bogdanovich, *John Ford,* 104.

7. Grau did the main title, and Brant may have done much of the rest. Apparently, when the credits were prepared, it was not clear who would orchestrate the film, and an orchestration credit was not included. Victor Blau, letter to Dick Pearse, April 9, 1964, Warner Bros. Archive, University of Southern California, Los Angeles.

8. These included the books *Navajo Legends, The Indian's Book, Cheyenne and Arapaho Music,* and *Drums, Tomtoms and Rattles* and the recordings *American Indians of the Southwest, Folk Music of the United States, Indian Music of the Southwest, Songs and Dances of the Flathead Indians, Songs and Dances of Great Lakes Indians, The Sioux and Navajo,* and *Plains: Comanche, Cheyenne, Kiowa, Caddo, Wichita, Pawnee.*

9. Alex North, music notes, *Cheyenne Autumn,* Alex North Papers, Margaret Herrick Library, Academy of Motion Picture Arts and Sciences, Beverly Hills, California.

10. North often relies on woodwinds and percussion rather than the full resources of a symphony orchestra, although that may have been an economic rather than aesthetic decision.

11. Mark Hockley, review of Alex North's *Cheyenne Autumn, Film Music on the Web,* October 2000, www.musicweb-international.com/film/2000/Oct00/north_alex.html (accessed October 18, 2006).

12. Alex North, music notes, *Cheyenne Autumn,* Alex North Papers, Margaret Herrick Library, Academy of Motion Picture Arts and Sciences, Beverly Hills, California.

13. Warner Bros. memo to Helen Schoen, September 1, 1964, Warner Bros. Archive, University of Southern California, Los Angeles.

14. Victor Blau, memo to Helen Schoen, April 14, 1964, Warner Bros. Archive, University of Southern California, Los Angeles.

15. Victor Blau, letter to J. L. (Jack) Warner, December 3, 1963, Warner Bros. Archive, University of Southern California, Los Angeles.

16. Kurt Wolff, memo to Victor Blau, September 11, 1963, Warner Bros. Archive, University of Southern California, Los Angeles.

17. Ken Curtis quoted in Michael Munn, *John Wayne: The Man Behind the Myth* (New York: New American Library, 2003), 131.

Select Bibliography

BOOKS AND ARTICLES ABOUT JOHN FORD
Individual entries in anthologies devoted to Ford are not listed separately.

Anderson, Lindsay. *About John Ford* . . . . New York: McGraw-Hill, 1983.

Baxter, John. *The Cinema of John Ford*. London: A. Zwemmer; New York: Barnes, 1971.

Behlmer, Rudy. "Bret Harte in Monument Valley: *Stagecoach*." In *America's Favorite Movies: Behind the Scenes*, 104–18. New York: Frederick Ungar, 1982.

Bogdanovich, Peter. *John Ford*. Berkeley: University of California Press, 1968, rev. ed. 1978.

Buscombe, Edward. *Stagecoach*. London: British Film Institute, 1992.

———. *The Searchers*. London: British Film Institute, 2000.

Buscombe, Edward, and Roberta Pearson, eds. *Back in the Saddle Again: New Essays on the Western*. London: British Film Institute, 1998.

Carey, Harry Jr. *Company of Heroes: My Life as an Actor in the John Ford Stock Company*. Lanham, Md.: Madison Books, 1996.

Cowie, Peter. *John Ford and the American West*. New York: Abrams, 2004.

Davis, Ronald L. *John Ford: Hollywood's Old Master*. Norman: University of Oklahoma Press, 1995.

Eckstein, Arthur M., and Peter Lehman, eds. *The Searchers: Essays and Reflections on John Ford's Classic Western*. Detroit: Wayne State University Press, 2004.

Eyman, Scott. *Print the Legend: The Life and Times of John Ford*. Baltimore: Johns Hopkins University Press, 1999.

———. *John Ford: The Searcher, 1894–1973*, ed. Paul Duncan. Cologne: Taschen, 2004.

Flanagan, Thomas. "The Irish in John Ford's Films." In *The Irish in America,* ed. Michael Coffey, 191–95. New York: Hyperion, 1997.

Ford, Dan. *Pappy: The Life of John Ford.* Englewood Cliffs, N.J.: Prentice-Hall, 1979. Reprint. New York: Da Capo Press, 1998.

Gallagher, Tag. *John Ford: The Man and His Films.* Berkeley: University of California Press, 1986.

Giles, Paul. "John Ford and Robert Altman: The Cinema of Catholicism." In *Unspeakable Images: Ethnicity and the American Cinema,* ed. Lester D. Friedman, 140–66. Urbana: University of Illinois Press, 1991. Reprinted in Paul Giles, *American Catholic Arts and Fictions: Culture, Ideology, Aesthetics,* 296–323. Cambridge: Cambridge University Press, 1992.

Grant, Barry Keith, ed. *John Ford's Stagecoach.* New York: Cambridge University Press, 2003.

Henderson, Brian. "*The Searchers:* An American Dilemma." *Film Quarterly* 34, 2 (Winter 1980–81): 9–23.

Kirby, Lynne. *Parallel Tracks: The Railroad and Silent Cinema.* Durham, N.C.: Duke University Press, 1996.

Lehman, Peter. "Texas 1868 / America 1956." In *Close Viewings: An Anthology of New Film Criticism,* ed. id., 387–415. Tallahassee: Florida State University Press, 1990.

Leighninger, Robert D., Jr. "The Western as Male Soap Opera: John Ford's *Rio Grande.*" *Journal of Men's Studies* 6, 2 (Winter 1998): 134–48.

Lourdeaux, Lee. *Italian and Irish Filmmakers in America: Ford, Capra, Coppola, and Scorcese.* Philadelphia: Temple University Press, 1990.

McBride, Joseph. *Searching for John Ford: A Life.* New York: St. Martin's Press, 2001.

McBride, Joseph, and Michael Wilmington. *John Ford.* London: Secker & Warburg, 1974. New York: Da Capo Press, 1975.

———. "*Sergeant Rutledge.*" *Velvet Light Trap* 2 (August 1971): 16–18.

Maltby, Richard. "A Better Sense of History: John Ford and the Indians." In *The Book of Westerns,* ed. Ian Cameron and Douglas Pye, 34–49. New York: Continuum, 1996.

Manchell, Frank. "Losing and Finding John Ford's *Sergeant Rutledge.*" *Historical Journal of Film, Radio and Television* 17, 2 (1997): 245–60.

Morgan, Jack. "The Irish in John Ford's Cavalry Trilogy—Victor McLaglen's Stooge-Irish Caricature." *Melus* 22, 2 (Summer 1997): 33–43.

Neale, Steve. "Vanishing Americans: Racial and Ethnic Issues in the Interpretation and Context of Post-war 'Pro-Indian' Westerns." In *Back in the Saddle Again: New Essays on the Western,* ed. Edward Buscombe and Roberta Pearson, 8–28. London: British Film Institute, 1998.

Nolley, Kenneth J. "Printing the Legend in the Age of MX: Reconsidering Ford's Military Trilogy." *Literature/Film Quarterly* 14, 2 (1988): 82–88.

Palmer, Barton. "A Masculinist Reading of Two Western Films: *High Noon* and *Rio Grande.*" *Journal of Popular Film and Television* 12, 4 (1984): 156–62.

Peary, Gerard, ed. *John Ford Interviews.* Jackson: University of Mississippi Press, 2001.

Place, Janey. *The Western Films of John Ford*. Secaucus, N.J.: Citadel Press, 1974.

Poague, Leland. "All I Can See Is the Flags: *Fort Apache* and the Visibility of History." *Cinema Journal* 27, 2 (Winter 1988): 8–26.

Pye, Douglas. "Genre and History: *Fort Apache* and *The Man Who Shot Liberty Valance*." In *The Book of Westerns*, ed. Ian Cameron and Douglas Pye, 111–22. New York: Continuum, 1996.

———. "Miscegenation and Point of View in *The Searchers*." In *The Book of Westerns*, ed. Ian Cameron and Douglas Pye, 229–35. New York: Continuum, 1996.

Reed, Joseph W. *Three American Originals: John Ford, William Faulkner, Charles Ives*. Middletown, Conn.: Wesleyan University Press, 1984

Sarris, Andrew. *The John Ford Movie Mystery*. Bloomington: University of Indiana Press, 1975.

Sinclair, Andrew. *John Ford*. New York: Dial Press, 1979.

Spittles, Brian. *John Ford*. New York: Longman, 2002.

Stowell, Peter. *John Ford*. Boston: Twayne, 1986.

Studlar, Gaylyn, and Matthew Bernstein, eds. *John Ford Made Westerns: Filming the Legend in the Sound Era*. Bloomington: Indiana University Press, 2001.

Thomas, Debra. "John Wayne's Body." In *The Book of Westerns*, ed. Ian Cameron and Douglas Pye, 75–87. New York: Continuum, 1996.

Walker, Janet. "Captive Images in the Traumatic Western: *The Searchers, Pursued, Once Upon a Time in the West*, and *Lone Star*." In *Westerns: Films through History*, ed. id., 219–51. New York: Routledge, 2001.

Wexman, Virginia Wright. *Creating the Couple: Love, Marriage, and Hollywood Performance*. Princeton: Princeton University Press, 1993.

White, Armond. "Stepping Forward, Looking Back." *Film Comment* 36, 2 (2000): 32–36.

ABOUT MUSIC

Cohen, Norm. *Long Steel Rail: The Railroad in American Folksong*. Urbana: University of Illinois Press, 1981.

Darby, William. "Musical Links in *Young Mr. Lincoln, My Darling Clementine*, and *The Man Who Shot Liberty Valance*." *Cinema Journal* 31, 1 (Fall 1991): 22–36.

Dolph, Edward Arthur. *"Sound Off!" Soldier Songs from the Revolution to World War II*. New York: Farrar & Rinehart, 1942.

Donnelly, K. J. "The Accented Voice: Ethnic Signposts of English, Irish, and American Film Music." In *The Spectre of Sound: Music in Film and Television*, 55–87. London: British Film Institute; Berkeley: University of California Press, 2005.

Emerson, Ken. *Doo-Dah! Stephen Foster and the Rise of American Popular Culture*. New York: Da Capo Press, 1998.

Gorbman, Claudia. "Scoring the Indian: Music in the Liberal Western." In *Western Music and Its Others: Difference, Representation, and Appropriation in*

Music, ed. Georgina Born and David Hesmondhalgh, 234–53. Berkeley: University of California Press, 2000. Revised as "Drums along the L.A. River: Scoring the Indian." In *Westerns: Films through History,* ed. Janet Walker, 177–95. New York: Routledge, 2001.

Griffis, Ken. *Hear My Song: The Story of the Celebrated Songs of the Pioneers.* Los Angeles: UCLA Folklore and Mythology Center, 1974.

Hardy, Phil. "Music." In *The BFI Companion to the Western,* ed. Edward Buscombe, 193–95. New York: Da Capo Press, 1988.

Lomax, John A., and Alan Lomax. *Cowboy Songs and Other Frontier Ballads.* 1910. Rev. ed. New York: Macmillan, 1938, 1952.

Lott, Eric. *Love and Theft: Blackface Minstrelsy and the American Working Class.* New York: Oxford University Press, 1993.

Marcuse, Maxwell F. *Tin Pan Alley in Gaslight: A Saga of the Songs That Made the Gray Nineties "Gay."* Watkins Glen, N.Y.: Century House, 1959.

McClary, Susan. *Feminine Endings: Music, Gender, and Sexuality.* Minneapolis: University of Minnesota Press, 1991.

Ohrlin, Glenn. *The Hell-Bound Train: A Cowboy Songbook.* Urbana: University of Illinois Press, 1973, 1989.

Pisani, Michael. "'I'm an Indian, too': Creating Native American Identities in Nineteenth- and Early Twentieth-Century Music." In *The Exotic in Western Music,* ed. Jonathan Bellman, 218–57. Boston: Northeastern University Press, 1998.

Preston, Katherine K., ed. *Irish American Theater.* New York: Garland, 1994.

Roth, Lane. "Folk Song Lyrics as Communication in John Ford's Films." *Southern Speech Communication Journal* 46 (Summer 1981): 390–96.

Sandburg, Carl. *The American Songbag.* New York: Harcourt Brace, 1927.

Scheurer, Timothy E. *Born in the U.S.A.: The Myth of America in Popular Music from Colonial Times to the Present.* Jackson: University Press of Mississippi, 1991.

Stanfield, Peter. *Horse Opera: The Strange History of the Singing Cowboy.* Urbana: University of Illinois Press, 2002.

Tinsley, Jim Bob. *He Was Singin' This Song.* Orlando: University Presses of Florida, 1981.

White, John I. *Git Along, Little Dogies: Songs and Songmakers of the American West.* Urbana: University of Illinois Press, 1975.

Williams, William H. A. *'Twas Only an Irishman's Dream: The Image of Ireland and the Irish in American Popular Song Lyrics, 1800–1921.* Urbana: University of Illinois Press, 1996.

FILMOGRAPHY

Gallagher, Tag. *John Ford: The Man and His Films,* 501–46. Berkeley: University of California Press, 1986.

ARCHIVES

Alex North Papers. Margaret Herrick Library, Academy of Motion Picture Arts and Sciences, Beverly Hills, California.

Archive of Popular American Music. UCLA Music Special Collections, Los An-
   geles.
Argosy Pictures Business Papers. L. Tom Perry Special Collections, Harold B. Lee
   Library, Brigham Young University, Provo, Utah.
George Duning Papers. Cinema-Television Library, University of Southern Cali-
   fornia, Los Angeles.
John Ford Archive. Lilly Library, Indiana University, Bloomington.
John Ford Phonograph Disk Collection. L. Tom Perry Special Collections,
   Harold B. Lee Library, Brigham Young University, Provo, Utah.
Louis Gruenberg Papers. Lincoln Center Library for the Performing Arts, New
   York Public Library, New York.
Max Steiner Music Archive. L. Tom Perry Special Collections, Harold B. Lee Li-
   brary, Brigham Young University, Provo, Utah.
Radio City Music Archive. New York.
Republic Pictures Music Archive. L. Tom Perry Special Collections, Harold B.
   Lee Library, Brigham Young University, Provo, Utah.
RKO Music Archive. UCLA Arts Special Collections, Los Angeles.
Twentieth Century–Fox Archive. UCLA Arts Special Collections, Los Angeles.
Victor Young Collection. Robert D. Farber University Archives and Special Col-
   lections, Brandeis University, Waltham, Massachusetts.
Walter Wanger Collection. Wisconsin Center for Film and Theater Research,
   Madison.
Warner Bros. Archive. University of Southern California, Los Angeles.

Index

Lanchbery, John, 32, 38
Larkin, Margaret, 212n39
Last Frontier, The (Fast), 195–96, 205n9,
    232n4
Last Hurrah, The (1958), 91, 94, 183,
    204n6
"Last Roundup, The," 106
"Laura," 163
Laura (1944), 163
Lee, Anna, 136
Lee, Duke, 15
Lehman, Peter, 160, 169, 171
Leighninger, Robert D., 147, 150
Leipold, John, 56, 211nn20,21
leitmotifs: and *Cheyenne Autumn*, 198;
    and *The Grapes of Wrath*, 120; and
    The Informer, 162; and *The Iron
    Horse*, 32; and *The Man Who Shot
    Liberty Valance*, 91–92, 98–99; and
    My Darling Clementine, 89; and *Rio
    Grande*, 151; and *The Searchers*, 2,
    160, 164–65, 167, 169, 173–74; and
    Stagecoach, 59–60, 63, 146; and *3
    Godfathers*, 105; and *Two Rode To-
    gether*, 186; and *Wagon Master*,
    115, 117, 120; and *Young Mr. Lin-
    coln*, 91–92
LeMay, Alan, 159, 161, 205n9
Levy, Beth E., 51
Libby, Fred, 188
light heavyweight boxing, 46, 47
"Lilly Dale," 57, 63
"Listen to the Mockingbird," 208n32
Little Bighorn, 123, 129, 134, 136
"Little Brown Jug," 78, 83, 91, 199,
    204n6
Little Jesse James (1923), 58, 60
"Little Joe, the Wrangler," 57, 62, 106
"Little Mother," 17
Livingston, Jerry, 190
location shootings, 14; and cavalry tril-
    ogy, 146; and *Cheyenne Autumn*,
    140; and *The Iron Horse*, 18–19,
    24–25, 36–37, 208n47; and *3 Bad
    Men*, 40; and *Wagon Master*, 112,
    146
Lomax, John, 67, 95, 117, 212nn39,40,
    215n27
"Londonderry Air," 135, 221n36
Long Gray Line, The (1955), 13, 183,
    204n6
*Long Steel Rail: The Railroad in Amer-
    ican Folk Song* (Cohen), 28–29
Long Voyage Home, The (1940), 13, 18,
    20, 100–101
"Lorena," 2, 13, 161, 165–69, 166, 172,
    174, 180, 226n23

Lorentz, Pare, 53, 216n5
Lost Horizon (1937), 102
Lost Patrol, The, 162
Lott, Eric, 175
Lowry, Robert, 81
Lucky U Ranch, 114
lynchings, 36, 182
Lyons, Cliff, 111

Macarthy, Harry, 180, 228n49
MacDowell, Edward, 50
Maltby, Richard, 206n3
Manchell, Frank, 190, 229–30n22
mandolin, 51, 137, 184
Manifest Destiny, 23, 25, 37, 39–40, 65,
    175
Man Who Shot Liberty Valance, The
    (1962), 6, 13, 20, 76, 90–99, 123,
    204n6, 215nn24,25, 216n32
"Maquita," 18
"March of the Iron Horse, The," 30–32,
    31
"March of the Outcasts," 54, 55
mariachi band, 22, 74, 139, 185–86
"Marianina," 92
Marked Men (1919), 111
Marley, Bob, 230n27
Martin, Chris Pin, 72
Martinez, Ray S., 80
"martyrology," 228n50
Mary of Scotland (1936), 162
masculinity, 4, 137–39; and cavalry tril-
    ogy, 7, 122, 139, 157, 222n46; and
    The Iron Horse, 23, 34, 38–39; and
    The Searchers, 160; and *3 Bad Men*,
    5, 23, 38–39, 42–44, 46–48; and
    Wagon Master, 120. *See also* gender
Maté, Rudolph, 228n5
matinee idols, 42–44
Mature, Victor, 76
Maybrick, Michael, 217n26
Maynard, Francis Henry, 107
Maynard, Ken, 95, 107
Mazurki, Mike, 199
McBride, Joseph, 3, 175, 214n18,
    224nn74,76, 229–30n22
McClary, Susan, 138
McConnell, H. H., 129
McCracken, Harold, 189
McDaniel, Hattie, 17
McDonald, J. Farrell, 35, 40
McLaglen, Victor, 132–33, 145, 154,
    162, 218n1
Medford, George, 15
"Meditation" (Massenet), 105
Meek, Donald, 65
Melody Time (1948), 218n41

Text: 10/13 Sabon
Display: Sabon
Compositor: Binghamton Valley Composition, LLC
Indexer: Sharon Sweeney
Printer and binder: Maple-Vail Manufacturing Group